DEVIL'S DEALBOOK

DEVIL'S DEALBOOK

Who's Really Pulling the Strings?

BOBBY RAKHIT

© Copyright - Bobby Rakhit 2025 - **All rights reserved.**

The content contained within this book may not be reproduced, duplicated or transmitted without direct written permission from the author or the publisher.

Under no circumstances will any blame or legal responsibility be held against the publisher, or author, for any damages, reparation, or monetary loss due to the information contained within this book. Either directly or indirectly. You are responsible for your own choices, actions, and results.

> **LEGAL NOTICE:**
>
> This book is copyright protected. This book is only for personal use. You cannot amend, distribute, sell, use, quote or paraphrase any part, or the content within this book, without the consent of the author or publisher.

> **DISCLAIMER NOTICE:**
>
> Please note the information contained within this document is for educational and entertainment purposes only. All effort has been executed to present accurate, up to date, and reliable, complete information. No warranties of any kind are declared or implied. Readers acknowledge that the author is not engaging in the rendering of legal, financial, medical or professional advice. The content within this book has been derived from various sources. Please consult a licensed professional before attempting any techniques outlined in this book.

By reading this document, the reader agrees that under no circumstances is the author responsible for any losses, direct or indirect, which are incurred as a result of the use of the information contained within this document, including, but not limited to, errors, omissions, or inaccuracies.

2nd Edition, 2025 - Updated and Revised version of "30 Minutes to Sales Greatness". Visit the Author's website at www.rakhitcapital.com.

Paperback ISBN: 978-1-0681557-1-0
Hardcover ISBN : 978-1-0681557-2-7
eBook ePub ISBN : 978-1-0681557-3-4
Audio ACX ISBN : 978-1-0681557-4-1

I dedicate this book with all my heart to my late mother, Asha Rakhit, whose boundless love and selflessness were the bedrock of my journey towards my dreams. Her sacrifices, unwavering support, and sage guidance have been the guiding light of my life. Though she is no longer with us, her influence remains an enduring source of inspiration and strength.

I also honor my grandfather, the extraordinary Santosh Chatterjee, whose unwavering faith in my potential ignited my pursuit of greatness. His wise words, gentle encouragement, and heartfelt kindness have left an indelible mark on my soul. I am deeply grateful for the privilege of having known and cherished him.

May this book serve as a testament to the profound love, sacrifice, and belief instilled in me by my mother and grandfather. Their legacy is woven into the very fabric of these pages and the life I lead.

May this book inspire you to never give up, no matter the obstacles you face. Remain positive in every situation, and live life to its fullest, true to your own dreams rather than others' expectations. Embrace each day with the urgency and joy of living it as if it were your last. May it help you be FUM© in sales.

Who is Bobby Rakhit

Hey there,

I'm Bobby Rakhit, your Chief Everything Officer, finance wizard, investment enthusiast, and sales junkie. My journey to this point has been a rollercoaster of wins, personal challenges, and a whole lot of not giving up. I've got a CFA charter and proudly flaunt my McGill University degree, which combined with my MBA in Finance, has made me a bit of a big deal in the finance world. I even launched Rakhit Capital, a family venture born from my business and investment triumphs.

But let's be real— I'm not just a spreadsheet nerd (even though I do love me a good Excel formula). I've also got a flair for sales. At FactSet, I led a sales and consulting team across the Middle East, Asia, and Africa, scoring big wins that not only boosted the company's international revenues but also its global swagger.

Before that, I was grinding away in investment banking and equity research at HSBC, U.S. Bancorp Piper Jaffray, and Morgan Stanley. I even managed to sneak my way onto CNBC, NDTV Profit, Al Jazeera, and Bloomberg TV.

What's my secret? It's a mix of stubborn perseverance and a deep appreciation for my mentors— my grandfather, Colin Rogers, Garrick Killbery, and Richard Bilotti. These legends saw something in me and shared their wisdom every step of the way. Their guidance, my drive, and a never-give-up attitude have shaped who I am today.

Oh, and here's a fun fact: my true calling in sales began when I was 11 and sold my bike for more than I bought it. Little did I know that this would turn into a lifelong gig. This book is all about sales and how to excel as a salesperson while staying true to yourself. I'm here to share my experiences and the tools needed to help you thrive in your own journey.

You might spot me dropping knowledge as a guest lecturer or sharing war stories as a speaker at conferences. I'm also hands-on as a board member for a bunch of tech and real estate firms.

So, in a nutshell, I'm here living the finance and sales dream, constantly evolving, and hopefully inspiring fellow hustlers. This book aims to help you find your own path in business and life.

Enjoy the ride!

Rakhit Foundation

As a firm believer in giving back, I am proud to announce the launch of the Rakhit Foundation, a non-profit enterprise aimed at fulfilling dreams and launching upliftment projects. Our first project will focus on selecting a small group of young orphans in Africa and providing them with much-needed assistance with their daily needs, health, and education.

I am excited to share that the proceeds from the sales of my book series, including "The Devil's Dealbook," will go directly towards supporting this project and future initiatives of the Rakhit Foundation. You can see some of the initiatives on my website - https://fkyoumoney.org. By purchasing a copy of the book, you'll not only gain valuable insights into sales mastery, but also contribute towards making a positive impact in the world.

I believe that it's our responsibility to give back to our communities and make a difference in the lives of those less fortunate. Through the Rakhit Foundation, I am committed to making a positive impact and inspiring others to do the same. Together, we can create a brighter future for all.

Table of Contents

Prelude 1

Introduction: Getting Back to Basics 17
   A Brief History of Sales 19
      Prehistoric Times (7 million years - 12000 BCE) 19
      Early Agrarian Societies and Early Civilizations
      (11000 BCE - 2nd Century AD) 21
      Dark and Middle Ages: 3rd Century AD - 14th Century AD 27
      Renaissance to Early Modern Period: 15th to 18th Century AD 29
      Modern Period to the Present: 19th Century to Date 30
   Today's World of Sales 41
   The Art of Making Connections 46
   The Dangers Associated with Today's Sales Tools 51

PART I: Hell's Baggage - What's Inside the Devil's Dealbook? 59

Chapter 1: The Good, the Bad and The Ugly -
The Tools of the Devil's Dealbook 65
   The Tools in the Dealbook 67
      1. Ambition 67
      2. Persuasion 73
      3. Networking 81
      4. Confidence 86
      5. Knowledge 93
      6. Empathy 100

    7. Passion.. 104
    8. Persistence 108
    9. Technology and Social Media... 113
  Key Takeaways.. 117

Chapter 2: The Devil's Dealbook Can Bring the Devil's Results 119
  Your Upbringing as the Foundation of Values................................ 120
  Family Dynamics – Their Influence and Support............................ 124
  Your Daily Life and Routines Play a Role 126
  Cultural and Social Influences 131
  Your Environment Creates You... 132
  Riches to Rags 134
  The Law of Marginal Productivity 139
  Key Takeaways.. 140

Chapter 3: Enter FUM© - The Rule of Law.. 143
  A Beautiful and Revolutionary Melody.. 144
  A Life of Constant Change 149
  Working the FUM© Way.. 152
  Say No to Conformity 153
  The FUM© Way of Selling.. 159
  Key Takeaways.. 162

Chapter 4: Will the Real Deal Maker Stand Up? 163
  Why Mentors Matter.. 164
  Great People Who Were Shaped by Mentors 165
  What Makes a Good Mentor?... 173
  Ineffective Mentors to Watch Out For 175
  The Negatives of Not Having a Mentor 178
  Key Takeaways.. 180

Chapter 5: The Law of Attraction.. 181
  What the Law of Attraction is About.. 182
  Positivity Draws People to You 186
  The Law of Attraction at Work in Sales.. 187

Table of Contents

Live In the Present 188
    Start each day with a positive mindset 191
    Cultivate gratitude 192
Key Takeaways 191

Part II: Live and Let Die - My Journey Through Sales 193

Chapter 1: Where it All Begun - The Environment That Shaped Me 195
Roots in Motion – A Nomadic Childhood 197
Other Early Influences 201
I Wanted to Make as Much Money as Possible 202
Key Takeaways 206

Chapter 2: A Time to Kill 207
The Philosophy I Embraced 207
Getting Higher Education 212
The Influence of Garrick Killbery 215
Working in Canada's Wall Street - Bay Street 218
Key Takeaways 222

Chapter 3: The Mistake 223
Climbing the Ladder of Success 223
Working at US Bancorp 227
The Burst of the Internet Bubble 228
The Hero's Journey 231
Chasing Only Money – The Mistake 235
Key Takeaways 237

Chapter 4: Stepping Into My Future 239
The Events Leading to My Sabbatical 239
Traveling Through Europe 242
Meeting Colin Rodgers 243
Reflecting on My Journey 249
Opportunity Strikes 253
Working at FactSet 255

Working Hard, Playing Hard 261
Key Takeaways 265

Chapter 5: The Final Chapter 267
Business Person, Entrepreneur & FUM© Architect 268
My Walk Continues 270
Key Takeaways 275

Part III: Trial By Fire – The Deal 277

Chapter 1: Into the Spotlight - Getting into Sales as a Young Buck 279
The Crisis 281
Using the Devil's Dealbook 283
Henry Becomes a Salesperson 288
Key Takeaways 290

Chapter 2: Embracing Change – Entering Sales in Your Industry 291
The Environment Changes 294
The Pivot 297
A New Sales Consultant 300
Key Takeaways 302

Chapter 3: Uncharted – Getting into Sales from an Unrelated Field 303
Changing Course 306
The Action Plan 308
Growing into Herself 309
Key Takeaways 309

Chapter 4: Selling Against All Odds - From Ex-Con to Salesperson 311
The Turning Point 313
Creating a Plan for the Future 316
Becoming a car salesperson 317
Key Takeaways 319

Chapter 5: Reinventing Yourself – A Retiree's Guide to Sales 321
Heeding the Call to Sales 325

Table of Contents

    Making the Leap 327
    The Outcome 328
    Key Takeaways.. 331

Part IV: Putting it All Together - Unlocking Your Sales Potential 333

Chapter 1: Are You Fit for Sales? 335
    Understanding Your Score 338

Chapter 2: What's In Your Hand? - Do You Have the Tools
in the Devil's Dealbook? 345
    Interpret Your Score... 351
    Combining Your Scores 355

Chapter 3: It is Not Set in Stone 359
    Moving Up the Categories 359
    Moving Down the Categories 362

Part V: The Sales Commandments 367
    Prep Like a Pro 368
    Shine During the Show 370
    Wrap It Up Right 371

References 373

Prelude

From the moment you take your first breath, you start to die. You begin on a path shaped by genetics, environment, and the influence of those around you. You learn to crawl, walk, and speak. You begin to explore the world more independently. You enter a broader social environment, form friendships, acquire knowledge, and your sense of identity takes shape. As an adult, you fully engage in the complexities of life. You have a career, apply your skills and talents in ways that contribute to society. You go through a series of milestones: entering the workforce, forming romantic relationships and, for many, starting a family of your own. You busy yourself with building your legacy, both personal and professional. Then old age comes in. You likely shift your focus from ambition to reflection. Your body starts to disintegrate. You are saying goodbye to the strength of youth. Then, you die.

Perhaps the shortness of life is the reason humanity has always been fascinated by the idea of living forever. From ancient myths and legends to modern scientific pursuits, the quest for immortality has been a common theme. Ancient Egyptians practiced elaborate burial rituals, believing in an afterlife where they could live eternally. Alchemists in the Middle Ages sought the mythical Philosopher's Stone, which was said to grant eternal life.

In contemporary times, this pursuit has shifted from mythology and magic to science and technology. Scientists are always looking into advancements in medicine, genetics, and biotechnology to extend human life expectancy. They are exploring ways to slow down aging, regenerate damaged tissues, and even upload human consciousness to digital platforms. Companies like Calico, founded by Google, are investing heavily in research to understand the biology of aging and develop interventions that could extend human life.

But is it truly possible for mankind to achieve eternal life? And even if it were, should we aspire to become like gods?

Despite our advancements, the answer remains no, we cannot achieve immortality, and in many ways it might not be desirable even if we could. What if instead we could learn to make the best of the life we have instead? What if we could thrive and be happy, and content to leave that to the next generation when our time to leave this earth comes?

I think that our mortality is what gives life meaning. The finite nature of our existence drives us to make the most of our time, to seek purpose, and to build relationships. Immortality could lead to a sense of ennui, a perpetual existence without the urgency that inspires creativity and growth. Death, not immortality, is the inevitable conclusion of your life cycle. It is the universal experience that transcends cultural, social and economic boundaries. The process of dying can vary widely, from sudden and unexpected to prolonged and gradual, but regardless of the circumstances, death is guaranteed. No one gets out of life alive.

One could say that, in all its complexity, life is composed of our daily experiences and the stark reality of death. Every moment, from the mundane to the extraordinary, is underscored by the undeniable fact that death is the only certain outcome – for all of us. Whether on a conscious level or not, this awareness of mortality shapes our actions, dreams, and desires, driving us to seek meaning and legacy in our brief existence. We go through our routines and rituals, from the morning coffee to the evening wind-down, all of them in an effort to survive – to stave off death, or to live the years we have with meaning and purpose.

An inevitable consequence of the truth that we all die is the instinct to survive.

Survival is an instinct in all living things, influencing actions that ensure the continuation of their genes. In the animal kingdom, this instinct is particularly evident in the ways animals "sell" themselves to attract mates. You will see it in how animals display a variety of behaviors and physical traits to appeal to potential mates.

Peacocks, for example, are renowned for their extravagant tail feathers. During mating season, peacocks fan out their colorful plumage, showcasing beautiful eyespots in a mesmerizing display. The peacock's tail display is a direct advertisement of his genetic fitness- the size, color, and condition of the feathers signal health and vitality to potential mates. *It is his sales pitch and his way of survival.* Females then select mates based on these visual cues, since vibrant feathers often correlate with strong genetics and the ability to evade predators and secure resources. By choosing males with superior traits, peahens ensure that their offspring have a better chance of survival.

Survival is also a fundamental human instinct. It is deeply embedded in our genetic code and has been a driving force behind the human journey from the primordial muck to modern civilization. This instinct has been honed over millions of years. Eons ago, our earliest ancestors emerged from a harsh and unforgiving environment. Life was precarious and survival depended on a keen awareness of surroundings, the ability to find food and the need to avoid predators. In those days, the survival instinct manifested as basic responses to environmental stimuli: the fight-or-flight reaction, the pursuit of sustenance, and the instinct to reproduce.

As we evolved, our survival strategies became more sophisticated. Early humans developed tools and learned to harness fire, significantly improving their chances of survival. These advancements were not only physical but also cognitive. We began to form social groups, share knowledge, and cooperate for mutual benefit. We gained the ability to think abstractly, plan for the future, and communicate effectively. Language, in particular, became a powerful tool for survival, allowing for the transmission of knowledge across generations and the coordination of group activities.

As human societies grew, so did the need for more complex social structures. The survival instinct drove us to create communities, develop agricultural practices, and build civilizations. These advancements ensured a more stable food supply, improved shelter, and improved protection against external threats.

But what does death and the survival instinct have to do with sales? I would go so far as to say that the way we survive is by selling ourselves.

The sales pitch is a natural phenomenon. We are always selling whether we know it or not, and the truth of the matter is, only the best sellers survive. In 1859, Charles Darwin shook the world with his book, "On the Origin of Species." His theory of evolution by natural selection changed how we see the natural world.

As we have already seen, in the wild, animals (and plants) produce many offspring, but not all of them survive. They face dangers like predators, harsh weather, and limited food. The ones that are best suited to their environment, the ones that sell themselves best, survive and reproduce, passing on their advantageous traits to the next generation. This process is what Darwin called natural selection.

Darwin's idea of natural selection can also be applied to modern life, where the ability to adapt and promote oneself often determines success. Modern writers confuse what Darwin meant by the term "fittest" in 'Survival for the fittest.' They equate it with our modern concept of being "fit" as in being strong and good in the gym. What Darwin in fact meant was the one who is the best fit for their environment. The best salesman is NOT the one who is best in the gym but rather the one who, in mastering the techniques I cover in this book, is the best fit in the environment of sales.

As you will see in this book, even in the prehistoric times it was not necessarily the strongest caveman who won the mate, but rather the one who had strength combined with cunning, fight when necessary but also the ability to be part of a social group. The way Darwin intended the use of the phrase is a very good description of how the modern salesperson, using the tools I cover in the book, can win in the sales environment. The best salespeople are not the strongest, they are the best at the techniques I provide.

Today, and throughout history, only those who can effectively market themselves and their ideas get ahead, much like how the best-adapted animals survive in the wild. This is true in all areas of life, because we are always selling ourselves. *Regardless of your profession or role in life, whether you are aware of it or not, we are all salespeople.* Whether you're trying to attract customers to your product, secure investments for your business venture, inspire your team, or even negotiate with your teenager to do household chores, your effectiveness hinges on your capacity to influence, persuade, and ultimately "close the sale".

Think about when you want to find a mate, for example. The desire to find a mate is deeply rooted in our biological imperative to reproduce and pass on our genes. This instinct drives a range of behaviors (sales) aimed at making us more attractive to others. We will often enhance our physical appearance to attract potential mates; this can include grooming, dressing well, and adopting fitness routines to improve health and aesthetics, all to signal good health, vitality, and genetic fitness. *We do all this, to sell ourselves.*

At its core, selling is about communication and persuasion. It's about conveying ideas, values, and propositions in a compelling manner that resonates with your audience. As I write this, it is 2024 and we live in a competitive landscape where attention spans are short and there are countless options for goods, services and products. The ability to articulate your message persuasively can mean the difference between success and obscurity, between survival and death.

Let's say you're leading a team within a company. Your ability to "sell" your vision and goals to your team members is crucial for fostering alignment, motivation, and productivity. Just like a salesperson, you must understand your audience's needs, concerns, and aspirations, and tailor your communication accordingly to secure buy-in and commitment.

Or perhaps, you own a startup; you are hoping to bring your innovation into the market and change how things are done. You need the ability to sell to secure funding and support. Whether you're pitching to venture capitalists, angel investors, or crowdfunding platforms, your capacity to articulate your business idea, market opportunity, and growth potential persuasively can make or break your chances of securing the resources needed to bring your vision to fruition.

Just as natural selection favors those who can adapt to their environment, human society often rewards those who are skilled at self-promotion. At work for example, people who are good at networking and branding themselves often advance more quickly - that's natural selection at work.

I have become convinced over time that there is a vicious part in our survival instinct that drives us to want better for ourselves and for our children and calls us to sales (whatever form the sales may take).

Take myself, for example. Across many circumstances, I have had to adapt and reinvent myself to survive. Like everyone else, my heredity and genetics determined my situation at birth. I was born in a maternity home in Germany. Second to my mother, the Germans were my earliest influences, they sparked my love for people. My parents had left India so that my father could pursue a new career while studying in Europe, and we ended up moving around the world before eventually settling down, and each of these environments shaped me.

We moved through many places and ended up in Montreal in the state of Quebec, Canada. This move meant I left a school where I was doing very well, surrounded by a great circle of friends and satisfied with life. I had to adapt and develop the skills I needed to survive in this new environment.

For context, 40 years ago, in the early 1980s, Quebec was a province deeply rooted in its French heritage and culture, which made it distinct from the rest of Canada. This period followed the 1977 enactment of Bill 101, the "Charter of the French Language," which established French as the official language of Quebec and made it the primary language of government, business, and education. One of the biggest challenges for a non-French-speaking child relocating to Quebec at that time would have been the education system. Bill 101 mandated that children of immigrants attend French-language schools unless their parents had received their own elementary education in English within Quebec. As a result, a child like me who did not speak French would have been immersed in a school environment where French was the language of instruction. This, of course, was difficult; social integration was a challenge and my cultural identity was challenged. Even navigating everyday life was difficult at first since I didn't speak French.

My father put us in a situation where most of the people were French-speaking Canadians and then basically disappeared from our lives. My mother had to survive and so did I. We had to adapt. We had to learn to sell ourselves anew. The flip side is that these moves all over the world introduced me to the civilized world and provided an opportunity for me to get the best kind of education.

I think education is a big deal because at its core, it equips us with the tools to get a job, to survive, and to sell ourselves in the real world. It is, in essence, a survival technique. One of the primary reasons we pursue education is to gain the skills and knowledge necessary to get to the point of financial freedom.

Anyway, my journey from that 11-year-old boy in Montreal to the man I am today was not smooth sailing. I worked at a Holiday Inn and watched who I am as a salesperson take shape. I went through a period where I wanted to be a doctor just like my grandfather, then my academic achievements got me into John Abbott College and McGill University, where a series of events caused me to switch to financial studies. Still, I was learning to adapt, sell and survive. Garrick Killbery, a mentor I met along the way, helped to shape the career path I followed, and I got to see how important mentors are. By the time I was 23, I was working as an investment analyst in Mergers & Acquisitions (M&A) on Bay Street Toronto.

I was still learning, adapting and surviving, but my ambition was helping me succeed. I learnt to communicate. I learnt to sell like a pro. In Canada's equivalent of Wall Street, I was in job heaven. Until I made another change and joined the world's best Equity research team- I will provide more details about my story in the book. But I can say that all my jobs have required some level of learning, which I have embraced and applied myself to diligently. They have required that I adapt. They have required persuasion. Everything I have done has been backed by that desire to live better and provide a better future for my kids – the need to survive. My skills, techniques and philosophies have changed over time, but that drive has always been there.

Which brings me to the crux of this book and why I am writing it.

We've already established we sell to survive. We educate ourselves so we can sell ourselves, and only the ones who sell themselves survive. Now what? Do we go ahead and sell ourselves by whichever means possible? Do we become like those unscrupulous salespeople who do everything they can, without a care for ethics, just to close the deal, and is that sustainable?

A couple of years back, in 2015, I published my first book, "The Deal Maker." The book offered a thrilling expedition into the world of sales. It debunked the myth that elite sales professionals are solely born, not made - although I've always held that an innate spark plays a role. The book is all about mastering the trade and unveiling insights garnered from my personal sales escapades, which as you may already see from the bit of my story that I have shared so far, are many.

Since then, life has undergone a drastic overhaul, especially with the disruptive force of COVID, and my perspectives have evolved further after my mother's passing in 2020. I called some of my beliefs into question and I learnt lessons that have significantly shifted my views. This revised edition is an infusion of philosophy, the natural laws of the universe, life lessons, and fresh perspectives. It's not merely about product knowledge or sharp attire — it's about priming your mind. The first book had sales commandments such as showing value, asking questions, having a killer instinct, researching the people you see and many others. This revision will have similar commandments, all updated and edited to keep with the times and changes of our world today.

I have held many jobs since my first job in Halifax, shoveling snow. I have had to sell myself so many times and I can say without a shadow of doubt, the sales tools explained in the following chapters will keep you in the game for the long run. In this book, I will argue against using the tools in the devil's dealbook for evil. I will argue for reinventing the same tools to use them differently. I will also introduce the concept of FUM©, which is a philosophy of selling which respects all the people involved in the selling process and guarantees longevity. I will provide examples in literature and in real life of people who have used these tools and how they have influenced their lives. I will also provide examples of how different life is when you sell from the FUM© mindset. The goal? To make you a true and lasting sales guru, enjoying the fruits of FUM©.

I would be remiss if I did not mention the connection between all of these and the pursuit of happiness.

Throughout human history, the pursuit of happiness has been a perpetual quest. From the earliest civilizations to the present day, mankind has strived to unlock the secrets to a life of contentment and joy. Some civilizations have been more successful than others, but the desire for happiness has been a constant.

If we go as far back as Mesopotamia, the ancient Sumerians carved the first cuneiform tablets, recording transactions, keeping accounts and keeping track of goods and services. In preserving their present, they were assuring their future and participating in the universal quest for happiness. These were agricultural people who were very familiar with the uncertainties of existence. They sought solace in the bonds of community, the pleasures of art and music, and the reverence for divine forces that governed their world.

Years later, in the grandeur of ancient Egypt, the pharaohs erected towering monuments and temples, symbols of a civilization that prized harmony, balance, and the eternal pursuit of ma'at – the cosmic order that underpinned their universe. Across the oceans, in the cities of classical Greece, philosophers pondered the nature of happiness with Socratic zeal. They debated the virtues of eudaimonia – the flourishing of the human spirit – and the cultivation of wisdom, courage, and justice as pathways to a life well-lived. In ancient Rome, stoic philosophers preached the gospel of tranquility, teaching that true happiness lay not in external wealth or power, but in the mastery of one's own desires and the acceptance of fate's capricious hand.

Everywhere you look, as empires rose and fell and civilizations clashed and merged, the pursuit of happiness evolved, shaped by the currents of history and human ingenuity. In the age of globalization, the pursuit of happiness has become an ever more elusive and complex quest, as people and societies navigate the competing demands of work and leisure, duty and desire, tradition and innovation.

But for all our achievements and advancements, the quest for happiness remains as urgent and essential as ever.

Even though the pursuit of happiness is universal, only a few people have been able to talk about it and create a philosophy for it that rings true to the very base of our instincts, or one that can be tried across vast experiences and geographies. One of those people is Aristotle. Although we do not have any of Aristotle's own writings intended for publication, we have volumes of the lecture notes he delivered for his students; through these, Aristotle exercised profound influence through the ages.

According to Aristotle, happiness is a central purpose of human life and a goal in itself. He was the first scholar of his kind to devote as much space to the topic of happiness as he did. Living during the same period as Mencius (4th Century BCE Confucian philosopher), but on the other side of the world, Aristotle draws some similar conclusions. That is, happiness depends on the cultivation of virtue, though his virtues are somewhat more individualistic than the essentially social virtues of the Confucians.

Yet as we shall see, Aristotle was convinced that a genuinely happy life required the fulfillment of a broad range of conditions, including physical as well as mental well-being. Essentially, Aristotle argues that virtue is achieved by maintaining the Mean, which is the balance between two excesses. Aristotle's doctrine of the Mean is reminiscent of Buddha's Middle Path, but there are intriguing differences. For Aristotle, the Mean was a method of achieving virtue, but for Buddha, the Middle Path referred to a peaceful way of life which negotiated the extremes of harsh asceticism and sensual pleasure-seeking. The Middle Path was a minimal requirement for meditative life, and not the source of virtue itself.

The key question Aristotle seeks to answer in these lectures is, "what is the ultimate purpose of human existence?" What is that end or goal for which we should direct all of our activities? The Greek word that usually gets translated as "happiness" is eudaimonia, and like most translations from ancient languages, this can be misleading. For Aristotle, however, happiness is an end or goal that encompasses the totality of one's life. It is not something that can be gained or lost in a few hours, like pleasurable sensations. It is more like the ultimate value of your life as lived up to this moment, measuring how well you have lived up to your full potential as a human being. Happiness is a powerful tool in sales.

This is the timeless wisdom, upon which this book draws. It is central to the concept of FUM©. As we talk about sales, money and life, you will see that man's quest for happiness and sales cannot be divorced. You will see that true fulfillment only comes from realizing our highest potential as human beings. It comes from human connection and the best sales tools and techniques honor this. When it comes to sales, many believe that success is primarily driven by financial incentives and monetary gains, but my experience has shown me an even more powerful and intangible driving force for success

— positive energy. This concept is rooted in the Law of Attraction, which suggests that positive energy attracts positive outcomes. When people see and feel your positive energy, they are naturally drawn to you, creating better results in sales and beyond.

The Law of Attraction is a philosophical concept which asserts that like attracts like. It means that positive thoughts and feelings can attract positive experiences and outcomes. When, as a salesperson, you radiate positivity, customers are more likely to feel comfortable, valued, and understood, making them more inclined to make a purchase from you. Of course, positive energy is more than just a cheerful demeanor; it encompasses a genuine attitude of optimism, enthusiasm, and confidence. This energy is contagious. When as a salesperson you are genuinely happy and optimistic, it builds trust and rapport with customers. They feel that you have their best interests at heart, which is crucial in forming lasting customer relationships.

Happy salespeople tend to be more productive, creative, and resilient. They are better at handling rejection and setbacks, maintaining their positive attitude and bouncing back quickly, and are more likely to provide excellent customer service. Their enthusiasm and genuine care for the customer's needs foster a strong sense of loyalty and satisfaction. Customers are more likely to return and recommend the business to others, leading to increased sales and a robust customer base.

The tools in this book will help you to harness the power of positive energy in sales. I am cognizant of the fact that the kind of tools for selling products and services have undergone a dramatic transformation from traditional methods to the cutting-edge technologies of today. But many salespeople do not realize that traditional sales methods still hold value, particularly when integrated with modern tools. I write this book to show you that the key to successful selling today lies in blending old-school techniques with contemporary advancements to create a comprehensive, adaptable approach. It lies in building personal relationships.

This is a book about sales, philosophy and life. It is a book that is different from any other that you will find on the market today, and that is by design. I want to make you the best possible version of yourself as a salesperson. If that sounds like what you are looking for, keep reading.

Introduction: Getting Back to Basics

How far back into the history of man do you think sales goes? Did you know it goes as far back as the earliest civilizations, back when man relied on the barter trade system as a way to get the goods they needed? If you had a surplus of wheat but you needed clothing, you would simply exchange with someone that had need for wheat but had a surplus of wool. Only the most diligent people, the ones driven to get the most out of life, the ones with the hunter instinct, would have the surplus, and consequently, be able to trade. Of course, the disparity between some tribes having more of one good than others also meant war. It meant that people fought each other over these items- it meant conflict.

Even later, when gold emerged as the universally accepted store of value and medium of exchange, its pursuit drove conflict. It caused wars. Empires and kingdoms launched extensive military campaigns to conquer territories rich in gold and other precious metals. The Spanish conquest of the Americas in the 16th Century, driven by the quest for gold and silver, is a prime example. Everywhere you look in the history of man, commercial gain was always driving conflict. Sales was driving wars.

Even after some time passed and currency was introduced into the market, that remained to be the case. The introduction of currency revolutionized trade, allowing for more complex and long-distance transactions, but also more conflict. Marketplaces became hubs of economic activity, where merchants could sell their goods to a broader audience. With the introduction of currency, economies became more complex and interdependent. The need for raw materials and markets for goods drove colonial expansion, leading to wars of conquest and subjugation. The industrial revolution further amplified this trend, as nations sought resources to fuel their industries and maintain economic dominance.

This went on into the 15th Century. With the invention of the printing press, printed media such as newspapers, brochures, and catalogs emerged as powerful sales tools; businesses could reach a larger audience through advertisements and product listings. Still, wars were fought over commercial gain. Perhaps the types of wars changed, but sales was still driving conflict. The 20th Century saw the rise of telemarketing and direct mail, allowing companies to connect with potential customers directly in their homes. The telephone became an essential tool for sales professionals, facilitating real-time communication and sales pitches. Then the internet came in and it shifted things yet again, the advent of the internet in the late 20th Century marked a seismic shift in sales. E-commerce platforms like Amazon and eBay transformed how people buy and sell products, making it possible to reach a global audience with minimal physical infrastructure.

Today, platforms like Facebook, Instagram, Twitter, and LinkedIn have become common tools for sales and marketing. They offer businesses unparalleled access to a vast audience, enabling targeted advertising, customer engagement, and brand building. AI has introduced sophisticated tools that automate and enhance various aspects of the sales process- from chatbots that handle customer inquiries to AI-powered recommendation engines that personalize the shopping experience- but these advancements have also come with their own downsides. Chief among them is the disregard for philosophies and practices that have been time tested and found to work, such as relationship building. This introduction section traces that history, providing milestone events, the evolution of sales across time and highlighting notable people in sales history. It will give you an overview of how we got to where we are today.

A Brief History of Sales

Prehistoric Times (Seven million years - 12000 BCE)

In prehistoric times, sales was all about survival and relationship building- take a walk with me many years back. It is seven million years before any civilization, and Sahelanthropus is slowly transitioning from an ape-like movement. In the long interim to Homo sapiens, human species live, evolve, and die out. They intermingle and sometimes interbreed along the way. Their bodies are changing, and so are their brains and their tools. Their diet is mostly plant-based: leaves, fruits, seeds, roots, nuts, and insects. Their needs are few, but their survival often hinges on a critical aspect: the art of trade and competition, which in this era can be thought of as a primal form of "sales."

Survival is not just about finding food; it's also about securing mates and territory. In this raw and unforgiving world, the concept of 'sales' is intertwined with these fundamental needs. Once in a while, two males will fight it out to secure a mate. The strong, those who can best showcase their prowess in battle, secure the most desirable mates. This competition is their earliest form of "salesmanship," where the strongest and most skilled gain access to the most coveted resources, including mates and territory.

Their tools are simple, chunky wooden handled axes that serve them just fine. Occasionally, they encounter neighboring tribes over hunting grounds, leading to skirmishes. These conflicts push innovation- such as the creation of the thrusting spear- which, although used up close, offers a significant advantage over previous tools. This primitive form of tool trade and innovation is akin to a basic market exchange where the best tools win out.

As Homo sapiens emerge with modern anatomy, their needs evolve. They begin to eat meat, requiring collaboration to hunt effectively. This collaboration is another form of early "sales" and barter, where group efforts ensure that meat is acquired and shared. The successful tribes, those that are most efficient in their hunting and sharing, are the ones that thrive, as their surplus allows them to gain prestige and access to better resources.

Entering the Stone Age, man learns to use stone to craft advanced tools with flaked points, which enhances hunting prowess. This advancement can be seen as a leap in "sales strategy" better tools lead to better hunting outcomes, which translates to more food and greater survival chances. Tribes that master these new technologies and tools can hunt elusive prey and defend themselves more effectively, gaining more from their environment.

The changes extend to clothing, where the tribes that secure the most spoils from hunting can craft better items of clothing. Clothing, while functional, also becomes a symbol of status. The leaders of the tribe, adorned in the finest hides, represent the pinnacle of successful "salesmanship" in this era, showing off the best resources acquired through skill and strategy.

As the earth evolves, lower sea levels enable migration to new areas. This movement brings humans into contact with other tribes, leading to battles over resources, including women and meat. These interactions are another arena where early "sales" techniques come into play, as tribes vie for dominance and survival through strength, negotiation, and tactical prowess.

Homo sapiens, now the sole surviving human species, have mastered fire. Roasting game and using fire for warmth and protection adds another layer to their survival strategy. Here, the control of fire can be seen as a significant advancement in their "sales" ability, as those who can harness and manage fire gain a distinct advantage in survival.

In this era of primal survival, "sales" is not just about trade but about showcasing strength, acquiring resources, and ensuring the prosperity of one's tribe. It is about surviving and forming relationships. The concepts of competition, innovation, and strategic sharing are deeply rooted in the survival tactics of early humans.

Early Agrarian Societies and Early Civilizations (11000 BCE - 2nd Century AD)

During this period, sales was still about relationship building, but less about survival and more about utilizing different technologies - coins, roads, and so forth. Better roads and a more settlement-oriented way of life meant people had more time on their hands to explore.

As the tribes move around, they learn the weather patterns and they choose habitable places to settle for longer periods before they have to move again. They start domesticating grains and roots and the plants they were familiar with. History will call this the dawn of agriculture, but early man was just making do; surviving. He was tired of his nomadic hunter-gatherer lifestyle and was beginning to settle. The earliest farmers grew wheat, legumes and barley and learnt to tame sheep and goats and cattle. They experimented with tools like using fire to clear land and create fertile soil. They planted wheat one season and legumes the next, learning how to use crop rotation. They killed off the animals that were weak to allow the stronger ones to survive and breed.

Now picture a tribe of farmers, having done the work to produce wheat or barley. They have harvested and have a surplus of produce- they are well set in terms of food, but they need clothing too, and items to keep their huts warm and cover their children. And so they find another tribe with a surplus of clothing, and they measure value to the best of their ability in order to exchange products. A sale has just happened. Everyone is happy. Until someone decides that they need more wheat than they can trade cloth for, so they wait for nightfall and they attack. They win and go back to their settlement with their loot. It was a fast and brutal war, but depending on who you ask, it was necessary.

This is how life was for prehistoric civilizations. The beginnings of creativity sparked specialty goods like figurines and jewelry, which were added to the pool of tradable goods, triggering enough conflict and driving trade. Man was learning how to market and sell. Fast forward a few years, and tribes have gotten larger and societies have formed. They are growing in complexity. there are influential cultures like the Sumerians, Assyrians and Babylonians and these societies exist in very fertile lands. Agriculture is thriving because of the annual flooding of the Tigris and Euphrates rivers.

These societies are also strategically located. They are in places where man can pass through to access different areas and exchange goods. Now, technologies and ideas are also spreading fast because man is moving longer distances and interacting with more tribes. Cities are forming and are becoming centers of trade, it is common to travel many kilometers to converge at a certain place and exchange commodities. Meanwhile, the Sumerians have started to write. They have legal codes and complex administrative systems that are driven by trade and sales. They are mostly agrarian with irrigation techniques that give them a surplus of agricultural goods. Sales as an industry is in its teething years.

Thanks to this surplus, people can also specialize. Pottery, metalwork and textiles are thriving and up for exchange locally and internationally. The Sumerians use written records to make commercial contracts and to document goods and services, as well as their transactions. The Sumerians rose and peaked around 2000 BCE. They overexploited their land and resources which strained agriculture and created social unrest. It didn't help that their city-states- which had thrived under centralized rule- were now having internal power struggles over resources. Besides, the old Babylonian powers were also keen to fight the Sumerians, yet again, over commercial gain. They ended up conquering Sumerian territories and integrating them into a larger empire.

So, at around 1894 BCE, the Babylonian Empire had taken over and fully absorbed the Sumerians, building upon their achievements in writing and trade. One of the earliest pieces of evidence of marketing practices that happened at the time is clay tablets stored in the British Museum. These tablets are in cuneiform writing, featuring things like complaints over getting the wrong grade of copper delivered. Under Hammurabi, the Babylonian Empire rises to prominence with Babylon as its capital. The people live by the code of Hammurabi which regulates trade and commerce. It has standards for measures, prices and weights to make sure trade is fair. In the meantime, the empire is also establishing trade routes from the Persian Gulf to Anatolia to facilitate trade. Yet again, sales is driving civilization.

The Babylonian Empire rules the world until it is captured after a short siege by the Persian Empire. Cyrus the Great used alliances with local elites, who were unhappy that he focused on projects outside of the capital in the quest for commercial gain, to topple Babylon. The Assyrians soon followed, rising and falling within just as short a period. They relied on trade to sustain their military campaigns. None of these civilizations would have risen, developed as they did, and fallen, were it not for sales.

Around 3100 BCE, there was another global power, Egypt. Centered along the Nile River Valley, this civilization also thrived on agriculture. Within Egypt, trade and commerce were also central to the economy. They transported goods across the Nile, trade networks extended to Thebes and Memphis, but they also traded with eastern Mediterranean civilizations like the Minoans. Egypt exported luxury items like ebony, ivory, gold and exotic animals like ostriches, and imported timber, copper and tin. Egypt had markets where goods and everyday necessities were exchanged. Craftsmanship also thrived there, with things like pottery and statuary being high demand items. Trade and sales were regulated by the central government to make sure the economy was stable, and the pharaohs oversaw commercial activities by supplying legal codes and decrees to govern trade and protect the rights of the sellers.

Introduction: Getting Back to Basics

As was the trend, Egypt rose, stayed prominent for a while, and then gave way to another civilization. By the 8th Century BCE, the Greeks had the most influence in the globe. Greek city-states began colonizing other regions, not just for territorial expansion but primarily for commercial gain and influence. They spread their empire across the Black Sea and Mediterranean regions, establishing colonies like Cyrene, Byzantium, and Syracuse, which became bustling centers of trade. These colonies were not just outposts, but key nodes in a growing network of commerce that facilitated the exchange of goods, ideas, and cultures.

The Greek city-states, with their strategic locations and maritime capabilities, became the heart of an extensive trade network. They developed complex marketplaces where craftsmen and merchants would gather, trading goods and services. Greek merchants were adept at building relationships and networks, crucial for the commercial success of their enterprises. The spread of Greek language, culture, and marketing practices throughout the Mediterranean basin was deeply intertwined with their commercial activities. This era saw the establishment of early forms of "sales" techniques that relied heavily on personal relationships and strategic alliances.

The Greek civilization was renowned for its cultural achievements in philosophy and literature, with luminaries like Aristotle, Plato, and Socrates leaving a lasting impact. Greek pottery, with its signed vases like the one by potter Nikias stored in the British Museum, is a testament to their craft and commerce. Such vases often bore inscriptions indicating their significance, such as the 'one of the prizes from Athens' vase awarded after a footrace, linking material culture directly with commercial and social activities.

Trade and commerce were integral to Greek life, and their decline was also connected to these activities. As internal conflicts between city-states like Sparta, Corinth, and Athens drained resources, the Greek empire's commercial dominance waned. This fragmentation made it easier for the Macedonian Kingdom, led by Alexander the Great, to seize control, leading to the gradual decline of Greek influence.

By the 2nd Century BCE, the Roman Empire began to exert increasing influence over Greece. Rome's expansion, which began as a small settlement on the Italian peninsula around 753 BCE, eventually encompassed much of Europe, North Africa, and the Near East. The rise of Rome was driven by military conquest, strategic alliances, and, notably, by the integration of advanced commercial practices.

The Romans capitalized on the existing Greek trade networks and expanded them significantly. They imported goods such as olive oil, wine, grain, silk, and spices, and exported valuable items like pottery, metalwork, glassware, and textiles. The Romans understood the value of efficient trade routes so they invested heavily in infrastructure, building a vast network of roads, bridges, and harbors. The most famous of these roads- the Appian Way- connected Rome to its southern territories and exemplified the Roman commitment to facilitating commerce.

Roman cities thrived with vibrant marketplaces where goods were actively traded. The Roman legal system, codified in the Twelve Tables and based on principles like "ius gentium" (law of nations), provided a stable framework for commerce, influencing legal systems far beyond the Roman Empire. It was during this transition from Greek to Roman rule that the barter trade system began to give way to the use of coins as a medium of exchange, marking a significant evolution in commercial practices.

Coins revolutionized trade by providing a standardized medium of exchange, which simplified transactions and fostered a more complex economic environment. This development was a direct result of the increasing sophistication of trade and the need for a reliable, efficient method of facilitating commerce across the expanding Roman Empire. Thus, the evolution from barter to coinage represents a pivotal moment in the history of sales and trade, driven by the need to support and manage growing commercial activities.

Dark and Middle Ages: 3rd Century AD - 14th Century AD

During the Dark Ages and the Middle Ages, the structure of careers and the ability to sell skills underwent a significant transformation due to the rise of apprenticeships and guilds. Apprenticeships were essential for professional development, allowing people to learn trades under the guidance of experienced masters. This system was crucial in transitioning from a society largely based on barter to one where skilled professions could be formally recognized and monetized.

Apprenticeships provided a structured path for career development. For example, in 12thCentury Paris, aspiring tradespeople would enter into apprenticeships with master artisans to learn skills such as blacksmithing, tailoring, or brewing. These apprenticeships typically lasted several years, during which the apprentice would acquire not only technical skills but also a deep understanding of the trade. Upon completion, the apprentice could set up their own shop or join a guild, becoming a recognized member of their profession.

Guilds played a pivotal role in formalizing careers and ensuring quality in various trades. The guild system regulated everything from the quality of goods produced to the pricing of services, protecting both consumers and practitioners. For instance, the Worshipful Company of Goldsmiths, established in London in the 14th Century, set stringent standards for goldsmithing and provided a formal structure for its members. Similarly, the Guild of Stonemasons, responsible for overseeing the construction of cathedrals and castles, ensured that only skilled and certified masons were employed.

Craftsmen and tradespeople could now sell their services and products more effectively within this organized framework. The weavers' guild in Flanders, for example, was instrumental in regulating the quality of textiles and ensuring fair trade practices. Weavers who completed their apprenticeships and were accepted into the guild could sell their high-quality cloth at fairs and markets, gaining access to broader markets and higher profits.

The creation of guilds also enabled specialized professions to flourish. For example, the medieval guild system supported the development of professions such as bakers, butchers, and brewers, each of whom had to meet specific standards set by their respective guilds. This standardization ensured that only skilled and qualified individuals could practice these trades, further establishing the importance of professional qualifications and craftsmanship

The rise of trade fairs further facilitated the exchange of services and goods. The Champagne fairs in France, held from the 12th to the 13th centuries, were major commercial events where artisans, merchants, and tradespeople from across Europe gathered. These fairs allowed craftsmen to showcase their skills and sell their goods to a wider audience, enhancing their career prospects and expanding their business opportunities.

Overall, the formalization of apprenticeships and the establishment of guilds were crucial in shaping medieval economies and career structures. They provided a framework for people to learn trades, gain recognition, and sell their skills effectively, laying the groundwork for modern sales professions and economic systems.

Renaissance to Early Modern Period: 15th to 18th Century AD

The Renaissance marked a profound shift in exploration, intellectual awakening, and economic systems, leading to the rise of consumerism and the formalization of careers. This era witnessed a transformation in sales practices driven by new inventions and global trade.

During this period, exploration opened up new lands and trade routes, expanding markets and driving the growth of consumerism. The mercantile system, which emphasized wealth accumulation through trade, fostered competition and innovation. Sales evolved into an art form where persuasion, branding, and the allure of exotic goods became crucial.

One notable example of early sales organization was the East India Company, established in 1600. This pioneering enterprise traded a diverse array of goods obtained through colonial ventures in Asia, including textiles, spices, and tea. Their sales approach included a basic catalog on parchment, which facilitated transactions with affluent customers such as nobility and foreign traders. This method laid the groundwork for modern sales practices by formalizing product presentation and customer interaction.

The Renaissance also saw advancements in technology and communication that significantly impacted sales. For instance, Johannes Gutenberg's invention of the movable type printing press around 1450 revolutionized information dissemination, making printed materials more accessible. This innovation enabled the mass production of promotional materials, including flyers and posters, which businesses used to reach broader audiences and enhance their branding efforts.

In the 18th Century, the Industrial Revolution further transformed the landscape. Significant technological advancements- such as the steam engine and mechanized textile production- centralized manufacturing and increased efficiency. This era saw the rise of factories, which mass-produced goods at lower costs, expanding domestic and international trade. The rapid urbanization that accompanied industrialization created new markets and consumer bases, further driving sales and marketing innovations.

The profession of sales also evolved during this time. The Philadelphia Contributionship, founded in 1752 by Benjamin Franklin, was one of the earliest examples of organized sales teams. This fire insurance company employed door-to-door sales and community engagement strategies, demonstrating early practices in customer acquisition and branding.

Another milestone in the development of sales and advertising was the establishment of the first advertising agency by William Taylor in 1786. Taylor's agency focused on selling advertising space in newspapers and periodicals and marked a significant shift from earlier, less formal advertising methods. By managing advertising placements and negotiating with publishers, Taylor's approach laid the foundation for the modern advertising industry.

Modern Period to the Present: 19th Century to present

The biggest advancement in the modern period regarding sales has to be branding. Sales became formalized and commercialized. Sales efforts were now about reaching more and more people; billboards came up and so did more targeted printing. Sales was becoming a science. All of this paved the way to the internet toward the end of the 20th Century.

The Industrial Revolution earlier on had marked the dawn of mass production, turning sales into a science driven by marketing and strategy. As cities grew and economies expanded, sales shifted from reaching a few people to targeting numbers. In the 1830s, the advent of billboards marked a seismic shift in the advertising landscape. These oversized posters and painted signs began sprouting up in major cities like New York, capturing the attention of bustling urban centers. The Ringling Brothers, famous for their circus, were among the first to harness the power of these large-scale advertisements. By 1835, they had strategically positioned billboards in high-traffic areas to draw crowds and boost ticket sales. This innovation transformed how businesses reached their audience, using the visibility and strategic placement of billboards to make a direct impact on pedestrian and vehicular traffic.

Billboards weren't just about catching the eye; they represented a significant leap in printing technology, allowing for large-format posters that were both economically viable and highly effective. As cities expanded and transportation networks grew thanks to railways and horse-drawn carriages, billboards became a practical tool for capturing the attention of an increasingly mobile population. From their humble beginnings, billboards evolved with the introduction of electric lighting, digital displays, and interactive features, proving their enduring relevance in the world of advertising.

Another intriguing development came in 1839 with the introduction of "Sandwich Men" in London, particularly on Oxford Street. This creative and slightly controversial method of advertising emerged as a solution to the growing clutter of stationary advertisements. With numerous posters overwhelming the street's visual appeal, public sentiment and legal resistance began to mount against these stationary ads.

In response, businesses turned to Sandwich Men— individuals hired to wear large placards strapped to their bodies, advertising on both the front and back. These walking billboards roamed busy streets, engaging passersby and distributing promotional materials. This approach was not only innovative but also highly effective in capturing attention. By bringing advertising directly to the streets and interacting with the public, Sandwich Men were able to reach a broader audience and drive more foot traffic to businesses, all while bypassing the static clutter of traditional ads.

The sight of Sandwich Men became a familiar aspect of urban life in London and other major cities. It reflected the growing importance of advertising in consumer culture and the increasing competition among businesses to capture the public's attention. While initially contentious due to its intrusive nature, the practice of using Sandwich Men eventually became accepted as a legitimate advertising strategy, paving the way for further innovations in outdoor advertising and marketing tactics.

Ernst Litfaß, a notable figure in the history of advertising, introduced the 'advertising pillar' (known as the "Litfaß Säule" in German) in Berlin, Germany in 1854. His invention revolutionized the way advertisements were displayed and managed in urban environments. Before the invention of the advertising pillar, printed announcements and advertisements were often haphazardly posted on walls, buildings, and other public spaces in cities. This ad-hoc method resulted in cluttered and disorganized advertising displays. Litfaß sought to provide a structured and regulated space for advertising in Berlin. The advertising pillar was designed as a cylindrical column made of stone or metal, with panels for affixing advertisements. By establishing designated spaces for advertisements, Litfaß aimed to reduce visual pollution, maintain urban aesthetics, and provide advertisers with a legal and organized platform to promote their goods and services.

The first advertising pillars were installed in prominent locations throughout Berlin, and the cylindrical columns allowed advertisements to be displayed securely and prominently. Advertisers could rent space on these pillars to showcase their advertisements, which ranged from commercial promotions to public notices and cultural events. Litfaß worked closely with city authorities to gain approval for his advertising pillars. His initiative was supported by municipal governments seeking to regulate advertising practices and improve urban cleanliness and orderliness.

Toward the end of the century, sales had changed so much that it was not as strange for people to sell ideas, in the same way that Thomas Edison did. An example of someone who was so good at selling ideas is Aimee Semple McPherson (1890-1944). She revolutionized the way evangelical Christianity was sold to the public. Moving beyond one-on-one interactions and small groups, she leveraged radio broadcasts and large stadium events to reach massive audiences. In doing so, she became arguably the modern world's first religious celebrity, with millions following her life closely.

1902, Edward David Jones introduced the first academic marketing course at the University of Michigan, which marked a significant milestone in the formalization and study of sales and marketing as a discipline within higher education. The world witnessed significant developments in economic thought, particularly influenced by the German Historical School. This school of thought emphasized understanding economic phenomena within their historical and social contexts, departing from the more abstract and theoretical approaches of classical economics. Scholars like Wilhelm Roscher and Gustav von Schmoller, associated with the German Historical School, advocated for a holistic and empirical study of economic activities- including commerce and trade- which laid the groundwork for modern marketing principles.

In the meantime, companies like New York-based Multi-Mailing Co. were introducing the concept of lead lists. They did so by compiling lists of potential prospects from researched phone books across 13 states, totaling 600,000 people. These prospects were considered affluent by virtue of owning a telephone, a luxury that categorized them among the "elite" in their communities. Although these early leads were utilized for catalog and mail-based advertising, they do not qualify as the first instance of an inside sales team, they were simply pre-cursors.

Secondly, cinema advertising was becoming a thing. Advertisers began to recognize the potential of reaching captive audiences in movie theaters. Cinemas provided a unique environment where large numbers of people gathered to watch films, presenting an opportunity to showcase advertisements to a broad and engaged audience. Initially, cinema advertising took the form of slides projected onto the screen between screenings or during intermissions. These slides featured static images and text promoting products, brands, or upcoming events. As technology advanced, advertisers started creating short films specifically for screening in cinemas. These "cinema shorts" were typically brief, engaging clips designed to capture the audience's attention and deliver promotional messages effectively.

Unlike earlier forms of advertising that viewers could easily ignore or skip, cinema advertising benefited from a captive audience that was actively engaged and focused on the screen. It used the immersive environment of the movie theater, combining compelling visuals with sound, to create memorable and persuasive advertising experiences. Cinema advertising quickly gained popularity among advertisers due to its ability to reach a diverse demographic of consumers, including both urban and rural audiences. Advances in film production and projection technologies further enhanced the quality and effectiveness of cinema advertising, allowing for more creative and visually stunning advertisements. It was against this backdrop that people like Aimee Semple McPherson were coming up, shaping their message of redemption with warnings to 'avoid cinema' and perhaps go to study instead as the 'holier' option.

But McPherson was by no means the only person who knew how to sell ideas. Another example of this would be Ronald Reagan. Reagan (1911-2004) was the first politician who truly understood the need to sell ideas. Unlike previous politicians who merely followed public opinion, he articulated his beliefs and goals clearly, convincing people to support his vision. His genial demeanor, crisp communication style, consistency of message, and commitment to delivering results are a model for building long-term customer relationships. He goes to show that selling isn't just peddling; it's leading the way.

In 1919, the Bauhaus was founded by the German architect Walter Gropius in Weimar, Germany, making it a pioneering institution that revolutionized modern art, architecture, and design. Walter Gropius envisioned the Bauhaus as a school that would unify art, craftsmanship, and technology under one roof. He aimed to break down traditional barriers between disciplines and foster a collaborative environment for creative experimentation. Bauhaus embraced an interdisciplinary approach where students and faculty from creatively diverse backgrounds— architecture, painting, sculpture, crafts, and industrial design— worked together to explore new forms, materials, and techniques. The goal? To create functional, aesthetically pleasing designs that were also accessible and practical for mass production. Despite its closure by the Nazi regime in 1933, Bauhaus's influence spread globally through its alumni and the dissemination of its ideas in design schools, architecture firms, and cultural institutions worldwide. It still influences how posters and billboards are designed for advertising.

Then, in 1940, Rosser Reeves introduced the concept of Unique Selling Proposition (USP), which revolutionized advertising and marketing strategies by emphasizing distinctiveness and clarity in messaging. Reeves was an advertising executive working at Ted Bates & Company when he coined the term "Unique Selling Proposition" to describe a unique and compelling proposition that sets a product or service apart from its competitors. According to Reeves, a USP should be a clear, specific, and memorable benefit that addresses a consumer need or desire in a way that competitors cannot replicate.

A USP must highlight something distinct and different about the product or service that is not easily found elsewhere in the market. It should focus on a compelling benefit that persuades consumers to choose the product over alternatives, and the USP should be a proposition or promise that communicates value and relevance to the target audience. Reeves's USP encouraged advertisers to identify and articulate the most compelling reason why consumers should buy their product. This clarity helped in crafting more effective and persuasive advertising campaigns. The idea is that emphasizing what makes a product unique and valuable, enables brands to differentiate themselves in crowded marketplaces and gain a competitive edge. It shifted advertising from emphasizing features to focusing on benefits and outcomes that mattered most to consumers, thereby enhancing relevance and resonance of marketing messages.

Examples of USPs today are Domino's Pizza; "You get fresh, hot pizza delivered to your door in 30 minutes or less— or it's free." Or FedEx; "When it absolutely, positively has to be there overnight." The concept of USP remains foundational in marketing and branding strategies and is still guiding businesses to communicate effectively to target audiences, some great salespeople who seem to understand these things by instinct. No matter, people like Jordan Belfort, Joe Gerard, Anita Krizasan and many others exemplified these truths in their sales and ended up making their own mark.

Jordan Belfort, immortalized in the semi-historical film "The Wolf Of Wall Street," was not just a character on screen but one of the most adept sellers of the 20th Century. Despite his controversial methods, Belfort orchestrated a process that enabled his company to handle over $1 billion in assets at its peak. Ben Feldman (unrelated to the actor from "Superstore"), holds the title of selling more life insurance than anyone in history. His lifetime sales at New York Life exceed $1.5 billion in face value, with notable feats like selling over $20 million worth of policies in a single day and reaching $100 million in sales within a year, earning him annual commission checks in the seven figures.

Within the same field of insurance sales, Clement Stone comes to mind. Clement Stone (1902-2002) is considered one of the world's greatest insurance salesmen. He realized early on that successful selling requires finding people who are ready to buy. As a newsboy, he sold newspapers in restaurants rather than on the streets, targeting locations where people had time to read. Similarly, his insurance sales efforts focused on downtown offices, where there were affluent people with families to protect. He was the embodiment of the sales lesson, sell in places where there are customers who want to buy.

As life would have it, progress could not be stopped. Man was still inventing and adapting. The first TV advertisement is attributed to Bulova, a watch company, and it aired in the United States in 1941 during a Major League Baseball game between the Brooklyn Dodgers and the Philadelphia Phillies on NBC's WNBT (now WNBC) television station in New York City. The advertisement was brief, lasting only 10 seconds, and featured a simple image of a Bulova clock superimposed over a map of the United States. The voiceover famously declared, "America runs on Bulova time." This event marked the beginning of television advertising as a powerful medium for reaching mass audiences and promoting products directly into people's homes. The simplicity and directness of the Bulova advertisement set a precedent for future TV commercials, emphasizing the visual impact and succinct messaging that would become characteristic of television advertising.

In 1916, the First World Salesmanship Congress was held in Detroit, Michigan, marking a significant moment in the professionalization of sales. This event brought together sales professionals and industry leaders to discuss best practices and emerging trends. A key focus of the congress was on building trust with customers, signaling a shift from the high-pressure, exaggerated claims of earlier sales techniques to a more ethical and relationship-based approach. This change underscored the importance of credibility and genuine connections in successful sales.

Introduction: Getting Back to Basics

This was a period where one man, well positioned, could make a big impact. I'm thinking of men like Dale Carnegie. Carnegie, a pioneer in personal development and sales training, published his seminal book, "How to Win Friends & Influence People," in 1936. This book quickly became an essential resource for salespeople and remains influential today. Carnegie's principles emphasized the importance of empathy, active listening, and building authentic relationships. His teachings encouraged sales professionals to focus on understanding their customers' needs and motivations, fostering a more customer-centric approach to sales.

The post-World War II era saw a proliferation of formal sales training programs. Companies recognized the need for structured education to equip their sales teams with the skills necessary to thrive in increasingly competitive markets. Organizations began to invest heavily in training initiatives, ranging from in-house programs to external workshops and seminars. These programs covered various aspects of sales, including product knowledge, communication skills, and advanced sales techniques.

The 20th Century saw other major events in sales such as the first Cannes Lions Festival (the most successful festival for the advertising industry in the world), the introduction of the 4P's of the Marketing Mix by E. Jerome McCarthy, the recognition of the most successful marketing book, and the rise of salespeople all over the world. Madonna Louise Ciccone for example, remains one of the most popular singers and entertainers on the planet. Despite having a relatively modest singing talent and a limited acting range, Madonna has sold over 300 million records worldwide. Recognized by the Guinness World Records as the world's top-selling female recording artist of all time, she has also established herself as a formidable deal maker in Hollywood and the music business. She proves that if you're good enough at selling, product quality is not an issue.

In 1973, another area of sales was born – sports advertising. The case of Eintracht Braunschweig and Jägermeister in 1973 represents a significant milestone in the evolution of sports advertising, particularly in soccer (football) sponsorship. During the 1950s and 1960s, sports sponsorships were primarily limited to individual endorsements or small-scale sponsorships in various countries. By the early 1970s, sports clubs and organizations began exploring more substantial sponsorship deals as a means of generating revenue beyond traditional sources like ticket sales and merchandise. Eintracht Braunschweig, a German soccer club competing in the Bundesliga (the top-tier football league in Germany), entered into a pioneering sponsorship agreement with Jägermeister, a prominent spirit company known for its herbal liqueur.

To circumvent the German soccer league's regulations on commercial advertising at the time, which restricted prominent display of sponsor logos on jerseys, Eintracht Braunschweig replaced its own club logo with the iconic Jägermeister stag logo on their jerseys. The decision to prominently display the Jägermeister logo on their jerseys significantly increased the brand's visibility among soccer fans, both domestically and internationally. The sponsorship deal provided Eintracht Braunschweig with additional revenue streams, allowing the club to invest in player development, facilities, and other operational aspects. The success of this sponsorship arrangement prompted leagues and governing bodies to revisit and eventually revise their rules regarding commercial advertising on sports uniforms, paving the way for more expansive and lucrative sponsorship deals in the future.

Today, sports players are brands, and individual players get sold for lucrative amounts of money.

Today's World of Sales

By 1978, the digital revolution was beginning, thanks to the internet, and today, sales is shaped by the internet - data, algorithms, and the relentless pursuit of customer satisfaction in an ever-connected world. But how did we get here?

In the 1980s, email, short for electronic mail, which had emerged as a form of digital communication in the late 1960s and early 1970s with the advent of ARPANET (Advanced Research Projects Agency Network, the precursor to the modern internet), was picking up. ARPANET facilitated the exchange of messages between computers connected to the network, laying the foundation for the widespread use of email as a communication tool. So, in 1980, Digital Equipment Corporation (DEC), a prominent computer manufacturer at the time, sent one of the first known commercial email advertisements. The email campaign targeted approximately 400 recipients and promoted DEC's new line of computers. Despite its limited reach compared to today's standards, the campaign reportedly generated an impressive return on investment (ROI) of $13 million, proving the potential effectiveness of email as a marketing channel even in its early stages.

Following DEC's pioneering effort, other companies began experimenting with email as a marketing tool, recognizing its ability to deliver targeted messages directly to potential customers. As internet infrastructure and email platforms evolved, email marketing became more sophisticated, enabling businesses to segment audiences, personalize messages, and track campaign performance metrics. The growth of email advertising also led to regulatory developments, such as the implementation of laws like the CAN-SPAM Act in 2003 in the United States, aimed at regulating commercial email messages and protecting consumer privacy.

Email marketing is now integrated with customer relationship management (CRM) systems, allowing businesses to automate campaigns, nurture leads, and maintain ongoing communication with customers. Advanced analytics and data-driven insights enable marketers to tailor email content based on subscriber preferences, behaviors, and demographics, enhancing engagement and conversion rates. Email marketing is often integrated into broader multichannel marketing strategies, complementing social media, content marketing, and other digital advertising efforts.

The latter half of the 20th Century saw the integration of psychological principles into sales training. Concepts such as Maslow's hierarchy of needs and cognitive-behavioral techniques were applied in order to understand consumer behavior better and refine sales strategies. This period also saw the rise of consultative selling, where salespeople acted as advisors, helping customers solve problems rather than just pushing products.

One pivotal moment in the evolution of sales technology was the introduction of the Metaverse concept. First introduced in 1985 with the video game Habitat by Lucasfilm Games (now LucasArts), the Metaverse laid the groundwork for virtual interactions and commerce which would become integral to modern sales strategies. Habitat envisioned a digital world where players could engage in social interactions and virtual transactions, featuring customizable avatars and a graphical representation of a shared space. This early experiment in virtual environments introduced the idea of digital commerce within a persistent online setting, allowing players to buy and sell virtual goods using in-game currency.

As the Metaverse concept evolved, so did its implications for sales. Today's Metaverse encompasses interconnected virtual worlds and augmented reality experiences where users navigate seamlessly between different digital environments. This evolution has opened up new avenues for sales and marketing, as companies explore immersive experiences for consumer engagement. From virtual storefronts to interactive product demos, the Metaverse is transforming how businesses reach and interact with their audiences.

In tandem with these advancements, the digital revolution has reshaped sales education. Platforms like Coursera, LinkedIn Learning, and Udemy now offer a range of sales courses accessible from anywhere, making training more flexible and interactive. Modern sales education incorporates social media and digital marketing, teaching professionals to leverage platforms like LinkedIn, Facebook, and Twitter. These skills are crucial for building personal brands, engaging in social selling, and utilizing analytics to drive sales strategies.

Looking to the future, the integration of AI and machine learning in sales is set to further refine how businesses approach customer interactions. Predictive analytics will enable more personalized sales strategies, while virtual and augmented reality will continue to enhance customer experiences. As we advance, discussions around privacy, data security, and the ethical use of these technologies will shape the next phase of sales innovation.

It was against this background that I wrote my first book. "The Deal Maker" marked my initial foray into the world of writing, embarking on a thrilling journey into the realm of sales. It boldly challenged the notion that elite sales professionals are exclusively born with innate talent, while acknowledging the crucial role of inherent spark. In the book, I drew inspiration from cinematic influences like the Rambo series, particularly a resonant line from "Rambo III," where Colonel Trautman asserts, "God didn't make Rambo. I made him." I highlighted how that line underscores the profound impact of mentorship and training in shaping exceptional salespeople.

In the book, my goal was simple – to help salespeople master the art of sales by providing insights I had gleaned from my personal sales exploits. The book has many strategies for cultivating positivity, harnessing energy and preparing to make a sale. Beyond meeting targets, it advocated for cultivating enduring relationships and getting referrals in order to be successful and stay in the game a long time. In the book, there were sales commandments such as:

- Show Value - Understand the process and put yourself in your client's shoes
- Maintain eye contact and good posture
- Understand the organizational structure and how decisions are executed
- Build relationships – the best salespeople don't stay in the office
- Stay persistent – never give up attitude
- Ask questions
- Always have a large goal and break it down into achievable benchmarks
- Killer instinct is key – go for the jugular
- Use your personality and humor – be yourself and find interesting things to talk about
- Research the people you meet, and many others.

Introduction: Getting Back to Basics

Since its initial release in 2015, life has undergone seismic shifts, particularly catalyzed by the disruptive influence of COVID-19 and more personally, the poignant loss of my mother in 2020. This revised edition represents a fusion of philosophical reflections, insights into the natural laws of the universe, life lessons, and fresh perspectives. It transcends conventional wisdom, emphasizing the importance of mental priming over superficial attributes like product knowledge or sartorial elegance. Why fret over minutiae when you can enter the professional arena brimming with positivity and resilience? In essence, "The Deal Maker" continues to evolve, reflecting not only personal growth but also a steadfast commitment to empowering others with the mindset and tools needed to excel in the ever-changing landscape of sales and beyond.

One of the primary criticisms of contemporary sales literature is its tendency to prioritize theory over real-world application. Sales books are often filled with a plethora of strategies and tactics, yet they frequently overlook the importance of practical experience. Sales is an inherently interpersonal endeavor, requiring people to navigate complex human interactions and adapt to diverse situations. Simply memorizing sales techniques from a book is insufficient; it is the application of these strategies in real-world scenarios that will truly hone your sales acumen.

Many sales books of today also propagate outdated or unrealistic advice that can be detrimental to both the customer and the salesperson. Some advocate for high-pressure tactics or manipulative techniques, which not only erode trust and damage relationships but also tarnish the salesperson's reputation in the long run. The marketplace today is increasingly transparent and socially conscious, therefore authenticity and integrity are necessary if you are to survive. Sales professionals must prioritize practices that center on the well-being and satisfaction of their customers.

As you know, social media has revolutionized the way businesses engage with customers. While platforms like Facebook, Instagram, and LinkedIn offer unparalleled opportunities for reaching and connecting with potential clients, there is a danger in relying too heavily on digital communication at the expense of genuine human interaction. Though social media can be an effective tool for prospecting and lead generation, it should complement, rather than replace, traditional face-to-face interactions. Over-reliance on social media may inadvertently dilute the authenticity of the sales process, undermining trust and credibility in the eyes of customers.

A significant part of social media which also impacts sales is the rise of the influencer. These are people who have significant influence over their followers' purchasing decisions and tend to be at the top of the social media hierarchy. They push products and promote brands through sponsored content and brand endorsements. They sway consumer behavior, sometimes towards products and services they have not even tried themselves. Unfortunately, the way people do sales today online, can rely too much on influencers. Salespeople end up treating social media as a panacea for all sales challenges, but this could not be further from the truth. Overall, digital communication risks diluting the essential element of sales, which is personal interaction and relationship building.

The Art of Making Connections

I believe sales education needs a paradigm shift. Rather than focusing solely on theoretical knowledge and the latest social media trends, we should emphasize the blend of hands-on experience and genuine human connections. While technology and sales tools like Salesforce have undeniably revolutionized the landscape, they sometimes risk replacing authentic interactions with efficiency-driven processes. In the next section of this introduction, I'll delve deeper into how this shift has impacted the field.

My goal in this book is to equip aspiring sales professionals with practical skills and relationship-building principles that combine the best of both worlds. Embracing social media as a tool for outreach is essential, but integrating it with the traditional art of making genuine human connections will create a far more effective approach to selling. This fusion of old-school relationship-building with modern technology will empower you to thrive in today's dynamic marketplace. The way I see it, and in an ideological yet practical sense, the sales landscape has undergone major changes that we all need to adapt to in four ways:

1. Embrace selling as helping

The reason we have come to dislike salespeople is because many of us have had experiences with pushy, manipulative sales tactics that leave us feeling annoyed or taken advantage of. They're using the tools from the Devil's Dealbook to get us to buy things we don't really need or want, hounding us with phone calls, bombarding us with emails, or following us around a store, trying to pressure us into making a purchase. It feels like they're not respecting our boundaries or giving us the space to make our own decisions. Other times they use sneaky tactics to manipulate us into buying. They'll use things like fake urgency or scarcity, saying things like "this offer is only available today" or "there are only a few left in stock" to make us feel like we have to buy now or miss out. They play mind games with us to get us to spend our money.

In a recent interview with Kendrick Shope, the CEO and founder of Authentic Selling emphasized the need to redefine the perception of selling and I think that's accurate. I am an advocate for "authentic selling," which revolves around the concept of providing solutions to people's problems rather than coercive persuasion. Ultimately, selling is about helping. Your potential customers are out there seeking solutions, and authentic selling focuses on bridging that gap. I believe that by aligning sales efforts with genuine help, salespeople can cultivate trust and create meaningful connections with customers.

2. Sell to yourself first

The outdated stereotype of salespeople pitching products they don't believe in no longer holds water in today's market. As a business owner or sales leader, you need to have unwavering confidence in the value your product or service offers. When you understand how your offering addresses genuine needs, you can convey its benefits with conviction and authenticity. Research indicates that genuine belief in a product or service enhances persuasive effectiveness, highlighting the importance of personal conviction in sales. Great salespeople are like Ronald Reagan; they don't peddle, they lead the way.

3. Understand how touch points have changed

Because of how sales have evolved over time, today, the journey from potential buyer to customer often requires multiple touch points with the brand. Research suggests that an average of seven to ten interactions are required before a prospect converts into a paying customer. However, it's essential to recognize that customers aren't just investing their money, they're also dedicating their time. Sales professionals need to prioritize and respect the valuable time of prospective customers to foster positive touch point interactions.

Advancements in technology have paved the way for innovative touch points that prioritize efficiency and convenience and have enabled touch points to be more considerate of a prospect's time. For example, webinars offer people the flexibility to engage with your presentation from the comfort of their own home, eliminating the need for them to physically visit your office. However, you need to leverage digital touch points that enhance convenience while staying true to the age-old principle of good people relationships.

4. Embrace individualization

Today, a one-size-fits-all sales approach is simply inadequate. Standard email funnels and generic sales follow-ups often miss the mark because they treat all customers as a homogeneous group, failing to address their unique preferences and needs. We are experiencing a time of unparalleled personalization, where customers seek choice and control in every aspect of their lives. In sales and service interactions, people desire varied engagement methods tailored to their preferences and timelines. We have to master the convergence of service and technology to offer customers multiple avenues that align with their individual needs and preferences. For example, there are many messaging techniques at your disposal, each catering to different customer segments. Whether you opt for conversational narratives, concise and direct pitches, or data-driven approaches with testimonials, each messaging style resonates differently with various groups. Besides, a single individual may respond differently to diverse messaging styles at different stages of their buyer's journey.

Sales isn't merely about closing deals; it's about forging lasting relationships that drive mutual success. Great salespeople excel in the art of making connections, which involves understanding and responding to customer needs, building trust, and leveraging technology to enhance these relationships. Great salespeople understand customer needs and take the time to listen to and learn about their customers' challenges, goals, and preferences. This customer-centric approach allows them to offer tailored solutions that genuinely meet those needs, rather than pushing generic products or services.

Effective sales professionals use empathy to put themselves in their customers' shoes. They actively listen to their concerns and goals so that they can better align their offerings with what the customer truly values. Successful salespeople customize their proposals, highlighting how their product or service uniquely benefits the customer. This personalization fosters a sense of care and consideration, enhancing the connection. They care about building trust, which is the cornerstone of any successful sales relationship. Without it, even the best product or service can fail to find a market. Trust is built through consistency, transparency, and reliability.

Great salespeople are honest about what their product can and cannot do. They set realistic expectations and avoid making exaggerated claims. This honesty builds credibility and trust over time. They consistently deliver on their promises; whether it's meeting deadlines, honoring agreements, or providing ongoing support, reliability strengthens trust. After the sale, these salespeople maintain communication and support which shows customers that they are valued beyond the initial transaction. They remember personal details about their clients such as birthdays, family events, and interests. It is this personal touch that turns business relationships into friendly partnerships.

All their interactions add value. Instead of just focusing on sales, great salespeople provide additional value through insights, industry knowledge, and helpful resources. This positions them as trusted advisors rather than just vendors. When they harness technology, great salespeople use it to enhance their connection with customers. Sales at its very essence is about making connections, and the best salespeople know this.

The Dangers Associated with Today's Sales Tools

As I write this, Taylor Swift has over 280 million followers on Instagram. She has approximately 90 million followers on Twitter and around 13 million followers on TikTok. Imagine that. In one tweet, or one press of a button, she can let more than 280 million people know what she had for breakfast or what the title of her next song will be. She has over 60 million monthly listeners on Spotify. Her songs are consistently among the most streamed, and she frequently appears on top playlists. Imagine that much influence!

We may be in an age where we can sell not just goods, but ideas, services and inventions, thanks to the internet, but the sales tools of today have many dangers attached to them.

For starters, influencers have become central figures in the digital marketing world, crafting communities, partnering with brands, and shaping trends. They hold considerable sway over our daily lives, affecting shopping habits, beliefs, and lifestyles. A 2022 Trust in Influencer Marketing report underscores their powerful reach: 50.7% of consumers reported buying products they saw endorsed by influencers. This demonstrates their significant impact on purchasing decisions and highlights their integral role in modern marketing.

Yet this influence carries significant risks, and with 83% of adults engaged by influencers, the potential for misuse is immense. While many find influencer content more engaging than traditional ads and trust it more than endorsements from celebrities, the power to shape opinions and behaviors can be dangerously exploited. For instance, influencers tend to create a false sense of urgency around products or ideas, potentially leading to misguided consumer decisions or spreading misinformation.

The trust people place in influencers can be leveraged for harmful purposes. Whether it's promoting dubious health products, spreading divisive political messages, or endorsing unethical practices, the consequences of misuse are profound. The same ability to drive sales and shape trends can also fuel deception and exploitation. As influencer culture continues to evolve, it's crucial to remain vigilant about the ethical implications of their influence and ensure that it is wielded responsibly.

Today's sales tools, while ostensibly designed to enhance efficiency and effectiveness, can inadvertently pose significant dangers when over-relied upon, particularly in their numerical metrics-driven approach- many modern sales tools emphasize quantitative metrics such as call volumes, conversion rates, and click-through rates. For example, a personal brand or influencer with a larger following on platforms like Instagram or TikTok can attract more attention to their products or services. Higher follower counts typically correlate with increased reach and exposure, potentially translating into higher sales volumes. Beyond follower count, engagement metrics such as likes, comments, and shares also contribute to sales success. The assumption is that brands with higher engagement rates can build stronger relationships with their audience, leading to higher conversion rates and sales, but does this last? What about the people who long for more connection? Is it enough that we touch base online, collect your information and call that 'knowing your customer?'

One of the primary reasons this is a big concern is our urge to belong and connect, which is being exploited by the 'influencer' culture in ways that diminish genuine human interaction. Social media platforms, while powerful for reaching broad audiences, also concentrate influence into the hands of a few. Influencers and automated systems can wield immense power, shaping opinions and driving consumer behavior with little personal engagement. This concentration of influence can lead to a superficial sense of connection, where interactions are driven more by algorithms and less by authentic relationships.

The reliance on technology and sales tools can create a false sense of connection. With the convenience of automated responses and data-driven marketing, the depth of personal interactions can be lost. Sales professionals may find themselves increasingly dependent on digital metrics and social media strategies, potentially neglecting the value of face-to-face communication and genuine relationship-building. This shift can lead to a detachment from the very human elements that foster trust and loyalty.

For e-commerce businesses, the number of visitors to their website is a crucial metric. Increased traffic driven through digital marketing efforts, SEO strategies, or social media campaigns, directly correlates with higher chances of conversions and sales. While traffic volume is essential, conversion rates (percentage of visitors who make a purchase) determine the effectiveness of sales strategies. Optimizing conversion funnels based on analytics and user behavior helps maximize sales from website visitors. And yet, the question remains, does a contact form on your email substitute really knowing the person you're selling to?

Sales today often revolves around leveraging numerical metrics to optimize strategies and drive results. Whether it's through social media influence, e-commerce traffic, email marketing, CRM analytics, or advertising metrics, businesses and personal brands utilize data-driven insights to enhance reach, engagement, and ultimately, sales conversions. And my question is, at what cost? While these metrics provide insights into performance, they often prioritize quantity over quality in customer interactions. Sales professionals may focus excessively on meeting numerical targets, sacrificing the depth and authenticity of client relationships. This can lead to transactional interactions that fail to foster genuine trust and long-term loyalty.

Platforms such as Salesforce prioritize data aggregation, often at the expense of personalized client relationships. Sales professionals may rely too heavily on automated features, neglecting the nuances of individual client needs and preferences. While automation streamlines processes, it risks reducing client interactions to impersonal transactions. Automated follow-ups and templated responses end up undermining the authenticity of client engagement, leading to superficial connections.

Tools like telemarketing scripts or automated social media ads can depersonalize sales efforts. Pre-scripted messages and automated responses alienate customers who want personalized attention and genuine engagement. Mass emails and automated outreach strategies dilute the sincerity of client interactions, potentially alienating clients seeking personalized attention. Technology-driven sales tools often overlook the importance of face-to-face interactions and personalized gestures that build trust and rapport.

These sales tools prioritize speed and volume, which whilst important, can diminish the importance of human empathy and understanding in the sales process. Genuine rapport-building and tailored solutions end up taking a backseat to efficiency-driven tactics. Someone who does not fall into this trap however, is MrBeast (Jimmy Donaldson). Known for his extravagant stunts, viral challenges, and philanthropic endeavors, MrBeast has revolutionized content creation and marketing by leveraging the immense reach of digital platforms. His success is largely attributed to his ability to rapidly capture attention and drive engagement through high-volume, eye-catching content. For instance, his videos often feature large-scale giveaways or elaborate projects that draw millions of viewers and generate substantial buzz.

However, this focus on speed and scale can sometimes diminish the nuances of personal connection. While MrBeast's content is designed to engage and entertain on a massive scale, the efficiency-driven nature of his approach may overlook the importance of building deeper, more individualized relationships with his audience. The sheer volume of content and the rapid pace at which he operates prioritize attracting attention and maximizing reach, potentially sidelining the more subtle aspects of empathy and tailored communication.

It is also true that relying solely on numerical metrics can paint an incomplete picture of sales performance; high call volumes or click-through rates do not necessarily translate into meaningful conversions or satisfied customers. Sales strategies driven by technology may prioritize closing deals over nurturing lasting client partnerships, jeopardizing loyalty and repeat business. While technology facilitates immediate efficiencies in sales processes, it may sacrifice the patience and dedication required to cultivate enduring client relationships. Quick wins through automated strategies may undermine the cultivation of trust and mutual understanding over time.

Over-reliance on data and algorithms can lead to a disconnect between sales strategies and genuine client needs, in the same way that automated insights and predictive analytics oversimplify complex client relationships, losing the ability of nuanced decision-making and adaptive sales strategies. Couple that with the rapid evolution of CRM technologies and you have the perfect storm. They may encourage a dependence on tools rather than cultivating intrinsic sales skills and intuition. Sales professionals may become reliant on technology-driven solutions, diminishing their ability to adapt and innovate in dynamic market environments.

As if that's not enough, social media and digital devices have become akin to a new drug, fostering an addiction that can undermine productivity and well-being. These platforms, designed to captivate and engage, often lead to compulsive behavior where the quest for likes, shares, and instant feedback becomes an endless cycle. Just as substances can alter mood and perception, constant exposure to social media can distort a salesperson's sense of reality, creating a reliance on superficial metrics of success rather than meaningful customer relationships and genuine achievements. This digital addiction not only hampers concentration and work-life balance, but also distracts from the core principles of salesmanship such as understanding customer needs and building trust.

Then, there are the ethical concerns surrounding these tools. Automated sales tools may inadvertently breach customer privacy or violate consent standards if not carefully managed. In March 2018, a collaborative effort between The New York Times, The Observer of London, and The Guardian led to the acquisition of a trove of documents from within Cambridge Analytica, a data firm primarily owned by right-wing donor Robert Mercer, in the US. These documents provided concrete evidence that the firm, which counted former Trump aide Stephen K. Bannon among its board members, had used data acquired improperly from Facebook to construct voter profiles. This revelation triggered investigations into Cambridge Analytica's practices and catapulted Facebook into its most significant data crisis. According to the Times, in 2014, employees and contractors of Cambridge Analytica gathered private Facebook data from tens of millions of users in order to sell the psychological profiles of American voters. The leak happened despite Facebook having been warned by its lawyer, Laurence Levy. Reporters found that there was a lot of raw data that the company could not control.

The Cambridge Analytica scandal ended up revealing Russian interference in the 2016 elections. The company suspended its chief after he was shown in an undercover video participating in bribery and seduction to entrap politicians and influence foreign elections, however one wonders whether that was enough. User data was still abused. The dangers of social media still exist; if anything, it seems like they are getting worse. Today, there is also the danger of social manipulation through AI algorithms. Politicians now rely on social media platforms to promote their perspectives, like Ferdinand Marcos Jr., with his TikTok troll army looking to get the votes of younger Filipinos during their 2022 election.

Besides this, unsolicited communications or overly aggressive sales tactics can damage brand reputation and erode consumer trust. Customers increasingly value transparency and authenticity in their interactions with brands. Sales tools that prioritize metrics over ethical considerations risk undermining these crucial aspects of customer relationships.

The final danger I will note is that sales tools which rely heavily on numerical data may overlook nuanced contextual factors influencing customer decisions. Understanding the unique needs, challenges, and motivations of clients requires a more holistic approach beyond quantitative metrics. Besides, over-reliance on standardized sales tools stifles creativity and innovation in sales strategies. Adaptive selling requires flexibility and responsiveness to evolving customer expectations and market dynamics.

Then, there is the additional issue of using technology for social surveillance. A prime example of this is the way China is using facial recognition technology in schools and offices. Besides having the ability to track a person's movements, the Chinese government can gather enough information to monitor a person's political views, relationships and activities. How intrusive is that? In the US, the police departments are using predictive policing algorithms to anticipate crime. The problem is that those algorithms are influenced by arrest rates which disproportionately impact black communities, so the police end up doubling down on those groups. They end up turning this technology into an authoritarian weapon. This begs the question: how much does predictive technology affect our communities, and what constraints should be put on it?

The list of risks is too long, and the fact is these risks are weakening goodwill and ethics. Along with the journalists, technologists and political figures who are protesting the unethical use of technology, religious leaders are also concerned. In 2024, Vatican Pope Francis called for nations to form a binding international treaty to regulate the use and development of AI. He warned against its ability to be misused and create disinformation, distrust in communication and interference with elections, increasing the risk of conflict. To these risks, I add that these dangers also make sales more difficult in the long run, because how do you sell to a people whose trust has been constantly abused and whose concerns have been consistently ignored? The human capacity to make moral judgments and choose ethically is more complex than algorithms can learn. It cannot be reduced to machine programming.

PART I

HELL'S BAGGAGE - WHAT'S INSIDE THE DEVIL'S DEALBOOK?

"Money is only a tool. It will take you wherever you wish, but it will not replace you as the driver." - **Ayn Rand.**

*I*n all my years working in sales, I've found one clear difference between those who excel and those who struggle: the top performers are incredibly hungry. Now, I'm not talking about craving a tasty Indian meal or a slice of cake (although who wouldn't enjoy that?). I mean a deep, intense hunger for success. They have an appetite for closing deals, smashing targets, and setting new records. These salespeople are simply more driven to sell and succeed than others.

There's a quote by Eric Thomas that says, "When you want to succeed as badly as you want to breathe, then you'll be successful." But here's the thing: while we all need to breathe, and we naturally want to breathe, it's not something we actively think about every day. Hunger, on the other hand, is a feeling that stirs deep inside us, fueling real emotion and motivation. Think about those moments when you're hungry before a meal, or you pass by a tempting cake shop, or even when you watch a food show on TV. Now, imagine having that same level of hunger when it comes to making a sale. How much more effort would you put in? How much further would you go to seal the deal?

The best salespeople are motivated, focused, and driven. They have a relentless appetite for closing sales, which gives them the energy and determination to overcome objections, make extra calls, and go the extra mile needed to secure a deal. When I hear salespeople complain about obstacles like objections, economic conditions, prospects, or leads, I have to wonder: how hungry are they really? While these challenges are real, salespeople with a true hunger for success find ways to push past them.

That's the difference between someone who dreams about ideas and someone who turns those ideas into reality. It's their hunger to make things happen that drives them forward. Entrepreneurs who start their own businesses often have an insatiable appetite for success compared to those who merely talk about it but never act. The same principle applies to salespeople who don't put in the effort to meet their targets, invest in their skills, adapt to new technologies, or challenge the status quo. They simply lack the hunger needed to close that sale.

But then there is the other end of the spectrum – salespeople whose hunger drives them to do whatever it takes to make a sale, even at the expense of the long-term relationship and their own reputation and credibility. These are the people who use manipulative tactics and bait and switch techniques among potential buyers. To them, hunger is not the prescription; discernment is. These ones need the reminder that money is only a tool- as Ayn Rand put it, it will take you wherever you wish, but it will not replace you as the driver They need to be reminded that money can open doors and create opportunities, but it cannot be a substitute for relationships. In simpler terms, money can facilitate success, but it's the person behind the decisions who ultimately determines the journey's direction and operational standards. Customers value honesty and authenticity, and when they feel manipulated, it erodes trust and can lead to lost opportunities in the future. True success in sales comes not just from closing deals, but from building enduring partnerships based on mutual respect and transparency.

In essence, while ambition and drive are essential in sales, they must be tempered with relational considerations and a focus on sustainable success. Sales professionals who embody these principles understand that genuine success stems from genuine relationships and a commitment to integrity, ensuring that their hunger for achievement aligns with long-term, mutually beneficial outcomes. This is what this first part of the book will show you. You will understand the tools inside the Devil's Dealbook and the results they bring, then I will introduce you to the FUM© way of selling and how you can use the law of attraction to become a true sales virtuoso.

And why the title 'The Devil's Dealbook?' I have named this book that way for a reason. The Devil, often referred to as Satan, Lucifer, or Beelzebub, is a figure that appears in various religious, mythological, and cultural traditions, representing evil and opposition to good. The concept of the Devil varies widely across different belief systems, but several common themes and attributes can be identified. In Christian theology, the Devil is typically seen as a fallen angel who rebelled against God. Lucifer's pride led him to rebel against God, seeking to usurp divine authority. As a result of his rebellion, he was cast out of heaven, along with other angels who sided with him; this event is often referred to as the Fall. In Islam, the Devil is known as Iblis or Shaytan. The Quran provides a similar yet distinct narrative - Iblis was a jinn, a type of being created from smokeless fire. When God created Adam, He commanded all the angels to bow to Adam. Iblis refused out of pride and arrogance, believing himself superior because of his fiery origin, compared to Adam's creation from clay.

The concept of the Devil or an equivalent evil entity appears in various other religious and cultural contexts. In Jewish tradition, the figure of Satan is less developed than in Christianity and Islam, but it is there. Satan (ha-Satan) is often viewed as an accuser or adversary within the heavenly court, testing the faith and righteousness of humans. Even in Hinduism, there are various demons (asuras) who oppose the gods (devas). Ravana, for example, is a demon king who opposes Rama in the epic Ramayana.

Beyond religious texts, the Devil has been a prominent figure in literature, art, and popular culture. From John Milton's "Paradise Lost" to Goethe's "Faust," the Devil is often portrayed as a complex character, embodying themes of rebellion, temptation, and the struggle between good and evil. No matter where we look, we can all agree that the devil is bad. He is the embodiment of evil – all that is opposed to good. This book is in a lot of ways about the struggle between good and evil.

And his dealbook? Well, that's simple. His dealbook is filled with all the tools he uses to carry out his nefarious agenda. The tools range from monstrous and terrifying sales techniques to more subtle and cunning means of achieving his ends. The Devil's Dealbook is the collection of tools salespeople can use to conduct business. These tools have no moral charge, it is how you use them that determines the result - they can either be used for good or for evil. This section will help you see how you can use these tools to enter into a FUM© way of selling.

CHAPTER 1

THE GOOD, THE BAD AND THE UGLY - THE TOOLS OF THE DEVIL'S DEALBOOK

Nature is about balance. All the world comes in pairs - Yin and Yang, right and wrong, men and women; what's pleasure without pain?
–Angelina Jolie.

*I*n sales, every day begins with the promise of opportunity, a chance to connect, persuade, and achieve. It's a career path defined by its highs and lows, and success hinges not just on determination, but on the tools that empower sales professionals to excel. From the early morning grind to late-night strategy sessions, the tools we use in sales play a pivotal role in shaping our journey. In this chapter, we explore the spectrum of these tools and how they amplify our efforts, streamline processes, and sometimes challenge us to adapt, as well as how the same tools, if used incorrectly, can have a negative impact on our ability to sell.

You will see that balance is a fundamental concept in sales, just as in life. Angelina Jolie eloquently captures this idea with her reflection that nature is about balance. All the world comes in pairs - Yin and

Yang, right and wrong, men and women, good and bad. This chapter explores the dualities that define the sales profession. We talk about the positive and negative aspects of the sales tactics and tools in the Devil's Dealbook.

> *Any tool can be used for good or bad. It's really the beliefs of the artist using it.* – **John Knoll.**

A tool itself is neutral, it possesses no inherent moral quality. Whether it becomes a force for positive or negative outcomes depends entirely on the intentions and values of the person wielding it.

Imagine the brush and canvas of a painter. In the hands of one artist, these tools may be used to create inspiring paintings that provoke thought and uplift spirits- think Vincent van Gogh's 'Starry Night.' In the hands of another, they could be employed to spread propaganda or evoke negative emotions, like the government commissioned artists during World War II, who used paintings to dehumanize enemies. Or think of a knife; I could use it to slice a fruit and someone else could use it to commit murder. The tools remain unchanged, it is the artist's intent and beliefs that shape the outcome.

This is also true of any of the tools within the Devil's Dealbook. Ambition is good; it drives you to wake up early and do what you must to make your sales, but when it crosses to overambition, it can cause you to cross the line with your sales techniques and to compromise integrity in the pursuit of success. Persuasion is an excellent sales tool. It is what you use to win people over, but when it crosses to manipulation, it causes a loss of trust and damages reputations.

In this chapter, you will see how using any of the tools in the devil's dealbook depends on you. It will hopefully dissuade you from using these tools for nefarious means. The main point? Using these tools without respect to relationships will inevitably bring the devil's results – you will see damaged relationships, lost trust and ultimately, unsustainable success.

It's a journey through the strategies that build trust and long-term relationships. The good practices and the pitfalls of unethical behavior, and the bad practices that can harm credibility and reputation. Throughout this chapter, we'll examine real-life examples and practical insights to understand how sales professionals navigate these challenges. By understanding the delicate balance between legal conduct and achieving sales goals, you will gain valuable perspectives on making responsible choices in your own sales.

The Tools in the Dealbook

The Devil's Dealbook is a collection of enigmatic and powerful tools. Each item within it is laced with potential for both creation and destruction. The contents are as varied as they are potent, and their dual nature embodies the eternal struggle between light and darkness, good and evil. There are many tools within the Devil's Dealbook, but I have divided them into nine:

1. Ambition

The best salespeople are ambitious. They push boundaries, exceed targets and consistently deliver exceptional results. For them, it's not just about making sales, it's about striving for excellence, setting high goals, and relentlessly pursuing them.

Imagine if Steve Jobs, co-founder of Apple Inc., had not been as ambitious as he was. Would he have been responsible for innovation that revolutionized not just technology, but also consumer behavior worldwide? Probably not. Jobs envisioned products that didn't just meet market demand but anticipated it, driving Apple to unparalleled success through groundbreaking products like the iPhone and iPad. As of August 2024, Apple Inc. is valued at over $2.8 trillion, making it one of the most valuable companies globally. In fiscal year 2023, Apple reported revenues of approximately $411 billion. This figure highlights the scale of Apple's operations, and the significant financial impact of the innovative products Jobs helped create.

His ambition wasn't just about profits, it was about pushing the boundaries of what technology could achieve and creating experiences that captivated millions. Launched in 2007, the iPhone revolutionized the smartphone industry. As of mid-2024, Apple had sold over 2.2 billion iPhones worldwide since its inception. The iPhone continues to be a market leader, with recent models like the iPhone 15 series contributing significantly to Apple's revenue. The iPad, introduced in 2010, changed the tablet market and contributed to Apple's ecosystem. As of early 2024, Apple had sold over 600 million iPads globally, with the device remaining a top choice for consumers and professionals alike.

Ambition will push you to the top of the food chain and will make you exemplary if well harnessed. This is true even in industries like sports- I'm thinking of Michael Jordan's ambition here. Beyond his unparalleled skills on the basketball court, Jordan's ambition drove him to become a global icon and pioneer in sports marketing. He has leveraged his ambition to transcend boundaries, establishing the Jordan brand that continues to dominate the athletic apparel industry.

- In 2023, the Jordan Brand generated approximately $5.1 billion in revenue. This figure represents a substantial portion of Nike's overall revenue.

- Jordan Brand holds a commanding 11% share of the global athletic footwear market.
- The brand is renowned for its iconic Air Jordan sneakers, which have remained at the forefront of sneaker culture since their debut in 1985. The Air Jordan 1, for instance, continues to be a best-seller and is frequently re-released with new colorways and limited editions.
- Jordan Brand's products are sold in over 100 countries worldwide, with significant market presence in North America, Europe, and Asia. The brand has an incredible global footprint.

Michael Jordan's 'Jordan Brand' has leveraged his ambition to transcend the boundaries of sports, establishing a lasting legacy in the athletic apparel industry. It is his relentless pursuit of excellence and his ambition that has continuously elevated his game and cemented his legacy as a symbol of determination and success.

This is what ambition can do for you. But, left to run wild, it also has its downsides. The ugliest side ambition manifests when its use becomes greed. Consumed in excess, it can warp a salesperson's personality, turning them into a hollow shell driven solely by a relentless need to achieve. Relationships crumble, morality fades, and humanity is lost. The once-inspiring drive morphs into a monstrous force, leaving behind a trail of broken dreams, shattered lives, and a legacy of destruction. Salespeople driven by excess, untampered ambition have been known to use techniques like 'bait and switch' sales tactics or high-pressure sales tactics, when the sale is all they see.

Just think of men like John DeLorean. His remarkable success in the automotive industry was fueled by his visionary ambition, but this same ambition also led to his downfall when it turned into overambition. DeLorean began his career at General Motors (GM) in 1956, where his ambition and innovative thinking quickly propelled him to prominence. By 1965, he became the youngest division head in GM's history, leading the Pontiac Division. Under DeLorean's leadership, the Pontiac GTO- often credited as the first muscle car- was introduced in 1964. This model became immensely popular, selling over 32,000 units in its first year alone and establishing a new market segment.

In 1973, DeLorean founded the DeLorean Motor Company with the goal of revolutionizing the automotive industry. His ambition was to create a car that would combine innovative design with cutting-edge technology. The DeLorean DMC-12, introduced in 1981, featured a distinctive design with stainless steel panels and gull-wing doors. Despite its unique features, the DMC-12 faced production challenges and financial challenges. By 1981, the company was in severe financial distress, with debts exceeding $175 million. In a desperate attempt to keep his company afloat, DeLorean became involved in a drug trafficking scheme to raise money. He was arrested in 1982 and accused of conspiring to smuggle $24 million worth of cocaine to save his failing company, but was acquitted of all charges later on. However, the scandal destroyed his reputation, and the DeLorean Motor Company went bankrupt.

Imagine if the man had paced himself. Imagine if he had checkered his ambition and put guard rails in place, like taking calculated risks. How different would the story be?

Everywhere you look, you see people who cross over to overambition end up paying for it. Maybe if Adam Neumann had checked his greed, the story would be different. Adam Neumann's vision for WeWork was nothing short of audacious. Launched in 2010, We-

Work aimed to revolutionize the concept of shared workspaces, providing flexible, community-oriented environments for businesses and freelancers. Initially, Neumann's vision captured the imagination of investors and the public alike. The company's growth trajectory was meteoric, with Neumann aggressively expanding WeWork's footprint across global markets. However, this rapid expansion was driven more by overambition than by sustainable business practices, setting the stage for a dramatic downfall.

Neumann's ambitious plans led to a series of costly decisions. The company pursued an aggressive expansion strategy, opening new locations at an unprecedented rate. WeWork's global footprint grew rapidly, but this expansion was accompanied by high operational costs and insufficient revenue to offset them. The company leased large properties, often at premium rates, and spent heavily on creating lavish and appealing office spaces. While this expenditure was intended to attract high-profile clients and investors, they also contributed to significant financial strain.

Neumann's overambitious vision extended beyond WeWork's core business. In an effort to position the company as a transformative force, Neumann ventured into various unrelated sectors, including real estate and education. This diversification, while innovative on the surface, diluted the company's focus and stretched its resources thin. Instead of consolidating its core business and achieving stability, WeWork found itself entangled in a web of disparate ventures that compounded its financial woes.

The culmination of these issues became evident in 2019, when WeWork attempted to go public with an initial public offering (IPO). The IPO was anticipated to be a major milestone for the company, but it quickly unraveled. The financial statements revealed massive losses, questionable business practices, and a bloated valuation that seemed disconnected from the company's actual performance. Investors and analysts were alarmed by the disparity between WeWork's soaring valuation and its unsustainable business model. The IPO was eventually postponed and later canceled, leading to a dramatic drop in the company's valuation.

In response to the mounting pressure and financial instability, Neumann was forced to step down as CEO. The company, once valued at $47 billion, saw its valuation plummet to a fraction of that amount. WeWork was forced to scale back its operations significantly, lay off employees, and rethink its business strategy. Neumann's fall from grace should be a cautionary tale about the dangers of unchecked ambition.

The WeWork debacle highlights several critical lessons about the perils of overambition. Firstly, rapid expansion without a solid financial foundation can lead to disastrous outcomes. While ambition can drive growth, it must be tempered with realistic planning and sustainable practices. Secondly, diversifying into unrelated areas can weaken a company's core business, making it vulnerable to financial instability. Focus and strategic alignment are crucial for maintaining organizational coherence and stability.

Finally, the WeWork story illustrates the importance of balancing visionary goals with practical execution. Neumann's grand vision for WeWork was not inherently flawed, but the execution was marred by excessive ambition and a lack of pragmatic oversight. Successful salespeople must navigate the fine line between ambition and overreach, ensuring that their goals are achievable, and their strategies sustainable. They must take calculated risks. They must temper their ambition with pragmatic oversight and realistic planning. They should diversify their portfolios, but do this wisely.

2. Persuasion

The great salesperson has persuasion in their toolbox. They have mastered every step of the sales process, from prospecting the sale to maintaining it and closing it. They know how to use language and the knowledge they have in their favor, and have the ability to influence others ethically and effectively. Think of people like Elon Musk, the visionary entrepreneur known for his persuasive abilities. Musk's presentations and product launches are masterclasses in persuasion, whether unveiling Tesla's latest electric vehicle or SpaceX's groundbreaking missions. His compelling stories not only captivate audiences but also inspire confidence and investment in his ambitious ventures. He is able to rally support and propel innovation in a very competitive market because he is persuasive.

Or think of Sara Blakely, the founder of Spanx. She has managed to grow from a door-to-door saleswoman to billionaire entrepreneur because of persuasion. Blakely's ability to communicate the benefits of her revolutionary shapewear product- initially rejected by many retailers- eventually led to its widespread adoption and global success. Her persuasive pitch resonated with consumers and investors alike, making Spanx into a household name and reshaping the fashion industry.

Even in politics, it is the persuasive politicians who manage to do well. They can connect with voters through persuasive rhetoric and compelling storytelling to secure their terms in office. They know how to use persuasion to galvanize support, inspire action and drive change on a national and global scale. Persuasion helps you build trust and close deals. It is not just about convincing someone to buy a product or serve, but creating a relationship with them, solving their problem and creating value. But, like all the other tools in the devil's dealbook, it has a dark side – emotional manipulation.

Sales is a fierce battleground, and salespeople often feel compelled to do whatever it takes to win over customers, even if it means straying from the widely accepted International Code of Ethics for Sales and Marketing. In a market brimming with brands, products, and services, persuasion can easily become a manipulative tactic to boost sales figures. Emotional manipulation leverages customers' feelings in order to drive sales, techniques include playing on fears, desires, or insecurities. For example, a salesperson might suggest that not purchasing a product could result in dire consequences ("your family's safety is at risk without this alarm system") or exploit a customer's aspirations and status concerns.

Here, I have in mind things like the 2008 Bernie Madoff Ponzi scheme. Bernie Madoff was a prominent financier and former chairman of NASDAQ who operated an investment advisory firm. Over several decades, Madoff lured investors into his scheme by promising steady and high returns. He presented an image of legitimacy and trustworthiness, which helped him manipulate institutional investors, charitable organizations, and even celebrities into investing billions of dollars. Then, in December 2008, amidst the financial crisis, Madoff confessed to his sons that his investment business was actually a Ponzi scheme. This scheme involved paying returns to existing investors using the capital of new investors, rather than from actual profits earned through legitimate investments. It was horrible, and the scale of Bernie Madoff's fraud was enormous. Investors were defrauded of approximately $65 billion in principal investments. Many people lost their life savings and retirement funds, and charitable organizations lost significant endowments. The financial losses were widespread and had far-reaching consequences for numerous families and institutions.

Bernie Madoff was arrested in December 2008 and in 2009 was sentenced to 150 years in prison after pleading guilty to 11 federal felonies including securities fraud, investment advisor fraud, and other related charges. His actions not only destroyed the financial well-being of many but also shattered his reputation and led to a profound loss of trust in the financial industry. The Madoff scandal highlighted major shortcomings in financial regulation and oversight. It underscored the need for stronger investor protections, transparency, and accountability in financial markets. The scandal also led to reforms aimed at preventing similar frauds in the future and improving regulatory supervision.

Beyond the financial losses, the Madoff scheme had significant psychological and emotional impacts on its victims. Many faced feelings of betrayal, anger, and disbelief after discovering they had been manipulated and deceived by someone they trusted.

Manipulation doesn't always look the same in all circumstances, but it is characterized by unethical behavior that strips buyers of their ability to make informed choices, whereas persuasion may sway a buyer's decision while still allowing them agency. Manipulators often distort reality, withhold truths about products, or conceal crucial features from customers. They behave a lot like Volkswagen did in what became the 2015 scandal. This scandal not only exposed ethical breaches of a global automotive giant, but also demonstrated how manipulation, initially employed as a tool of persuasion, can spiral into a monumental failure with far-reaching consequences.

At its core, the Volkswagen emissions scandal revolved around the deliberate manipulation of vehicle emissions data. Volkswagen, a leading automobile manufacturer known for its engineering prowess and commitment to environmental sustainability, was found to have installed sophisticated software in its diesel vehicles. This software was designed to detect when vehicles were undergoing emissions testing and subsequently alter the performance of the engine to pass the tests. Under normal driving conditions, however, these vehicles emitted pollutants far exceeding the legal limits.

The decision to employ such deceptive practices was driven by a desire to position Volkswagen as a leader in environmentally friendly technology. The company's marketing campaigns prominently featured the eco-friendly attributes of their diesel engines, promising customers both high performance and reduced environmental impact. Volkswagen's strategic use of manipulation— presenting their vehicles as more environmentally friendly than they were— was intended to bolster their market position and attract environmentally conscious consumers.

The initial success of this manipulation was striking. Volkswagen's diesel vehicles were lauded for their fuel efficiency and low emissions, and the company enjoyed a significant boost in market share and consumer trust. However, this success was built on a foundation of deceit. When the deception was uncovered, it had a catastrophic impact on Volkswagen's reputation and financial stability.

The scandal came to light in September 2015 when the Environmental Protection Agency (EPA) and California Air Resources Board (CARB) discovered discrepancies between the emissions data reported by Volkswagen and the actual emissions produced by their vehicles. The revelation triggered a series of investigations, legal battles, and regulatory actions. It was found that the software had been installed in approximately 11 million vehicles worldwide, affecting a substantial portion of Volkswagen's diesel fleet. The fallout was dire. Volkswagen faced billions of dollars in fines, legal settlements, and compensation costs. The company was forced to recall millions of vehicles, leading to significant financial losses and operational disruptions. The scandal also prompted a broader scrutiny of the automotive industry's environmental practices, leading to increased regulatory oversight and a loss of consumer trust in diesel technology.

Of course, the scandal also had profound implications for Volkswagen's brand image. Once celebrated for its innovative engineering and commitment to sustainability, Volkswagen's reputation was severely tarnished and the scandal goes to show how manipulation can lead to disastrous outcomes. While the company's intent was to persuade consumers of their environmental commitment, the use of deceptive practices undermined their credibility and led to severe legal and financial repercussions.

The Wells Fargo fake accounts scandal unfolded between 2011 and 2016 and is proof of how manipulative actions intended to achieve sales targets can spiral into a profound ethical and financial disaster beyond the involved party.

Central to the Wells Fargo scandal was a widespread practice of creating unauthorized accounts. The scandal began to take shape in 2011 when employees, under immense pressure to achieve unrealistic sales goals, resorted to creating fake accounts without the knowledge or consent of customers. These unauthorized accounts were often linked to existing accounts or opened using fabricated information. The practice was not only a violation of customer trust but also an illegal manipulation of the financial system intended to boost the bank's performance metrics and incentivize employee bonuses. This manipulation was driven by a toxic corporate culture that prioritized sales figures over ethical conduct and customer trust.

It did achieve its intended result in the short term: Wells Fargo reported impressive growth in new accounts and credit card sign-ups, which appeared to validate the company's sales strategies and performance metrics. But this success didn't last. Customers began to notice discrepancies in their account statements, unexpected fees, and unauthorized transactions, which led to complaints and eventually drew regulatory scrutiny.

In September 2016, the Consumer Financial Protection Bureau (CFPB) and other regulatory agencies fined Wells Fargo $185 million for fraudulent practices. The bank was required to pay additional settlements and compensation to affected customers, bringing the total cost of the scandal to over $3 billion. The scandal also eroded public trust and led to a series of leadership changes, including the resignation of CEO John Stumpf.

As it turns out, this tactic of fooling customers into a purchase is losing its appeal. It's time to shun the old "always be closing" mantra, especially with millennials poised to become the dominant consumer force in many Western countries. They gravitate towards businesses that uphold ethical standards and engage with them on an equal footing.

Millennials are inherently more skeptical and demanding, scrutinizing businesses' motives with a discerning eye. According to Deloitte, 54% of them believe that businesses lack ambition beyond profit-making, underscoring the importance of ethical conduct in today's sales. Today, being perceived as a manipulative seller can have serious repercussions. That's why I am drawing a clear distinction between positive and negative influence, ensuring that you can cultivate satisfied customers whom you'll never hesitate to face.

When engaging with hesitant prospects, every sales pitch inherently involves influencing their decisions, and every form of influence can be classified as either persuasion or manipulation. If you've ever dealt with manipulative salespeople, you're likely familiar with their tendency to blur the line between persuasion and manipulation, often citing the lack of clear definitions. Essentially, it boils down to a mindset of "who cares about morals? I closed the deal!"

Alternatively, some sellers, in a genuine attempt to differentiate between the two, focus solely on intent. Their rationale? "If I genuinely believe the prospect needs or wants my product, my intentions are pure. I can't possibly manipulate them." According to this perspective, even bending the truth in a pitch is justifiable as long as the seller believes the prospect will benefit from the product. This approach hinges on the assumption that both the prospect and the seller accurately discern what's best for the prospect. But what if they don't? What if, for example, the prospect expresses admiration for a car's panoramic sunroof, not considering that that they live in a region where it rains almost daily?

Encouraging your prospect to opt for an additional feature may seem like a good idea, as you know they desire it and it could momentarily enhance their experience. However, it's also not in their best interest, considering they won't have much use for it most of the time. In this situation, even with the best of intentions, it's challenging to ensure you're truly acting in your prospect's best interest. So, the question arises: are you persuading or manipulating? Intent alone isn't sufficient, especially when dealing with indecisive prospects. You're essentially banking on them feeling satisfied with their decision later on. If your product isn't truly suited to their needs and they regret their purchase, they'll likely view your sales efforts negatively in hindsight and question your motives.

Let's break down some scenarios to make it all clearer:

- Catering to your prospect's unwanted subjective desires can make them feel betrayed → *manipulation*
- Convincing the prospect there's an issue worth addressing (via your product) when it doesn't affect them → *manipulation*
- Presenting your product as a solution for a problem it can't actually solve → *manipulation*
- Portraying your product as a permanent fix when it's only temporary → *manipulation*
- Claiming scarcity of a product that addresses the prospect's problem, knowing there are similar options available → *manipulation*

Examining these scenarios reveals two overarching principles:

- Any sales action that diminishes your prospect's ability to attain maximum value for what they're willing to pay, or restricts their freedom of choice, constitutes manipulation.
- Any sales action that aligns with what the prospect genuinely values and comfortably uses as the basis for their purchasing decision, constitutes persuasion.

Taking a similar approach focused on technological products like apps, Nir Eyal introduced the concept of the "Manipulation Matrix" in his article "The Morality of Manipulation." The core premise revolves around the idea that app creators or vendors should essentially be the ideal users of their own products. Consequently, the seller's genuine evaluation of the product serves as a benchmark to gauge its usefulness for customers as well. Nir Eyal outlines four categories of sellers within this matrix:

- *Facilitator*: These sellers offer products that significantly enhance the user's life, and they themselves would use the product → persuasion
- *Peddler*: These sellers may deceive themselves into believing that their product enhances the user's life, but when pressed, they wouldn't find it valuable enough to use personally → unintentional manipulation
- *Entertainer*: These sellers provide products that are enjoyable to use but don't necessarily enhance the user's life materially → persuasion if the prospect is aware of this aspect
- *Dealer*: These sellers offer products that they believe do not improve the user's life, and they wouldn't use the product themselves → manipulation

You don't need to be in tech to understand these categories; you want to be selling the types of products that you are also interested in as a consumer. Use the Manipulation Matrix to help you decide where you fall.

3. Networking

Networking is a vital skill for salespeople which enables them to build relationships, create opportunities, and establish credibility in their industries. A prime example of effective networking is Richard Branson, the founder of Virgin Group. Branson's ability to forge connections with influential people and industry leaders played a pivotal role in the expansion of his diverse business ventures, from music and airlines to telecommunications and space travel. His knack for networking allowed him to gain valuable insights, secure partnerships, and navigate challenges, illustrating how cultivating a robust network can fuel entrepreneurial success.

It's true everywhere you look- whether it's in tech, sports, pharmaceutical, real estate or industrial sales– the ability to network is a goldmine. You can leverage your networks throughout your career; networks give you referrals, enhance your reputation and when well used, give you a competitive edge. Of course, effective networking goes beyond collecting business cards; it involves cultivating genuine connections, offering support, and exchanging valuable insights. Successful salespeople understand that networking is a reciprocal process where mutual trust and respect are essential. They know that investing time and effort in building relationships can lead to long-term success, professional growth, and a robust pipeline of opportunities.

Think of Sheryl Sandberg and what her networks helped her achieve. She graduated from Harvard Business School and initially worked at McKinsey & Company as a management consultant. During this time, she cultivated a strong network of colleagues and mentors. In 2001, Sandberg joined Google as Vice President of Global Online Sales & Operations. At Google, she not only excelled in her role but also expanded her network significantly within the tech industry, establishing connections with key leaders and influencers.

Then, in 2008, Sandberg was recruited by Mark Zuckerberg to join Facebook as its COO. This move was facilitated in part by her existing relationships in Silicon Valley and her reputation for strategic leadership and operational expertise; i.e. her network. At Facebook, Sandberg played a pivotal role in scaling the company's operations and revenue growth. Her leadership was instrumental in turning Facebook into a profitable enterprise and navigating complex challenges as the company expanded globally.

Beyond her operational responsibilities, Sandberg's network and relationships allowed her to advocate for important initiatives, such as diversity and gender equality in tech. She authored the best-selling book "Lean In," which sparked a global conversation about women in leadership. Its impact was amplified by her network, and the thing with these networks is that whilst they didn't always yield results immediately when formed, they definitely did in the long run.

Unfortunately, networking can also facilitate the rise of unethical alliances and power cliques, and like everything else in life, it has a dark side. When networking is used to exclude, manipulate, or exploit others, it becomes a tool for reinforcing inequality and corruption. Here, think of pyramid schemes and multi-level marketing organizations. Of course, not all pyramid schemes or MLMs are scams; some operate legitimately within the boundaries of the law. However, the lines between legitimate MLMs and deceptive schemes can often blur, particularly when companies promise extraordinary rewards for recruitment rather than for actual product sales. Here are some examples of how networking can cross into unethical territory:

- Mary Kay is a well-known MLM company that operates legally, but has faced scrutiny over its business practices. According to a 2012 Harper's Magazine article, Mary Kay avoids being classified as an illegal pyramid scheme by using specific language and practices. The company doesn't require salespeople to purchase inventory, yet there are benefits to doing so. The FTC considers commissions based on actual product sales as legal, but a significant portion of transactions occur between

the company and its salespeople rather than between salespeople and end consumers. This internal sales focus can skew the business model towards recruitment rather than genuine product sales.
- During the Great Recession, Business in Motion promised Canadians the chance to earn substantial income by selling vacation club packages. New members paid a $3,200 entrance fee but were promised a $5,000 commission for each package sold. This red flag highlighted a classic scheme where commissions were unsustainable compared to the actual cost of the product, leading to a fraudulent scheme that duped about 2,000 investors.
- Fortune Hi-Tech Marketing was deemed a pyramid scheme by the FTC in 2013. The company's model focused on recruiting rather than selling products. Roughly 100,000 Americans were affected, paying fees to participate while earning more from recruitment than actual sales.
- In 2015, the FTC accused Vemma of operating a pyramid scheme, where rewards were primarily based on recruitment rather than sales of energy and weight-loss drinks. New recruits, often students, paid high fees for starter packs and ongoing purchases, with 93% of distributors reportedly earning less than $6,169 annually.

These examples demonstrate how networking, when misapplied, can lead to exploitation and unethical practices. Networking, like MLMs and pyramid schemes, can either build genuine connections and opportunities or become a tool for reinforcing inequality and corruption. In corporate environments, this can manifest as favoritism, nepotism, or backdoor dealings that undermine meritocracy and fairness. When misapplied, networking can become a tool for exploitation and unethical practices. The FIFA corruption scandal is an example of how networking, when corrupted, can lead to widespread unethical behavior, legal repercussions, and systemic reform. This scandal, which came to light in 2015, highlights the dangers of leveraging professional connections for corrupt purposes and the extensive impact such misconduct can have on an organization and its stakeholders.

FIFA, the global governing body for football (soccer), has long been one of the most influential sports organizations in the world. Responsible for overseeing international competitions such as the World Cup, FIFA's decisions hold significant weight in the global football community. The scandal revealed that many of FIFA's top officials engaged in a complex network of corruption that compromised the integrity of the organization's operations.

The scandal was driven by a network of bribery and kickbacks orchestrated by high-ranking FIFA officials. These officials used their positions to manipulate the decision-making processes related to the awarding of World Cup hosting rights and other football-related contracts. The system of networking within FIFA was corrupted by unethical practices, as officials exchanged bribes for votes and influence. This manipulation extended to the awarding of lucrative sponsorship deals and broadcasting rights, further entrenching the corruption.

The misuse of networking in this context involved the cultivation of relationships for personal gain without the advancement of the organization's mission. Officials engaged in a web of deceit, using their connections to secure financial benefits and control over the allocation of football's most prestigious events. This exploitation of networking not only undermined the fairness of FIFA's decision-making but also eroded public trust in the organization's ability to operate with integrity. In May 2015, the U.S. Department of Justice (DOJ) and Swiss authorities launched a series of high-profile investigations and arrests, leading to indictments against several FIFA executives. The investigation unveiled a vast conspiracy of bribery, money laundering, and racketeering, implicating multiple officials and associated entities.

Perhaps, the ugliest side of networking is when it facilitates systemic corruption and abuse of power. Networks can become exclusive clubs that perpetuate inequality, racism, or other forms of discrimination. When powerful people and groups use their connections to shield themselves from accountability or to oppress others, the network becomes a tool of tyranny. The abuse of networking in political arenas, where lobbyists and influential figures manipulate policies for personal or corporate gain at the expense of the public, exemplifies this ugly aspect.

For salespeople, the goal is to use your networks to benefit yourself and others; not to benefit yourself at the expense of your clients, employer or other stakeholders. Ethical networking involves adhering to principles of fairness, transparency, and accountability, ensuring that one's actions contribute positively to the industry and society. It is building and maintaining genuine relationships based on trust and mutual respect, which fosters a healthy sales environment and supports long-term success.

4. Confidence

The best salespeople have audacity. They are confident. They dare to think big, take bold actions and challenge the status quo to achieve remarkable results. Salespeople need confidence because it fuels their ability to push beyond limits and seize opportunities. It is confidence that empowers salespeople to step outside their comfort zones and embrace challenges that others might avoid. Whether it's cold-calling a high-profile client or pitching a bold new idea, audacious salespeople are willing to take risks to achieve breakthroughs.

In a crowded marketplace, confidence sets salespeople apart. It allows them to innovate, propose unconventional solutions, and create compelling value propositions that resonate with clients. Audacious sales tactics can capture attention, spark interest, and ultimately win business. Not only that, but confidence builds resilience in salespeople. It gives them the courage to persevere in the face of rejection, setbacks, and challenging sales cycles. Confident sales professionals understand that failure is part of the journey and use it as fuel to propel them toward future successes.

Confidence fosters a mindset of innovation. Confident salespeople are more likely to explore new markets, pioneer creative sales strategies, and adapt quickly to changing industry trends. This proactive approach drives continuous growth and keeps them ahead of the competition. People like Beth Comstock; the former Vice Chair of General Electric (GE) was known for her innovative approach to sales and marketing. Comstock's audacious initiatives, such as pioneering GE's digital and clean energy efforts, positioned the company at the forefront of industry trends. Her willingness to embrace risk and drive transformative change within a traditionally conservative, corporate environment showcases how audacity can drive innovation and market leadership.

Or imagine people whose confidence allows them to step out of unfavorable environments and create a future that is better suited for them, people like Mary Kay Ash. She started her career in direct sales but found herself consistently overlooked for promotions in favor of men she had trained. Frustrated, she retired in 1963 with the intention of writing a book to assist women in navigating the male-dominated business world.

She had begun her career in direct sales in the 1930s and 1940s, selling books door-to-door. She later moved into selling home goods and then cosmetics for another direct sales company. In 1963, confident that she could do more and deserved to be paid for it, Mary Kay retired with the idea of writing a guide to help women succeed in business. Her husband encouraged her to turn this idea into a business instead. Later, with a $5,000 investment, Mary Kay Ash founded Mary Kay Cosmetics in Dallas, Texas, in 1963. She established the company with the principles of offering women an opportunity to achieve personal and financial success through direct selling of cosmetics. None of these things would have been possible if she didn't have that audacity that pushes salespeople to go above and beyond.

Mary Kay's direct selling model was unique for its time, empowering women to start their own businesses as independent beauty consultants. Consultants could earn commissions on their sales and on the sales of others they recruited into the company. She fostered a culture within her company that celebrated women's achievements, provided extensive training and support, and promoted a positive and uplifting environment. The company's motto, "God first, family second, career third," reflected her values of faith, family, and work-life balance. The company grew rapidly and became one of the largest direct sellers of cosmetics in the world. See what confidence can do!

And yet, confidence has a dark side too. Overconfidence can also lead to reckless behavior and dangerous business practices. When confidence crosses the line into hubris, it can result in catastrophic failures. The 2008 financial crisis, partly fueled by the audacious risk-taking of financial institutions, demonstrates the destructive potential of unchecked audacity.

In personal relationships, excessive boldness can come off as arrogance, damaging trust and respect. You start to think yourself better than everyone else. In business, overconfidence will often lead to decisions that appear logical on the surface but ultimately result in significant losses and setbacks. The Quaker Oats acquisition of Snapple in 1994 is a compelling example of how overconfidence can derail strategic initiatives. The $1.7 billion purchase, driven by the belief that Quaker Oats could replicate the success they had achieved with Gatorade, turned into a costly miscalculation, culminating in a $1.4 billion loss when Snapple was sold just three years later.

Let me backtrack. In the early 1990s, Quaker Oats was riding high on the success of Gatorade, the sports drink that had transformed the beverage industry. With Gatorade, Quaker Oats had established itself as a formidable player in the beverage market, and the company's executives were eager to replicate this success with other brands. This ambition led them to Snapple, a quirky and popular beverage brand known for its unique flavors and distinctive marketing approach. Snapple seemed like a promising addition to Quaker Oats' portfolio, offering an opportunity to diversify their beverage offerings and capitalize on the growing trend of specialty drinks.

The decision to acquire Snapple for $1.7 billion was based on an overconfident assumption that Quaker Oats could leverage its successful marketing and distribution strategies to replicate Snapple's market performance. It stemmed from the belief that their track record with Gatorade demonstrated an innate ability to manage and scale beverage brands effectively. But this assumption overlooked several critical factors that ultimately led to the failure of the acquisition.

Firstly, Quaker Oats underestimated the complexities of managing Snapple's brand and distribution network. Unlike Gatorade, which was a product with broad appeal and a clear market niche, Snapple was a more niche brand with a unique identity and a loyal but specific customer base. The integration of Snapple into Quaker Oats' existing operations required a nuanced understanding of the brand's culture and consumer base, something that the executives underestimated.

Secondly, Quaker Oats struggled to align Snapple's distribution and marketing strategies with their own. Snapple's success was driven by its grassroots marketing and distinctive brand image, which contrasted sharply with Quaker Oats' more traditional, broad-based marketing approach. The company's efforts to impose its own distribution and marketing strategies on Snapple led to a dilution of the brand's unique identity and alienation of its core customer base.

To top it all, the acquisition was marked by operational and strategic missteps. Quaker Oats made several changes to Snapple's distribution model, including shifting it from a direct-to-store delivery system to a more centralized distribution approach. This change led to distribution inefficiencies and supply chain issues that adversely affected Snapple's market presence and consumer satisfaction.

Unsurprisingly, the financial performance of Snapple under Quaker Oats was disappointing, failing to meet the high expectations set by the initial acquisition. The brand's market share declined and sales underperformed relative to projections. Faced with mounting losses and a declining brand value, Quaker Oats made the decision to sell Snapple in 1997, just three years after the acquisition. The sale, which was completed for $300 million, resulted in a substantial financial loss of $1.4 billion, a stark contrast to the $1.7 billion investment made just a few years prior.

Do you see how much damage overconfidence can do? It makes you unwilling to do the necessary work behind success and causes you to overestimate your capabilities. Another example of this is Blockbuster. Blockbuster was once the titan of the video rental industry, commanding a dominant position with its expansive network of physical stores. At its peak, Blockbuster's business model appeared invincible. The company's reliance on a vast inventory of physical rentals, late fees, and store locations seemed well-suited to the video rental market. However, Blockbuster's overconfidence in its business model led to a critical misjudgment: the dismissal of Netflix and the broader shift towards digital media consumption.

In the early 2000s, Netflix emerged as a disruptive force in the video rental industry, initially offering a DVD rental-by-mail service and later pioneering a subscription-based streaming model. Netflix's innovative approach promised greater convenience and a shift away from physical media, a trend that was gaining traction among consumers. Despite Netflix's growing popularity, Blockbuster's leadership- confident in their established business model- underestimated the potential impact of digital media.

Blockbuster had opportunities to adapt to the changing market. In 2000, Netflix co-founder Reed Hastings proposed a partnership with Blockbuster, suggesting that the video rental giant acquire his fledgling company. Blockbuster's management, however, dismissed the offer, believing that their extensive store network and established customer base provided a sustainable competitive advantage. This overconfidence in their traditional model led them to ignore the emerging threat posed by digital media.

As Netflix continued to innovate and attract a growing subscriber base, Blockbuster struggled to adapt. The company eventually launched its own online rental service and later a streaming platform, but these efforts were too little, too late. Blockbuster's late entry into the digital arena failed to overcome the advantages of Netflix's head start and superior technology. By the time Blockbuster attempted to reposition itself, the damage had been done. The company filed for bankruptcy in 2010 and overconfidence played a key role in its demise. Perhaps if the management had been willing to consider that they did not have it all figured out, things would have unfolded differently.

The ugliest side of overconfidence is seen when it fosters extreme risk-taking and callous behavior, leading to scandals and disasters like with Lehman brothers. As a major investment bank, Lehman Brothers was heavily involved in the housing market and financial derivatives. The firm's leadership exhibited profound overconfidence in their ability to manage and profit from increasingly risky financial products, including mortgage-backed securities and collateralized debt obligations (CDOs).

Throughout the early 2000s, Lehman Brothers, along with other financial institutions, aggressively pursued profits from the booming housing market. The firm's executives were confident that the housing market would continue its upward trajectory and that the risks associated with their investments were manageable. This overconfidence led Lehman Brothers to take on an enormous amount of leverage and invest heavily in subprime mortgages— loans made to borrowers with poor credit histories.

When the housing bubble burst in 2007, the value of mortgage-backed securities plummeted, exposing the vulnerabilities in Lehman Brothers' portfolio. The firm's overconfidence in their risk management strategies and the continued stability of the housing market blinded them to the growing signs of trouble. As the value of their investments eroded and the firm struggled to secure additional capital, Lehman Brothers faced an insurmountable financial crisis. In September 2008, Lehman Brothers filed for bankruptcy, marking the largest bankruptcy filing in U.S. history. The collapse of Lehman Brothers had far-reaching effects, triggering a global financial crisis that led to widespread economic turmoil. The firm's overconfidence in their financial strategies and the robustness of the housing market contributed directly to the severity of the crisis.

Confidence is a powerful asset for a salesperson, driving persistence and creating a persuasive presence that can inspire trust and secure deals. It enables sales professionals to approach challenges with a positive mindset, communicate effectively, and build strong relationships with clients. However, when confidence morphs into overconfidence, it can lead to significant pitfalls. Overconfidence often clouds judgment, leading to poor decision-making and an underestimation of risks or customer needs. It may result in ignoring valuable feedback, alienating potential clients, or making unrealistic promises. Striking the right balance is key: maintain a healthy self-assurance that empowers and motivates, but stay grounded and open to learning, adapting, and genuinely understanding your customers' needs.

5. Knowledge

Knowledge is one of the most powerful tools at a salesperson's disposal. It goes beyond simply knowing the features and benefits of a product or service; it encompasses a deep understanding of the market, the competition, the customer, and the broader industry. When used effectively, knowledge can transform the sales process building trust, credibility, and long-term relationships.

A salesperson who is thoroughly knowledgeable about their product or service can answer any question a potential customer might have. This depth of understanding not only helps in addressing objections but also allows the salesperson to tailor their pitch to highlight the most relevant features for each customer. For example in the technology sector, where products can be complex, a salesperson who understands the technical specifications can better communicate the value of those features to both technical and non-technical stakeholders.

Knowledge enables effective product demonstrations. Whether it's a software tool, a piece of machinery, or a service offering, the ability to showcase its capabilities in a live setting can significantly enhance the persuasiveness of a sales pitch. A well-executed demonstration that highlights key benefits directly relevant to the customer's needs can often be the deciding factor in closing a sale. HubSpot is a great example of this.

The company is a leading provider of inbound marketing and sales software and excels in leveraging knowledge as a sales tool through its comprehensive educational resources. HubSpot has developed an extensive library of free content, including blogs, eBooks, webinars, and courses through HubSpot Academy. This rich array of resources serves not only to educate potential customers but also to demonstrate HubSpot's expertise and thought leadership in the industry.

One of the key ways HubSpot uses knowledge to enhance their sales efforts is through live demonstrations and interactive webinars. By offering hands-on demonstrations of their software in real-time, HubSpot allows potential customers to experience firsthand how their tools can address specific business challenges. These live sessions are designed to highlight the unique features and benefits of HubSpot's software, showing how it can streamline marketing efforts, improve sales processes, and drive business growth.

During these demonstrations, HubSpot's sales representatives leverage their deep understanding of inbound marketing, CRM best practices, and sales strategies to provide tailored solutions. They use their knowledge to address the specific needs and pain points of each potential customer, offering personalized insights and solutions that resonate with the audience. This not only showcases the software's capabilities, but also builds credibility and trust with prospective clients.

Besides the live demonstrations, HubSpot's educational content plays a crucial role in the sales process. The company's well-crafted eBooks, white papers, and case studies provide in-depth information on various aspects of inbound marketing and sales. These resources often include practical tips, real-world examples, and success stories that illustrate the effectiveness of their software. By offering valuable knowledge that helps potential customers understand industry trends and best practices, HubSpot positions itself as a knowledgeable partner rather than just a vendor.

HubSpot also uses its extensive database of webinars and online courses to educate potential customers. These sessions often feature industry experts and thought leaders who share their insights on relevant topics. By hosting these events, HubSpot not only showcases its software but also demonstrates its commitment to providing ongoing value and support to its audience. This educational approach helps build long-term relationships with customers and reinforces HubSpot's reputation as a trusted advisor.

As you think of knowledge as a sales tool, its scope expands to the knowledge of the market landscape and the competition. A salesperson who understands where their product stands relative to competitors can better position it in the market. This might involve highlighting unique features, better pricing, or superior customer service. For instance, in highly competitive industries like consumer electronics, knowing how your product outperforms others can be the key to winning over a customer.

Awareness of current trends and future directions within an industry allows salespeople to align their offerings with what customers are looking for, before they even realize they need it. In the renewable energy sector, a salesperson who is aware of upcoming regulations and incentives may guide customers to products that will be compliant or more profitable in the long term.

Knowledge is also about customer insight. This includes understanding their pain points, needs, preferences, and their decision-making processes. With this insight, a salesperson can offer highly personalized solutions, which are more likely to resonate with the customer and result in a sale. For example, in B2B sales, understanding a client's business challenges allows the salesperson to present their product as the perfect solution to those specific challenges.

Beyond just making a sale, knowledge of the customer fosters long-term relationships. Salespeople who remember details about their customers such as past purchases, specific preferences, or even personal details like a customer's birthday, can create a connection that extends beyond the transactional. This kind of relationship-building can lead to repeat business, referrals, and strong customer loyalty.

Modern sales strategies often emphasize a consultative approach, where the salesperson acts more like a trusted advisor than a traditional seller. In this role, the salesperson uses their knowledge to educate the customer, helping them to make informed decisions. This approach is particularly effective in industries where customers may not have a full understanding of the product or service, such as financial services or healthcare. By providing valuable information, the salesperson builds trust, which can be instrumental in securing the sale.

Salespeople who position themselves as thought leaders in their industry can attract customers by sharing their knowledge. This can be done through writing articles, giving presentations, or engaging in industry discussions. By contributing to the knowledge pool, salespeople can build a reputation that precedes them, making it easier to attract and convert leads.

Finally, knowledge is important for overcoming objections. When objections arise, as they often do in sales conversations, knowledge is the key to overcoming them. Whether the objection is related to price, product features, or timing, a well-informed salesperson can address concerns confidently and convincingly. For example, if a customer is worried about the cost, a knowledgeable salesperson might explain the long-term cost savings that justify the initial investment, thus reframing the objection as a benefit.

Knowledge in sales is not just about information; it's about empowerment. It empowers salespeople to engage more effectively with customers, position products more strategically, and build lasting relationships. In today's highly competitive market, where customers are more informed than ever, the salesperson's knowledge can be the differentiator that turns a potential lead into a loyal customer. The more a salesperson knows, the more they can adapt, persuade, and ultimately succeed.

But, like all other tools in the Devil's Dealbook, knowledge has a downside. Too much knowledge can turn you into a salesperson who talks over your clients. Salespeople who are highly knowledgeable may be tempted to share too much information with customers, subsequently overwhelming the customer and making the decision-making process more difficult. A salesperson might dive too deeply into technical details, which could confuse or intimidate a customer who is not familiar with the product or industry. And of course, providing too much information can lead to "paralysis by analysis," where the customer becomes stuck in the decision-making process because they feel they need to consider all the information before making a choice. This can slow down the sales cycle or even lead to the loss of a sale.

IBM has faced challenges with an overly knowledge-driven approach to sales. While IBM's salespeople are experts in technology and can offer in-depth product specifications, the company has struggled with making this knowledge accessible and relevant to its clients. In the past, IBM's sales team have been accused of inundating customers with an overwhelming amount of technical detail, making it difficult for them to see the value of the solution in a simple, understandable way.

A key example of this issue occurred during IBM's push into cloud computing services. Salespeople, highly knowledgeable about cloud technology, would often dive deep into the intricacies of cloud architecture and server configurations. It turned out, customers were more concerned with understanding how IBM's solution could solve their specific business challenges- such as increasing efficiency or cutting costs- rather than the underlying technical specifications. As a result, some customers felt frustrated and overwhelmed, leading to slower sales cycles or even the loss of deals. Too much knowledge, when not communicated effectively, can alienate customers and hurt sales performance.

A salesperson who is extremely knowledgeable might unintentionally come across as arrogant or dismissive, especially if they are overly confident in their expertise. This can create a disconnect with the customer, who may feel belittled or undervalued. For example, if a salesperson corrects a customer too bluntly or dismisses their concerns without properly addressing them, it can damage the relationship. There is also a risk that a knowledgeable salesperson might underestimate the customer's understanding or needs. Assuming that the customer doesn't know as much can lead to oversimplification or failing to address important concerns that the customer might have.

Perhaps, the ugliest side of too much knowledge is the loss of empathy it could produce in some salespeople. You end up focusing too much on facts, figures, and technical details and overlook the emotional aspects of the buying process. Sales often involve more than just rational decision-making; customers also need to feel understood and valued. A salesperson who is too focused on demonstrating their knowledge might miss the opportunity to connect with the customer on a personal level. They might not listen as attentively to the customer's needs, concerns, or pain points. This can lead to a one-sided conversation where the salesperson talks more than they listen, potentially missing key information that could help close the sale.

A knowledgeable salesperson might become too rigid in their approach, relying heavily on their expertise and proven methods rather than adapting to the specific needs of each customer. This can be a problem in dynamic sales environments where flexibility and creativity are needed to respond to unique customer situations or unexpected objections. In fast-moving industries, what a salesperson knows today may be outdated tomorrow. A reliance on established knowledge can lead to complacency, where the salesperson is less motivated to stay up to date on new developments, trends, or innovative solutions. This can make them less competitive in the long run.

Alternatively, they might selectively present information that supports their sales pitch while omitting details that might not be as favorable. This can lead to biased presentations that mislead customers, which can hurt the relationship if the customer feels deceived after the purchase. This breach of trust can have long-term consequences, including negative reviews, diminished customer loyalty, and potential damage to the salesperson's reputation. Transparent and complete communication is crucial to building and maintaining strong, trustworthy relationships with customers.

Finally, relying too much on knowledge can lead to a more transactional approach to sales, where the focus is primarily on the exchange of information rather than building a relationship. While knowledge is important, relationships are often what lead to repeat business, referrals, and long-term success. A salesperson who focuses solely on their expertise might miss opportunities to connect with customers on a deeper level.

6. Empathy

Empathy is defined as the ability to understand and share the feelings of another person. In sales, empathy is not just a nice-to-have, it's a crucial skill that can significantly enhance customer satisfaction and drive higher sales. When you put yourself in the customer's shoes, you can better grasp their needs and concerns, leading to a more personalized experience that exceeds their expectations.

When salespeople demonstrate empathy, they end up building stronger relationships with customers. Empathetic salespeople actively listen to their customers' pain points to understand their desires, and tailor their approach to align with the customer's unique situation. They are able to create an atmosphere of trust and a rapport, making customers feel valued and understood.

Empathy always translates to better sales. This is true with companies and individuals alike. Zappos is renowned for its exceptional customer service, which is rooted in a strong culture of empathy. Their representatives are encouraged to spend as much time as needed on calls, even if it means not making an immediate sale.

For example, it is not uncommon for customers to call seeking advice on shoe size for a specific occasion. Instead of rushing to complete the transaction, a Zappos representative would then engage in a friendly conversation, asking questions about the event and making personalized recommendations. Perhaps this is why Zappos consistently ranks at the top of customer satisfaction surveys. According to the American Customer Satisfaction Index (ACSI), Zappos has maintained a high score (over 80) for years, directly correlating to their empathetic customer service approach. Happy customers lead to increased sales through repeat purchases.

A 2017 study by Zappos revealed that 75% of their customers would recommend the brand to others, largely due to the empathetic customer service they experience. Empathy creates word-of-mouth marketing that is invaluable for driving new sales. It also creates engaged employees who end up offering better customer service. It's a win-win for everyone involved.

Genuine concern for the customer's needs will always foster a high level of loyalty and satisfaction, resulting in repeat business and positive word-of-mouth referrals. During the pandemic, Airbnb showcased empathy by implementing flexible cancellation policies and providing support to hosts facing financial hardships. This responsiveness acknowledged the struggles both guests and hosts were undergoing during an uncertain time.

By prioritizing the well-being of its community, Airbnb reinforced trust and loyalty among its users, which maintained customer relationships and demonstrated that the company genuinely cares about its stakeholders, ultimately enhancing its reputation in a challenging market. No wonder 73% of users felt safe using the platform during the pandemic, largely due to its empathetic measures. High trust translates to higher conversion rates, as customers are more likely to book when they feel secure.

Of course, empathy in sales goes beyond simply making a sale; it's about creating a memorable experience that resonates with customers. When customers feel understood, they are more likely to return and recommend the business to others. Empathetic salespeople can identify underlying motivations that may not be immediately evident, allowing them to address concerns proactively and offer tailored solutions. This increases customer lifetime value. It is only when you are empathetic that you are able to mitigate potential objections to a sale.

However, like with the rest of the tools in the Devil's Dealbook, empathy has a downside. Salespeople who lack empathy may come across as pushy or insensitive, which can alienate potential customers and damage their reputation.

Have you heard stories of some banks which push customers into products that may not meet their needs, such as loans with high fees? They lack empathy. This kind of behavior often stems from sales targets rather than a genuine understanding of the customer's financial situation, leading to distrust and dissatisfaction. It is also a lack of empathy when telemarketing companies use pushy sales tactics, ignoring the preferences and responses of potential customers. For example, repeatedly calling people who have opted out can lead to a sense of annoyance and resentment, damaging the company's reputation.

In some cases, salespeople can take it too far. Comcast, for example, has been criticized for its customer service. Reports of pushy sales tactics and a lack of genuine concern for customer issues have led to negative experiences, such as long waiting times and aggressive upselling, which left customers feeling frustrated and undervalued. When customers call to resolve a simple issue, they are often presented with additional products or services they didn't ask for such as upgraded cable packages or internet services, despite the customer's clear indications that they don't want them. This lack of empathy for the customer's current needs and preferences leads to frustration and makes customers feel unheard and undervalued.

A 2014 survey from the American Customer Satisfaction Index ranked Comcast near the bottom for customer satisfaction, citing its "pushy" and "unhelpful" customer service. The sales tactics, which prioritize company revenue over customer needs, have led to negative customer experiences and significant churn.

Wells Fargo had a similar story. The company was caught in a scandal where employees opened millions of unauthorized accounts for customers in order to meet sales targets. The company's aggressive sales culture pushed employees to cross ethical boundaries, often convincing or pressuring them to sell products customers didn't need, such as credit cards, loans, and savings accounts.

In 2016, it was revealed that Wells Fargo had created over 2 million fake bank accounts, and many customers were unknowingly charged for services they never authorized. The sales tactics used by the bank were not driven by an understanding of the customer's actual needs or desires but by intense pressure to meet sales quotas. This resulted in widespread customer resentment and led to a significant loss of trust in the bank. Wells Fargo was fined $185 million by federal regulators and faced significant reputational damage.

As a salesperson, your role is to figure out how to feel the feelings of others, walk in their shoes for a bit and then recommend products that actually solve their problems. That's using empathy well.

7. Passion

Passion is an essential ingredient for success in sales. It is about loving what you do so much that you would do it for no pay. Studies show that only 40% of sales representatives remain with their company beyond the first year; these are the passionate salespeople, they prevail beyond whatever challenges they meet. Even with top-notch training, employers who are clear about the job's demands and who fully understand a candidate's capabilities, a salesperson without passion will still quit.

Unlike fields such as engineering or accounting, where specific degrees can predict job performance, there's no degree in sales that guarantees success. Simply knowing a product or the sales process doesn't equate to being effective in selling. To truly excel, sales professionals need a unique blend of skills and qualities, and chief among them is passion.

Passion fuels motivation and motivation is a powerful driver in sales. Passionate salespeople are motivated by the desire to achieve financial gain and independence. They are driven by a desire not just to achieve targets, but to connect with customers and create meaningful relationships. This intrinsic motivation often leads to greater success in sales roles.

When people are passionate about what they do, they naturally take initiative. Passionate salespeople are motivated to act, seek opportunities and explore creative solutions to challenges. They are proactive in engaging customers and follow up diligently, which significantly enhances their chances of closing deals. When guided effectively, their passion becomes a catalyst for success.

Passionate salespeople are also able to work well independently, as their enthusiasm drives them to manage all aspects of their role effectively. It is this independence that fosters the development of essential skills, from time management to strategic thinking. Passion creates a solid foundation upon which other talents and abilities can be built, enabling them to adapt and thrive in diverse situations.

Because passion is contagious, you will often find companies like Apple, that are founded on passion, having a culture that encourages passion in its employees and operations. The founder of TOMS, Blake Mycoskie, built the company around a passionate mission of social responsibility— "One for One," where every purchase helps someone in need. Salespeople share this mission with customers, often leading to an emotional connection that goes beyond the transaction. This is the kind of passion for making a difference that has propelled TOMS into a successful brand. As of 2024, TOMS reported revenues of approximately $400 million, and this growth is attributed to the brand's strong mission-driven approach and passionate marketing strategies.

Tesla's sales team embodies a passion for innovation that extends beyond just selling cars, it's about selling a vision for the future of sustainable transportation. Tesla salespeople aren't simply focused on making a sale, they are passionate about the technology, design, and environmental impact of the vehicles. Their enthusiasm is contagious, helping customers feel like they are part of something bigger than just purchasing a car. This passion for pushing the boundaries of electric vehicle technology creates a sense of excitement and loyalty among Tesla's customer base. As a result, many customers return for subsequent models, and Tesla's passionate salespeople often become key ambassadors for the brand. The passion for the product and its mission fosters a deep connection with customers, which drives long-term success and market growth.

As a final example, Patagonia- a leader in outdoor apparel- has built its brand around a passionate commitment to environmental sustainability. Their salespeople are not just selling jackets or backpacks, they are advocating for a lifestyle aligned with environmental responsibility. A customer who enters a Patagonia store is met with passionate employees who can speak deeply about the company's commitment to ethical sourcing, fair labor practices, and reducing the carbon footprint of their products. This passion resonates with customers, making them feel like they're part of a movement. For example, during Patagonia's "Worn Wear" campaign, salespeople actively encouraged customers to buy used gear or repair their existing items, which not only increased sales of secondhand products but also reinforced the brand's values of sustainability. Patagonia's passion for the environment has translated into loyal customers who align with the company's values, resulting in increased sales and an unshakeable brand identity.

On the flipside, passion goes wrong when the salesperson is only driven by the desire to make money. They become sad and stressed with whatever they make because it does not compare with their target goals. Timeshare presentations can exemplify passion taken to an extreme, where salespeople are driven primarily by commissions. The high-pressure tactics used during these presentations often leave potential buyers feeling overwhelmed and manipulated. While the salespeople may be passionate about their product, their focus on closing deals for financial gain often leads to negative customer experiences and high rates of buyer's remorse.

In luxury retail, salespeople will often exhibit a strong passion for the products they sell; in this case, let's consider perfume. This passion can sometimes go too far, leading to a situation where the salesperson's enthusiasm overshadows the customer's preferences. For example, in a high-end perfume boutique, a salesperson might be so passionate about a specific fragrance that they pressure a customer into buying it, even if the customer shows no interest. The salesperson's drive to close the sale, fueled by personal goals or commission, can make the customer feel uncomfortable or manipulated. This overzealousness can result in buyers leaving the store frustrated or making a purchase they later regret, damaging the brand's reputation. In this case, passion becomes counterproductive because the salesperson's emotional investment in the sale doesn't match the customer's needs or desires.

Herbalife, a multi-level marketing (MLM) company known for its nutritional supplements, has long been a polarizing example of how passion can go wrong. Salespeople within Herbalife often exhibit immense passion for the products they sell, driven by personal belief in the brand's health benefits and financial incentives tied to recruitment. However, this passion sometimes leads to aggressive, high-pressure tactics, especially when it comes to recruiting new distributors. Many critics have highlighted that the company's sales force, motivated by commission and the opportunity to recruit others, frequently pushes products on people who don't need them, or even to make exaggerated health claims.

In 2016, Herbalife settled a lawsuit with the U.S. Federal Trade Commission (FTC) for $200 million, agreeing to change its business practices after being accused of operating a pyramid scheme. The passionate salespeople, driven more by the potential to recruit others into the business than by any actual concern for the products or the health of consumers, caused many customers to invest large sums of money into the company. This created financial harm for many individuals who did not achieve the level of success promised to them, illustrating how passion without ethical boundaries and a focus on the customer's true needs can lead to significant harm. The company's sales force, fueled by passion and financial incentives, often crossed ethical lines, leading to widespread dissatisfaction and lawsuits.

The great salesperson is the one who learns how to channel their passion to make sales without sacrificing the relationship. Their passion is supported by other values.

8. Persistence

Every salesperson dreams of that perfect moment— finding the ideal prospect, making a great connection, and sealing the deal in one fantastic meeting. It sounds amazing, right? But the reality is quite different. In fact, studies show that only about 2% of sales actually close after the first meeting. That's a pretty low number.

So, what does this mean for you? It's simple: you need to keep reaching out to that prospect. A couple of calls just won't cut it. You have to stay on their radar until they're ready to buy, you have to persist. If only 2% of deals close in a single meeting, then not following up is a missed opportunity. You haven't really built a relationship or established trust yet; you probably don't know enough about the customer's needs or how your product can help them. That first meeting could've come at a bad time for them, they might have had budget issues, cash flow concerns, or any number of things on their mind that had nothing to do with your offering.

A great salesperson knows that it is about the long game. It might seem like there's a fine line between being persistent and being pushy, but that line is much clearer than you think. Research shows that it often takes about five contacts to close a significant sale. If you give up after one or two meetings, you're not even halfway there. Being persistent isn't just smart; it's necessary. You want to be on the right side of those statistics for your determination and resolve to pay off.

Salesforce, the world's leading CRM provider, offers a prime example of how persistence in sales can pay off, especially in the complex B2B space. One of Salesforce's sales strategies focuses on building strong relationships over time rather than closing a deal in a single meeting. For instance, sales teams at Salesforce are known for their persistence in following up with potential clients, sometimes for months or even years, before securing a deal. This approach is particularly effective in enterprise sales, where decisions often involve multiple stakeholders and long approval processes.

A notable example occurred when Salesforce pursued a large financial institution for nearly two years before closing a multi-million-dollar deal. The prospect initially wasn't ready to buy, but Salesforce continued to provide value through ongoing communication, offering webinars, sharing insights on how their CRM system could improve efficiency, and personalizing their outreach. By the time the company was ready to make a purchase, Salesforce had established itself as a trusted advisor, not just a vendor. The persistence, combined with providing value at every step, helped Salesforce close the deal and solidify a long-term relationship.

Being persistent demonstrates dedication and commitment. There are plenty of ways to stay in touch with a prospect— drop by in person, send a thoughtful note, shoot over an email, or make a quick phone call. Great salespeople know how to mix it up. Where necessary, they go beyond that magic number of five contacts to show the prospect that they genuinely care.

For anyone who wants long-term success, being persistent is non-negotiable. Great salespeople get creative with their outreach and keep their names fresh on the client's mind. They do not let refusals discourage them from pursuing great opportunities. Achieving success in sales takes drive, commitment, and a whole lot of motivation.

When Airbnb was first launched, the company's founders needed to convince people to list their homes on the platform. Early on, Airbnb's salespeople exhibited incredible persistence by constantly reaching out to potential hosts, even in the face of rejection or indifference. The sales team didn't simply make one or two calls; they persisted, showing hosts how Airbnb could offer an alternative to traditional rental models. Over time, Airbnb's salespeople would use follow-ups and personal stories from successful hosts to build trust and demonstrate the value of joining the platform. This persistence, combined with personalized outreach and education, allowed Airbnb to build its host base and become the global phenomenon it is today. Airbnb's early success shows that persistence in sales can be powerful when coupled with understanding the customers' needs and delivering value over time.

Persistence stops being useful when it becomes stalking and thoughtless pushiness. While it's important to follow up and stay engaged, there's a fine line between being persistent and being overly aggressive.

When you start bombarding a prospect with constant calls, emails, and messages without any regard for their responses or cues, you risk coming across as a nuisance. If a prospect has clearly indicated they're not interested or need more time, continuing to push can make you seem desperate or inconsiderate. This not only damages your reputation but also can turn potential clients away for good.

One of the most infamous cases of persistence gone wrong occurred with Dish Network, a satellite TV provider. In the mid-2000s, Dish Network became notorious for its aggressive telemarketing tactics. The company employed persistent calls, often multiple times a day, to potential customers, sometimes for months at a time. Even if a prospect expressed disinterest, the sales team would continue to push, not respecting the prospect's boundaries. In some cases, Dish Network even continued calling people who had requested to be removed from their calling lists.

The persistence of Dish's telemarketers, driven by sales targets, ultimately led to widespread customer frustration, complaints, and damaged reputation. In 2017, the company paid a record $280 million fine to settle a case with the Federal Communications Commission (FCC) related to these practices. While persistence is valuable in sales, Dish Network's example illustrates the downside of pursuing prospects without regard for their boundaries. Their lack of thoughtfulness and respect turned what should have been a sales strategy into a customer relations nightmare. It highlights the fine line between persistence and pushiness.

Thoughtful persistence means understanding when to back off. It's about respecting the prospect's time and space while still showing your interest. If you're not reading the room and adjusting your approach, your persistence can be perceived as pushy. Instead of building rapport, you could be creating resentment. To keep your persistence effective, focus on being strategic and considerate. Make sure each follow-up adds value, whether it's sharing helpful information, answering questions, or simply checking in to see how they're doing. This way, you show that you care about their needs rather than just pushing for a sale.

Early in its history, CarMax- a used car retailer- faced significant challenges in how it approached customers. CarMax is now known for offering a no-haggle, customer-friendly car buying experience. However, before the company refined its approach, some of its salespeople used overly persistent tactics that bordered on the aggressive side. Salespeople were driven by commission, and while they were taught to follow up with customers, many took this advice to an extreme. For example, sales staff would call customers repeatedly, sometimes several times a week, even after the customer had expressed no interest in buying a car. This type of persistence often led to negative customer experiences, where potential buyers felt harassed and manipulated into making a decision they weren't comfortable with. Over time, CarMax recognized that this persistence was driving customers away rather than building relationships. The company shifted to a more respectful, thoughtful approach to persistence, focusing on delivering value rather than just pushing for a sale. Imagine what could have happened if they didn't make the shift.

Ultimately, the goal of persistence should be to build relationships. When prospects feel valued and respected, they are much more likely to consider your offerings. So, remember: persistence is only beneficial when it's paired with thoughtfulness and respect for your prospect's boundaries. Striking that balance is necessary to turn persistence into a powerful tool for success, rather than a source of annoyance.

9. Technology and Social Media

Technology and social media are powerful tools that can significantly enhance sales efforts by expanding reach and providing a wealth of information. When used effectively, they offer unparalleled opportunities for generating leads, building relationships, and maintaining customer engagement. However, this abundance of information can sometimes become overwhelming, and when these tools are misused or wielded with harmful intentions, they can lead to detrimental effects, such as spreading misinformation or engaging in unethical practices. The challenge lies in balancing the advantages of broader reach and deeper insights with the need for integrity and responsible use.

According to HubSpot, as of 2024, approximately 54% of B2B marketers have reported using social media to generate leads. Social media platforms such as LinkedIn, Facebook, and Twitter, are particularly effective for this purpose. Companies like HubSpot and Salesforce use targeted social media campaigns and advanced analytics to identify potential leads and engage with them. For instance, LinkedIn's Sales Navigator tool helps sales professionals find and connect with potential clients based on detailed filters and engagement metrics.

A study by Sprout Social found that 77% of consumers are more likely to make a purchase from a brand they follow on social media, which further demonstrates the power of social media in nurturing customer relationships and driving sales. Starbucks leverages social media to build a community around its brand. Through interactive campaigns, user-generated content, and personalized responses, Starbucks maintains a strong connection with its customers, which in turn drives loyalty and repeat business.

Social media is also useful for maintaining contact with people you have formed relationships with to keep nurturing those relationships. Email marketing remains one of the most effective channels for maintaining contact with customers, with a reported ROI of $36 for every $1 spent, according to Litmus. Companies like Amazon use automated email campaigns to keep customers informed about new products, special offers, and order updates. This consistent communication helps maintain customer engagement and drives repeat purchases.

However the downsides of technology and social media are also glaring. It has often been used to spread misinformation. According to a study published in *Science* (2018), false information spreads significantly faster and wider on social media than true information, with misinformation 70% more likely to be shared. During the COVID-19 pandemic, misinformation about vaccines and treatments spread rapidly on social media platforms leading to confusion and public health risks. The spread of false claims undermined trust in health authorities and exacerbated the pandemic's impact.

A 2023 survey by the Better Business Bureau (BBB) found that 42% of consumers experienced deceptive or aggressive sales tactics through social media and online platforms. Multi-level marketing

(MLM) companies, such as those discussed earlier, often use social media to recruit new members by making exaggerated income claims. For instance, companies like Vemma and Herbalife have faced scrutiny and legal challenges for promoting business models that heavily emphasize recruitment over actual product sales, leading to widespread financial losses for participants.

As if that is not enough, there are numerous privacy violations attached to the use of social media. According to a 2024 report by Statista, 53% of internet users are concerned about their data privacy on social media platforms. The Facebook-Cambridge Analytica scandal of 2018 discussed earlier highlighted severe privacy issues, particularly around the use of personal data, which in this case was used to influence political campaigns, raising serious concerns about data misuse.

Imagine how harmful that is juxtaposed with the knowledge that people are spending more time on social media now than anything else. Social media platforms are designed to be captivating and engaging; algorithms tailor content to individual preferences, ensuring that users are continually presented with posts, images, and videos that align with their interests. This personalized feed creates a dopamine-driven feedback loop, where each notification, like, or comment provides a small but significant reward to the brain. The result is a cycle of instant gratification that can be incredibly addictive.

Research has shown that social media triggers the same brain areas as gambling and substance abuse, reinforcing the addictive nature of these platforms. The constant influx of new content and the need for social validation can make it difficult for users to disconnect, leading to prolonged usage and a compulsion to check devices frequently. This addiction can be especially pronounced in children and adolescents, whose developing brains are particularly sensitive to these reward mechanisms.

The rise of social media has coincided with a dramatic increase in screen time among children and teenagers. Studies have reported that the average teen spends several hours a day on social media, often exceeding the amount of time spent on other activities such as studying, exercising, or engaging in face-to-face interactions. It is as though social media is a new highly addictive drug. This trend is concerning for several reasons.

Firstly, excessive screen time can lead to physical health issues. Prolonged device use is associated with poor posture, eye strain, and disrupted sleep patterns. Many children and teenagers report difficulty falling asleep due to the blue light emitted by screens, which interferes with the production of melatonin, the hormone responsible for regulating sleep.

Secondly, the mental health implications are significant. Research has linked heavy social media use with increased rates of anxiety, depression, and low self-esteem. Social media platforms often present an idealized version of reality, leading users to compare themselves unfavorably to others. This constant comparison can erode self-confidence and contribute to mental health struggles.

The dangers of social media addiction extend beyond individual health issues. One major concern is the impact on social skills and interpersonal relationships. As children and teenagers spend more time interacting with screens rather than people, they may struggle with face-to-face communication and empathy. The superficial nature of online interactions can replace meaningful conversations, leading to weakened social bonds and a diminished ability to navigate real-world social situations.

Finally, social media and technology increase the risk of cyberbullying and harassment. The Cyberbullying Research Center reported in 2023 that approximately 37% of teenagers have experienced cyberbullying, and 40% of adults have encountered online harassment. Social media platforms like Twitter and Instagram have faced criticism for inadequate measures to prevent and address cyberbullying. High-profile cases, such as the harassment of public figures and influencers, demonstrate how technology can be misused to harm individuals both personally and professionally.

Technology and social media offer powerful tools for advancing sales and marketing strategies, generating leads, and fostering customer relationships. Salespeople that harness these tools effectively can achieve significant growth and customer loyalty. However, when these tools are misused, they can contribute to the spread of misinformation, unethical sales practices, privacy violations, and online harassment. It is crucial for us as salespeople to use technology and social media responsibly, adhering to ethical practices and safeguarding personal and professional integrity.

Key Takeaways

- Ethical influence (persuasion) builds trust and creates genuine connections, but its flipside, manipulation, can undo all the good work you've done.
- It pays to be confident because it drives calculated risks, but hubris will often result in deceptive messages or overpromising.

- Ambition drives excellence and growth, but unchecked it can lead to the use of illegal tactics to make sales.
- Your networks should support relationships, opportunities and collaborations rather than enable unethical practices and exploit connections only for personal gain.
- Knowledge is great, but too much knowledge, especially wielded by a salesperson without self-awareness, can take away empathy and interrupt relationship building.
- Social media has a lot of power to streamline the sales process, but in the wrong hands, it can cause a lot of damage.
- A great salesperson knows how to use their empathy, persistence and passion together, without being pushy and inconsiderate.

CHAPTER 2

THE DEVIL'S DEALBOOK CAN BRING THE DEVIL'S RESULTS

"I am not what happened to me. I am what I choose to become".
–Carl Jung.

There is an age-old question about nature vs. nurture. Some people argue that our innate qualities and natural talents define who we are and how we perform. Others contend that our experiences, upbringing, and the environment in which we live are more decisive in shaping our character and abilities. I think both nature and nurture have a role to play in shaping us. This chapter is about the influence of nurture.

We will explore a fundamental truth about personal and professional development: the environment in which you are raised and live has a profound impact on how you navigate the world, including how you engage with the tools and resources available to you. From the formative experiences of your childhood to the everyday interactions and societal norms you encounter, your surroundings play a crucial role in shaping your behavior, values, and identity.

In sales, this influence is particularly significant. Your environment molds not only your approach to using tools in the Devil's Dealbook but also how you interact with clients, manage relationships, and seize opportunities. Whether it's the values instilled in you by your family, the daily routines you follow, or the broader societal context in which you operate, each aspect of your environment affects how you apply your skills and navigate the sales landscape.

You will see that even though your environment shapes you, you have a role to play in the way it does. As Carl Jung once said, "I am not what happened to me. I am what I choose to become."

While your environment undoubtedly shapes who you are, it is ultimately your choices that define your success in sales. This chapter will help look at what influences you and see how you can leverage that to enhance your sales strategies and drive your success.

Your Upbringing as the Foundation of Values

Your upbringing is the bedrock upon which your values and behaviors are built, and these foundational elements play a critical role in shaping your career in sales. The family background, cultural traditions, and early education you experienced will all have contributed significantly to how you approach sales, interact with clients, and utilize sales strategies.

Consider the example of someone who grew up in a family that placed a strong emphasis on education and discipline. Such a person is likely to carry forward a high value for hard work and perseverance into their sales career. This background fosters a robust work ethic and a commitment to personal growth, which are crucial in the competitive field of sales. The discipline learned in childhood can translate into meticulous preparation for sales pitches, a consistent follow-up with prospects, and a dedicated effort to meet and exceed sales targets.

On the other hand, people raised in environments where resources were scarce or support was limited might develop a different set of values. For instance, a person who grew up facing financial hardships might enter sales as a way to escape poverty and improve their economic situation. This survival instinct can translate into a high level of motivation and determination. They might approach sales with a keen sense of urgency and a focus on achieving immediate results, driven by a personal need for financial stability.

Not only that, but cultural traditions and familial values also play a crucial role in shaping your sales approach. In many cultures, respect for elders and the importance of maintaining strong family ties are deeply ingrained. For example, someone from a culture where familial respect is paramount might approach client relationships with a higher degree of respect and consideration. They may prioritize building strong, long-term relationships with clients, valuing trust and mutual respect over transactional interactions. In contrast, a person from a culture that emphasizes individual achievement and independence might focus more on results-driven sales strategies. They might excel in competitive environments where personal performance and individual goals are highlighted.

Your early environment also teaches you how to navigate emotions and express interpersonal values. Sales is not just about pushing products; it's also about understanding and responding to the emotional needs of clients. If you were raised in an environment that emphasized empathy and emotional intelligence, you might excel in identifying client pain points and providing solutions that address their needs effectively. These early lessons in emotional expression and relationship management can translate into a sales approach that prioritizes active listening and personalized solutions. By drawing on your experiences of how emotions were managed and relationships were handled in your formative years, you can build stronger connections with clients and foster a more collaborative sales environment.

Let's bring it closer home. If you grew up in a slum, you may think of money and sales as a way to get out of poverty. Your experiences would have likely ingrained in you a sense that economic success is a primary route out of poverty. The harsh realities of living in impoverished conditions— limited access to quality education, inadequate healthcare, and scarcity of resources— can shape your worldview and drive your ambitions. For many, the aspiration to achieve financial stability becomes a powerful motivator.

This focus on money and sales is not just a personal inclination but also a practical response to the environment you were raised in. According to a study by the World Bank, people who grow up in low-income settings are significantly more likely to view economic success as a critical means of improving their lives. The research highlights that people from impoverished backgrounds often see financial success not only as a personal goal, but as a crucial step toward achieving broader social mobility and improving their communities.

The statistics support this connection between childhood environment and economic aspirations. Data from the Pew Research Center reveals that children from low-income families are less likely to attain higher education and experience upward economic mobility, compared to their peers from wealthier backgrounds. For instance, a 2018 report by the Brookings Institution found that only 14% of children from low-income families in the United States achieve the top income quintile as adults, compared to 42% of those from high-income families.

On the other hand, if you grew up in a financially stable household, your view of life and sales would be different. The stability and abundance of resources contribute to a different set of priorities and attitudes compared to those growing up in financial hardship. For starters, financial stability provides a foundation of security that allows for a broader range of experiences and opportunities. This stability often translates into access to quality education, extracurricular activities, and exposure to diverse fields of interest. You are more likely to attend college and complete higher education, achievements which open doors to various career paths and influences.

Without a doubt, your history will influence your story, but it does not have to define it in ways that are not life affirming.

Take a moment to think about it: in what ways has your upbringing shaped the way you do sales? What values do you embody that you think you carried along from your upbringing?

Remember that reflecting on your upbringing and early experiences is not about dwelling on past grievances but about recognizing how these factors influence your current behavior and sales strategies. Understanding your origins helps you identify why you might excel in certain aspects of sales or struggle with particular challenges. This self-awareness can lead to improved sales techniques and more effective client interactions.

Your upbringing is more than just a backdrop to your life; it is a powerful influence that shapes your values, behaviors, and approach to sales. By examining how your family background, cultural traditions, and early education have molded you, you gain valuable insights into your sales practices and professional growth.

Family Dynamics – Their Influence and Support

Family dynamics also play a pivotal role in shaping your personal development and influencing how you approach your career in sales. The presence, behavior, and values of family members can profoundly impact your ambitions, resource utilization, and professional conduct. Whether your family fosters a supportive environment or presents challenges, these dynamics affect how you engage with tools and opportunities in your sales career. Additionally, the nuances of your personal life such as being married, single, or having children, add further layers to how family dynamics influence your sales approach.

A supportive family can be a significant asset in your career development, particularly in sales, where motivation, skill development, and personal growth are crucial. Research has shown that family support is closely linked to professional success. According to a study published in the *Journal of Vocational Behavior*, people with strong family support systems are more likely to experience career satisfaction and achieve their professional goals. For example, if your family encourages you to pursue higher education and career development, they provide you with the confidence and resources necessary to excel in sales. This support might include financial assistance for education, emotional encouragement during challenging times, or practical advice on career strategies. A salesperson with a strong support system is more likely to seek advanced training, adopt innovative sales techniques, and maintain resilience in the face of setbacks.

Families that promote a growth mindset— believing that abilities and intelligence can be developed through dedication and hard work— instill in their members a drive to continually improve and achieve. In sales, this mindset translates into a willingness to learn new skills, adapt to changing market conditions, and persevere through challenges. Sales professionals who live in such environments might be more open to adopting new technologies, attending industry seminars, and pursuing professional certifications, leading to greater success in their careers.

Conversely, negative family dynamics or a lack of support can pose significant barriers to personal development and career success. People who live in family environments marked by conflict, instability, or discouragement might face difficulties in using their skills and resources effectively. A lack of familial encouragement can undermine your motivation and self-confidence. In sales, this could manifest as a reluctance to take on challenging sales targets, a lack of initiative in pursuing new opportunities, or difficulties in building client relationships. Without a supportive foundation, you might struggle to develop the resilience needed to succeed in a high-pressure sales environment.

Negative family dynamics can also impact how you manage resources and make decisions. For instance, if financial instability or family conflicts limit your access to professional development resources, such as training programs or networking opportunities, it can hinder your growth in sales.

The dynamics of your personal life, including whether you are married, single, or have children, also shape your approach to sales and influence how you navigate your career. Married salespeople might face different challenges and advantages compared to their single counterparts. Married people might experience additional responsibilities, such as balancing family commitments with work obligations. In sales, this can impact time management, work-life balance, and the ability to travel or attend networking events.

On the flip side, having a supportive spouse can provide emotional and practical support, helping to alleviate some of these pressures. A study by the University of Michigan found that spouses who provide encouragement and share responsibilities can contribute to higher job satisfaction and career success.

When children are introduced into the picture, it adds another layer. Salespeople with children face unique challenges, such as managing time between family and work commitments, and addressing the financial needs of their families. This can affect their ability to focus on sales goals, engage with clients, and maintain productivity if they are not careful. However, parents might also benefit from enhanced time management skills and a strong sense of responsibility, which can translate into effective sales strategies.

Single salespeople might have more flexibility to dedicate time and energy to their careers. They might be able to travel more frequently, attend networking events, and pursue professional development opportunities with fewer personal constraints. This flexibility can provide a competitive edge in a sales career, allowing for greater focus on achieving sales targets and building client relationships.

Your Daily Life and Routines Play a Role

Your daily life and routines have a profound impact on how you use the tools in the Devil's Dealbook, approach challenges, and ultimately navigate your career in sales. The environment in which you live, whether it's a bustling urban center or a tranquil rural area, profoundly influences the skills you develop, the tools you use, and the strategies you adopt.

Living in a bustling urban environment versus a rural setting creates different opportunities and challenges that shape how you approach sales, and research highlights these differences vividly. Urban dwellers often encounter fast-paced environments that necessitate quick decision-making and adaptability. According to a study by the Pew Research Center, urban residents tend to have higher levels of technology use and digital literacy compared to their rural counterparts. In cities, access to cutting-edge technology and the need to stay ahead in a competitive market foster skills in digital tools, social media, and data analytics.

For instance, sales professionals in urban areas might leverage advanced CRM systems, utilize data for market analysis, and employ digital marketing techniques to reach potential clients. The familiarity with technology in urban settings can lead to more innovative and efficient sales strategies. Research shows that 73% of high-performing sales teams in urban areas use advanced analytics and technology compared to only 47% in rural settings (HubSpot, 2022). This technological edge often translates into enhanced productivity and greater success in sales.

On the other hand, rural residents often develop strong practical skills due to their direct engagement with their environment. A study by the University of Nebraska found that people in rural areas often cultivate resourcefulness and problem-solving skills as they work with limited resources and infrastructure (Smith, 2019). These skills can be invaluable in sales, where creativity and adaptability can help in overcoming obstacles and finding unique solutions for clients.

A salesperson from a rural background might excel in personalized customer service, using a deep understanding of their community and practical problem-solving skills to build strong, trust-based relationships with clients. The hands-on approach developed in rural settings can lead to a more grounded and empathetic sales strategy.

What is more, the daily interactions and the societal norms you are exposed to further shape how you use today's sales tools and prioritize your goals. In countries with high levels of technological advancement, such as the United States or South Korea, there is a strong emphasis on utilizing technology to enhance productivity and creativity. A report by McKinsey & Company highlights that businesses in technologically advanced regions are 50% more likely to adopt digital tools and innovative practices (McKinsey, 2020). This widespread use of technology allows sales professionals to implement sophisticated tools for customer relationship management, automate repetitive tasks, and analyze data for better decision-making.

For instance, sales professionals in tech-savvy environments may use artificial intelligence-driven sales tools to predict customer behavior, optimize pricing strategies, and tailor sales pitches to individual needs. This integration of technology can significantly increase efficiency and effectiveness in sales processes.

Conversely, in areas with limited access to technology, people often rely on more traditional or resourceful methods. According to a study by the International Telecommunication Union (ITU), rural areas in developing countries have lower rates of internet access and technological adoption (ITU, 2021). In such environments, sales strategies might focus more on direct, personal interactions and face-to-face communication. Sales professionals in these settings might excel in relationship-building skills, relying on word-of-mouth referrals and community networks to generate leads and close sales. Their resourcefulness and ability to work with what's available can lead to innovative sales techniques that do not depend heavily on digital tools.

The influence of your daily environment gets more detailed than whether or not you live in an urban area. The companies you work with, the industry in which you work, the people you interact with every day, all say something to the kind of salesperson you are.

The culture of the company you work for plays a pivotal role in defining your sales approach and professional behavior. Company culture encompasses the values, norms, and practices that dictate how employees interact, make decisions, and conduct their work. Research shows that organizational culture significantly influences employee performance and job satisfaction. According to a study by Deloitte, organizations with a strong, positive culture experience 30% higher employee engagement and 40% higher job satisfaction (Deloitte, 2019).

For instance, if you work for a company that emphasizes aggressive sales tactics and high-pressure strategies, you might adopt these methods in your own sales approach. This environment can foster a competitive mindset and a focus on closing deals quickly. On the other hand, if your company values relationship-building and consultative selling, you are likely to develop skills in understanding client needs, offering personalized solutions, and building long-term partnerships.

The level of collaboration and support within your company also impacts on your sales performance. A company that fosters a collaborative environment where sales teams share knowledge and strategies can enhance your effectiveness.

The industry in which you work significantly affects your sales approach, strategies, and priorities. Different industries have unique characteristics, market dynamics, and customer expectations that shape how sales are conducted. For example, the tech industry often emphasizes rapid innovation, cutting-edge solutions, and technical expertise. Sales professionals in tech might need to stay updated with the latest advancements and be adept at explaining complex products. According to a report by Gartner, 75% of tech buyers prefer working with salespeople who understand their industry's challenges and offer tailored solutions (Gartner, 2020). This requires salespeople to continuously adapt and educate themselves about industry trends and technological developments.

In contrast, industries such as finance or healthcare are heavily regulated, and sales strategies must adhere to strict compliance and ethical standards. Sales professionals in these sectors must be well-versed in legal requirements and industry regulations. For example, the Financial Industry Regulatory Authority (FINRA) mandates specific compliance practices for financial sales professionals to prevent unethical practices and ensure transparency (FINRA, 2022). This regulatory environment shapes how salespeople approach their work and interact with clients.

Finally, the people you interact with daily, including colleagues, clients, and mentors, have a significant impact on your development as a salesperson. Your network provides feedback, support, and opportunities for growth, influencing your approach and performance.

Mentors and colleagues can offer valuable insights and guidance, shaping your sales strategies and professional behavior. Research from the Harvard Business Review indicates that employees with strong mentorship relationships are more likely to advance in their careers and achieve higher job satisfaction (HBR, 2018).

Your interactions with clients also shape your sales practices. Regular feedback from clients can reveal what works well and what needs improvement. For instance, if clients frequently express a preference for personalized service, you might focus on developing a more tailored approach.

The intricate details of your daily environment—from your company's culture and industry dynamics to your interactions and networking—play a crucial role in shaping your identity as a salesperson.

Cultural and Social Influences

The broader societal context, such as encompassing cultural norms, economic conditions, and social structures, also profoundly shapes how you are as a salesperson. This influence manifests in various ways, from how societal values dictate the approach to sales strategies, to the expectations placed on sales professionals by their cultural and social environments.

Societies with robust social safety nets and supportive community structures often foster environments where people leverage their skills for communal benefits. This can lead to an emphasis on social entrepreneurship and community service, where the focus is on creating value for the collective rather than solely for individual gain. An example of this is in Sweden and Denmark. Social entrepreneurs develop ventures aimed at addressing social issues and improving community welfare. Research from the *European Journal of Social Innovation* shows that social entrepreneurship is particularly prevalent in environments where there is strong community support and a focus on social impact.

In contrast, societies characterized by individualism- such as the United States- often emphasize personal success and self-reliance. This cultural orientation encourages people to pursue their own goals and ambitions, which can influence how they approach their careers and use their resources. In individualistic cultures, there is typically a greater focus on personal achievement and self-expression, which can lead to highly competitive sales environments where personal performance is closely linked to career advancement.

What's more, the cultural orientation of a society often dictates whether individuals prioritize collective well-being or personal gain, affecting their approach to professional opportunities and interactions. In collectivist cultures, where community and family are highly valued, people often prioritize actions that benefit the group over personal achievement. For example, in East Asian cultures such as Japan and China, there is a strong emphasis on harmony, respect for others, and group cohesion. This cultural orientation can influence how people in these societies approach their sales careers. Sales professionals in collectivist cultures might focus on building strong relationships with clients, fostering team collaboration, and contributing to the success of their organization as a whole.

As you move across cultures, and as the internet continues changing the nature of sales teams, we are continually encountering multicultural environments. When working in multicultural or international sales environments, it's crucial to adapt your approach to align with the cultural values and societal norms of your target audience. Whatever the case, recognizing and adapting to the cultural values and societal norms of your environment can make you more effective- or not- depending on you.

Your Environment Creates You

I often find myself reflecting on a crucial question: "Is my environment helping me advance or holding me back?" It's a question that, despite its importance, is often overlooked. As you have seen, our surroundings have a profound impact on how we think, feel, and act. They are not merely backdrops to our lives but active players in shaping our experiences and outcomes.

Consider the familiar saying, "you are the average of the five people you spend the most time with," often attributed to motivational speaker Jim Rohn. This idea underscores a powerful truth: the people we surround ourselves with significantly influence our trajectories. If you don't consciously evaluate and curate these influences, negative or limiting factors can subtly seep into your life, shaping your behavior and mindset in ways you might not even notice.

Your environment, comprising the people you interact with, the places you frequent, and the daily routines you follow, mirrors your internal state. If you want to change your life results, you must begin by understanding and managing this internal landscape. You have control over which influences you allow into your mind. When you don't actively manage these inputs, you risk becoming ensnared in repetitive patterns, feeling as though you're a victim of your circumstances.

As Napoleon Hill wisely stated, "without doubt, the most common weakness of all human beings is the habit of leaving their minds open to the negative influence of others." The energy you focus on dictates your path. What you concentrate on expands and grows, influencing your decisions, behaviors, and ultimately, your success.

Yet, beyond the tangible aspects of your environment, there is an elusive element— the *je ne sais quoi*— an indescribable drive within you that defies explanation. It might be the energy from the universe, a deep-seated passion, or an inner spark that propels you forward. This unique force is part of your environment, shaping your experiences and interactions in ways that are both profound and mysterious.

Take a moment to evaluate your current environment — the company you work for, the industry you're part of, and the clients you interact with. How are you letting them shape you?

A common thread I have seen among salespeople is that we let our environment steer us toward making sales all about money. This shift often occurs because the prevailing culture prioritizes profit over people, driving sales professionals to adopt tactics that might yield short-term results but damage their reputation and effectiveness in the long run.

Riches to Rags

The thing with many of us salespeople is that life hands us a hunger for success which makes it that we succeed at nearly everything that we do. We are often driven by the desire to get rich; we want to retire early and live out our golden years enjoying our money. But we fail to consider whether that's truly the idea of success we want for ourselves, or is a product of the influences around us.

I often tell people not to think of retirement as is traditionally portrayed in the media when planning their money. Just think about the way it happens in our society. You start saving for retirement many years before with the promise of travelling and sunning yourself on exotic beaches. Your only drive when working, and more specifically in sales, is to make as much money as possible so that you can make this a reality. But do you know how many rich people there are in the world? A snapshot of the global population of 8.2 billion people in 2024 proves the following statistics to be true.

- 2,755 billionaires - 0.00003487% of the world population
- 56.1 million millionaires - 0.710% of the world population
- 3.6 billion people living on less than $5.50 a day - 45.56%

That leaves the rest at 53.73%, all trying to be 'rich'! The world is driven, to its detriment, by an affliction few are willing to admit. Even the poorest of the poor are caught up in it and would never be satisfied, even if they came into a pile of cash by some stroke of luck.

The story with many salespeople, driven only by the desire to get rich, has been that their hunger for success (which is a good thing) drives them to succeed for a while, only to trip them over. It's the classic story of riches to rags. I could fill this book with sad 'Riches to Rags' stories from the daily shocks of the mighty who fall from grace, ending up in the poor house because of what too much money has done to them.

Think men like Jordan Belfort. Jordan Belfort, infamously dubbed the "Wolf of Wall Street," initially gained prominence in the 1990s as the founder of Stratton Oakmont, a brokerage firm that became notorious for its unethical and illegal practices. His firm specialized in pump-and-dump schemes, where they would artificially inflate the price of stocks through aggressive and deceptive sales tactics, only to then sell off their own shares at the inflated prices, leaving investors with worthless stocks.

Belfort's meteoric rise in the financial world was fueled by a combination of charisma, high-pressure sales tactics, and a blatant disregard for regulatory compliance. He was using the tools in the Devil's Dealbook for evil. His lifestyle reflected his success and excess— lavish parties, expensive cars, and a seemingly endless flow of money. This extravagant lifestyle was part of what attracted the attention of both the public and regulatory authorities.

Stratton Oakmont's operations eventually caught the attention of the Securities and Exchange Commission (SEC) and the Federal Bureau of Investigation (FBI). The investigations revealed a wide array of financial crimes, including securities fraud and money laundering. In 1999, Belfort pleaded guilty to charges of securities fraud and money laundering. He was sentenced to four years in prison but served about 22 months of his sentence before being released in 2004. In addition to his prison term, he was ordered to pay $110.4 million in restitution to the defrauded investors. His financial empire crumbled and he was left in a dire financial situation, far from the lavish lifestyle he once enjoyed.

Vijay Mallya had a similar story. Once celebrated as the "King of Good Times," Vijay Mallya was a prominent Indian businessman and the owner of Kingfisher Airlines. His rise to fame was marked by his extravagant lifestyle and a series of high-profile ventures. As the chairman of the United Breweries Group, Mallya was well-known for transforming the company into a global powerhouse in the alcoholic beverage industry, particularly with his flagship brand, Kingfisher Beer. His success in the beer business allowed him to branch out into other ventures, including the ambitious but ultimately troubled Kingfisher Airlines.

Launched in 2005, Kingfisher Airlines was Mallya's attempt to dominate the Indian aviation market. The airline was initially celebrated for its luxury and innovative services, embodying the high-flying image that Mallya had cultivated. However, despite the initial glamor and enthusiasm, the airline struggled with financial stability from the outset. Kingfisher Airlines faced a series of operational challenges, including a lack of funds, regulatory issues, and rising operational costs.

Mallya's financial troubles were compounded by his other ventures, which began to falter. The lavish lifestyle he was known for, including high-end parties, luxury yachts, and expensive properties, did little to help the situation. His once-thriving empire began to crumble under the weight of massive debts. The United Breweries Group itself was not immune to these financial strains, as Mallya struggled to manage and sustain his various investments.

By 2016, the financial strain became unbearable. Kingfisher Airlines ceased operations, and the company's debt load became a pressing concern. Mallya faced mounting pressure from creditors and financial institutions seeking to recover unpaid loans and outstanding dues. The Indian banking sector, reeling from the defaulted loans, pushed for legal action against him. In April 2016, facing intense scrutiny and legal challenges, Mallya fled India. He sought refuge in the United Kingdom, where he continued to face a series of legal battles. His departure from India was not just about evading financial creditors, but also about avoiding legal prosecution for alleged financial crimes including fraud and money laundering.

There are countless examples of people like this. There are even examples of stars who follow this trend - rock stars, film stars and sports stars who end up broke and addicted to drugs or alcohol or overdosed and dead. Charlie Sheen, who made it big as the star of Two and a Half Men, revealed his HIV-positive status in 2017. His ex-girlfriend slammed him with a lawsuit for exposing her to the disease that cost him a fortune. The death- knell came when Sheen had to pay nearly $5 million in unpaid taxes.

Oscar-winning Kim Basinger was one of the most successful Hollywood actresses in the 1990s, starring box office toppers like Batman, 8 Mile, and The Natural. Besides her movie fame, Basinger rose to fame through a scandalous lawsuit in the early 1990s when she pulled out of the controversial film Boxing Helena. The studio sued for her refusal to appear and walked away with $8.1 million, forcing her to file for bankruptcy protection. The once successful actress has unsuccessfully tried to claw her way back into the movies after making one poor decision because she thought she was bigger than the movie industry.

Mike Tyson became the youngest heavyweight boxing champion in history at age 20 in 1986. Throughout the late 1980s and early 1990s, he earned hundreds of millions of dollars from boxing purses, endorsements, and other ventures, but his downfall began with personal and legal troubles. He was convicted of rape in 1992 and served three years in prison. During this time, he spent lavishly on cars, mansions, and extravagant items. His financial advisors mismanaged his money, and by the early 2000s, Tyson was reportedly $23 million in debt. He filed for bankruptcy in 2003, with his financial difficulties exacerbated by continued legal issues and lavish spending habits.

Johnny Depp achieved worldwide fame and financial success through roles in blockbuster films such as "Pirates of the Caribbean," "Edward Scissorhands," and "Charlie and the Chocolate Factory." He earned tens of millions of dollars per film and was one of Hollywood's highest-paid actors. Depp's financial troubles became public in the mid-2010s. Despite earning vast sums, he faced significant financial strain due to extravagant spending habits. Reports surfaced of Depp spending $30,000 a month on wine, millions on private islands and art collections, and facing legal battles with former managers over mismanagement of his finances. In 2017, Depp sued his management company claiming financial mismanagement that left him facing debts and potential foreclosure on several properties. His lavish lifestyle and legal battles contributed to a decline in his financial stability, despite his previous earnings.

What was happening with them and what does it have to do with you as a salesperson? How can we learn from these stories?

The Law of Marginal Productivity

Imagine this situation: you're in sales, and at the beginning, every extra bit of effort you put in— like making more calls, meeting more clients, or refining your pitch— yields impressive results. You're building relationships, closing deals, and everything's looking up. This is the sweet spot where each additional hour or dollar spent on improving your sales strategy brings a noticeable boost in returns. This is what we'd call the law of marginal productivity in action: the more you put in, the more you get out, and it feels like you're on a winning streak.

But here's where things start to get tricky. As you continue to push harder, striving to do even more to get that same increase in sales, you might notice that the additional benefits aren't as great as they once were. Maybe your efforts start to feel like they're not paying off as much as they used to. This is a classic example of what's known as the principle of diminishing returns, or the law of diminishing marginal productivity.

In simpler terms, there's a point where more input— whether it's time, money, or effort— results in progressively smaller gains. Let's say you're pouring money into new marketing strategies or hiring more staff. At first, these investments yield great returns, but eventually, each new dollar or hour invested starts to bring in less and less additional revenue. You've hit a threshold where the efficiency of adding more input starts to wane.

So, what happens if you ignore this tipping point and keep pushing for more? Well, you might start experiencing diminishing results and eventually, even negative returns. Let's say you start getting a bit greedy with your newfound success, splurging on luxuries or expanding your lifestyle beyond what your increased earnings can support. This can lead to financial strain and stress, which might impact your performance and relationships negatively. You're essentially running into the law of diminishing returns, not just in your business, but in your personal life too.

This threshold, or "optimal result," is where you've maximized your efficiency with the resources you have. Beyond this point, merely increasing the input (like working more hours or spending more money) won't sustain the same level of output. To keep growing and achieving, you need to rethink your approach and perhaps expand or restructure your entire system, whether that means improving your strategies, diversifying your methods, or scaling your operations effectively.

In essence, understanding and applying the law of marginal productivity means recognizing that while initial efforts bring great rewards, there's a point where more of the same just won't cut it. It's about finding that balance between effort and reward and knowing when to pivot or adjust your strategy to keep thriving without falling into the trap of diminishing returns.

Key Takeaways

- Your upbringing shapes your values, which dictate how you use the tools in the Devil's Dealbook.

- Your daily life, routines and family dynamics play a role in the way you do sales.
- Getting rich is not necessarily the best goal for sales.
- There is a limit beyond which more hard work and more money do not bring you any measure of joy or success.

CHAPTER 3

ENTER FUM© - THE RULE OF LAW

To be content doesn't mean you don't desire more, it means you're thankful for what you have and patient for what's to come.
—**Tony Gaskins.**

The status quo tells us that riches are the same as power and influence. It is those with the most money who have the most political and societal influence. It tells us that the more goods and materials we have, the happier we are. It is normal to get into debt and to live by your credit score. According to conventional wisdom, few things are subject to the pursuit of money. You are always chasing the bag over every other pursuit. The status quo glorifies retirement as the ultimate goal to begin chasing from the moment you start making your own money. The relentless pursuit of financial success and the pressure to achieve societal norms regarding money end up contributing to stress, anxiety, and poor mental health outcomes. People experience burnout and dissatisfaction despite financial success. Is that a way to live?

Let's revisit some current statistics about wealth and poverty. As of 2024, there are approximately 2,710 billionaires worldwide, representing about 0.000034% of the global population. Meanwhile, around 0.72% of people globally are millionaires. The latest figures show that over 40% of the world's population lives below the poverty line. This leaves the remaining 59.28% of us aspiring to improve our financial status.

But what if we weren't striving for riches? What difference would it make if everybody strived for contentment, rather than simply being rich? How many people living on $5.50 a day aren't content? How many are? Some of them might already be enjoying FUM©. I know it sounds crazy, but what if the person owns the mud hut they live in? It is situated next to a perennial spring of crystal-clear water, they eat one meal a day (which costs around $1.50) and teach illiterate elderly people to read and write. They support their orphaned neighbor with $1 a day and have the most gratifyingly restful sleep every night. Isn't that a dream come true? It's the ultimate state of independent contentment.

The FUM© philosophy emphasizes that sales and financial success are tools to achieve this state of contentment, not the end goals in themselves. FUM© is the goal of sales. This chapter will introduce you to the FUM© concept, which you can explore further at fkyoumoney.org, and how to apply this mindset to excel in sales. It's not about abandoning ambition but about channeling it towards a meaningful end. As Tony Gaskins wisely said, "to be content doesn't mean you don't desire more, but that you are thankful for what you have and patient for what is coming."

A Beautiful and Revolutionary Melody

Picture a man- let's call him John. John is a 30-year-old entrepreneur who starts with a modest market stall selling handmade jewelry in his local community. Despite his initial lack of resources, John is determined to build a business that will eventually grant him financial freedom.

As John's business begins to grow, he invests his profits wisely, focusing on creating unique designs and developing a loyal customer base through personal connections and word-of-mouth. Over time, John's commitment pays off, and he achieves financial stability. Despite traditional advice from financial advisors suggesting that he needs a staggering $3 million in savings to retire comfortably, John discovers through careful analysis and current statistics that this figure is unrealistic for many. He realizes that he only needs $5,000 after-tax per month to live comfortably, whether in his town or even more luxuriously in a place like the Philippines. With his investments and passive income generating around $60,000 per year, John finds that he only needs approximately $800,000 in investments— about a third of the amount initially suggested. This strategic adjustment allows him the freedom to explore his passions and enjoy life without being confined to a traditional retirement model.

With his business thriving, John makes a strategic decision to diversify his income streams. He purchases a rental property with some of his savings, generating a steady stream of passive income from tenants. This investment provides him with additional financial security and stability. John also invests in other income-generating assets, such as royalties from a design patent he secured. His goal is not to retire early, but to work in a way that honors the strength he has as a young man and as he ages. He wants financial independence that allows him to adjust to the changes of age.

Interestingly, John's experience reflects a broader trend observed globally, where traditional notions of retirement are being redefined. In Singapore, for instance, the government has implemented the "Live

Well, Age Well" program, which highlights a shift towards integrating older adults more actively into society. The initiative- part of the Republic's 2023 action plan for successful aging- aims to empower seniors through health promotion, continued employment, and community engagement. As Singapore anticipates that one in four people will be aged 65 and above by 2030, the government is addressing this demographic shift with a focus on maintaining health and employment among older adults.

The "Live Well, Age Well" program offers various activities such as group exercise sessions and mental well-being education, and it supports extended working years through wage offsets for employers who hire older workers. The retirement age is being gradually increased, and efforts are being made to ensure seniors remain connected and active in their communities. This approach not only helps seniors remain financially stable but also enhances their overall well-being and fulfillment.

John's story mirrors this evolving perspective. By redefining his financial goals and adopting a flexible approach to work and retirement, he aligns with a global trend that values continued engagement and purpose over traditional retirement. The success of his business and investments generates sufficient money that allows John time to focus on his passions. He starts pursuing photography, a hobby he had always wanted to explore but never had the time for due to the demands of his business. With passive and multiple streams of income supporting his lifestyle, John enjoys the freedom to travel and capture stunning landscapes and cultures around the world.

John's journey illustrates how achieving financial independence through smart investments and passive income streams can offer the freedom to explore personal interests and passions. His story demonstrates that financial stability and freedom provide the opportunity to pursue the activities you've always dreamed of, all while enjoying the benefits of a well-rounded and fulfilling lifestyle. It is the FUM© lifestyle on display.

It's a lot like music. Isn't it incredible how music, crafted from just seven simple notes— C, D, E, F, G, A, and B— can create countless melodies? When played without skill, these notes can sound chaotic. Yet, in the hands of a trained musician, they flow effortlessly, akin to the familiar "do, re, mi, fa, sol, la, ti" from the classic film "The Sound of Music." This film helped many understand the essence of musical notes, even those not formally trained.

I'm not a musician myself, but I am creative. I've used three fundamental letters— 'F', 'U', and 'M'— to compose a melody that symbolizes a new cultural movement: FUM©. This movement aims to revolutionize how individuals lead content, productive, and meaningful lives. FUM©, much like music, is inclusive and only requires your commitment to shape its tune.

Reflecting on our progress, it's clear we've made strides since the days of early humans. Innovations such as fire, tools made from rocks and wood, and better food storage methods have significantly improved our lives. But despite our technological advancements today, our well-being seems to be declining. Mental health issues, particularly depression, affect a staggering 3.8% of the global population, or about 303.2 million people. This statistic is as large as the entire population of the United States. Imagine that.

We've become adept at treating the symptoms of mental illness but struggle to address its root causes effectively. It's a challenge reminiscent of the early struggles of our ancestors, who, like us, sought ways to enhance their lives and communities. We may have developed rapidly in many areas, but our understanding and approach to mental health and well-being still require significant evolution, but that's a subject for another book.

When it comes to managing our finances, the pace of evolution is largely stuck on a 'rinse and repeat' conveyer belt with minor changes introduced out of necessity rather than radical innovation. Another worrying fact from the World Health Organization is that a large percentage of the 303.2 million depressed souls are struggling with financial issues. It's time to treat this stagnation with a combination of F, U, and M to restore mental well-being and introduce practical, individual financial management for everyone. I am not throwing the baby out with the bathwater, but I want to shake things up for the baby to feel uncomfortable enough to hold on and wait for it to be replaced with fresh, warm water. This is where the culture of FUM©'s practical approach to creating a future life of well-being begins.

F$CK YOU MONEY is a culture that exists between the ancient wisdom of deep thinkers and modern capitalism. Not Socrates and Plato from 347 BC, I'm talking about 300 years earlier when Buddha the teacher, philosopher, and spiritual leader was around. Essentially teaching us that the ego must be dethroned from the misconception that it is an entity that exists by itself. Once we do this, we can have an authentic relationship with our true selves. Buddhism teaches us to put our ego in its rightful place as an advisor, not as our identity, and to have freedom from our conditioned thinking. This makes you a happier person. When you free your mind from a static identity, then you are open to change and external circumstances.

Fundamentally, as with most ancient wisdom, it teaches the basic precept of equality and reciprocity amongst our fellow humans. Biblical truth tells us we are all created equal and should do unto others as we would have them do unto us. Embracing this truth, you will find yourself flowing naturally into the disciplines of practicing concentration, meditation, and mental development to gain insight, wisdom, enlightenment, and well-being. If you combine this mindset with the worldly system of capitalism, understanding that the intrinsic value of money is finite, you will find yourself living in the culture of FUM©.

There is no question that we need money to survive in a capitalist society, but we must do things differently than our ancestors before us and the status quo today, because how they have always done things is no longer working. Are you ready to change your thinking to evolve with the ancient wisdom that promises an independent life of well-being?

A Life of Constant Change

FUM© is a flexible discipline that thrives on adaptation rather than rigid control, recognizing that change is the only constant in both life and the pursuit of contentment. For John, embracing this flexibility was crucial to his journey from a modest market stall to achieving financial freedom and personal fulfillment. Once John set his FUM© goals, he understood that his path would require regular adjustments as circumstances evolved.

Initially, his focus was on growing his jewelry business and achieving financial stability. However, as his business matured and he reached his financial goals more swiftly than anticipated, John realized that his initial retirement plan was based on outdated assumptions. Instead of adhering to the rigid $3 million target suggested by financial advisors, John adapted his strategy by reassessing his needs and discovering that $800,000 in investments was sufficient to generate the $60,000 annual passive income required for a comfortable lifestyle. This shift in perspective allowed him to enjoy a richer, more fulfilling life without being confined to traditional retirement expectations.

This need to adapt is true of everyone after setting your FUM© goals. Your journey will require regular adjustments as circumstances evolve. The nature of your goals and the path to achieving them will shift with the changing dynamics of your business, family, and the world at large. Embracing this fluidity is essential for maintaining progress towards your contented happiness.

Life is unpredictable, and numerous factors can influence your FUM© journey. For example, a sudden family emergency, such as the death of a loved one, or financial needs arising from a family member's situation can create significant shifts in your priorities and resources. Similarly, unexpected events like accidents or job loss can impact your financial stability and overall well-being. These events, while challenging, are part of the broader landscape that affects your FUM© potential.

The death of a loved one can be emotionally devastating and may disrupt your daily life, mental focus, and financial stability. The grief process can affect your ability to make decisions or engage in routine activities, which can indirectly impact your FUM© goals. If a family member, such as a sibling, requires financial assistance, it can place an unexpected burden on your resources. This situation may force you to reassess your budget and financial priorities, potentially diverting funds from your FUM© objectives.

Accidents or health problems can result in medical expenses, reduced income, or changes in lifestyle. These factors can affect your financial stability and ability to pursue FUM© goals. Losing your job can also have a significant effect on your financial security and sense of stability. It may lead to a sudden loss of income, affecting your ability to maintain your current lifestyle and pursue FUM© goals. Even broader economic conditions, such as inflation, market downturns, or changes in interest rates, can influence your financial landscape and FUM© potential. These factors can impact investment returns, purchasing power, and overall financial stability.

As you grow personally and professionally, your goals and priorities may shift. What once was important might become less relevant, or new opportunities might arise that change your direction. In each of these scenarios, the key to maintaining progress towards FUM© lies in your ability to adapt and remain resilient. By proactively managing these changes and adjusting your strategies as needed, you can continue to pursue a state of contented happiness, regardless of the obstacles you may encounter.

To effectively manage these changes, you will need to reflect on how they influence your FUM© goals and overall state of contentment. Then you need to develop strategies to adjust your goals and actions in response to the changes. This might involve reassessing your financial priorities, seeking new opportunities, or recalibrating your expectations. Flexibility is key.

As your FUM© landscape evolves, the tools and strategies you use to achieve your goals may need to be redefined. Sales techniques and tools that worked previously might need modification. Engaging with mentors can provide valuable guidance and support to help you navigate these shifts and stay aligned with your FUM© goals.

Working the FUM© Way

As it is, global life expectancy continues to rise as people are living longer and healthier lives. Advances in healthcare, nutrition, and technology have contributed to this increase, allowing people to enjoy extended years beyond previous generations. However, this demographic shift also brings with it new social challenges, particularly the growing issue of loneliness among older adults.

Loneliness has become a significant concern in many developed nations. According to a study published in *The Lancet Public Health* in 2020, loneliness is prevalent among the elderly, with about 33% of individuals aged 65 and older experiencing some level of loneliness. This can be attributed to various factors, including the loss of peers, physical limitations that reduce social interactions, and changing family dynamics.

The paradox of living longer but feeling more isolated highlights a critical need to rethink how we structure our lives and work. The traditional model of working for decades, followed by retirement, is increasingly being questioned as people seek more fulfilling ways to integrate work with life enjoyment. FUM© is an answer to this.

They may not call it that there, but Singapore is pioneering the FUM© way of working. This concept redefines the conventional work paradigm by emphasizing the importance of integrating work with personal satisfaction and leisure. In the FUM© way of working, work is a means, not an end. The model challenges the traditional notion of work merely as a financial necessity to be endured until retirement, and instead promotes the idea that work should be a means to enable a fulfilling life. This approach encourages people to view their careers as a part of a larger life plan that includes time for personal interests, hobbies, and relationships.

Rather than adhering to a rigid retirement age, the FUM© model suggests a more flexible approach. People are encouraged to continue working in ways that suit their interests and capabilities, even as they age. This flexibility helps to maintain a sense of purpose and engagement, reducing feelings of loneliness and disconnection. Based on FUM©, work should not dominate your life. Instead, you need to balance your professional responsibilities with activities that bring joy and satisfaction. It creates a culture where work and enjoyment coexist, to help you create a more fulfilling and balanced life.

Say No to Conformity

In a world saturated with messages and expectations, it's easy to feel overwhelmed by the pressure to conform to societal norms and ideals. From media and advertising to personal advice and societal expectations, we're bombarded with directives on how to live our lives and manage our finances. But it's crucial to recognize that not all of these directives are aligned with achieving true contentment and happiness. Embracing the FUM© philosophy means saying no to conformity and charting your own course based on what genuinely fulfills you.

Modern media and social media platforms often present a curated vision of success and happiness, frequently emphasizing consumerism and a particular lifestyle. Instagram influencers, YouTube celebrities, and other media personalities often showcase a life of luxury, new gadgets, and designer brands. These portrayals can create an illusion that happiness is tied to material wealth and social status.

Banks and financial institutions often push the narrative that you must save aggressively, invest in specific products, or follow certain financial strategies to secure your future. Advertising frequently promotes the idea that you need to accumulate vast amounts of money or own the latest products to be happy or successful.

Family members, like a well-meaning mother, and societal norms often come with their own set of expectations. Whether it's advice on career choices, financial planning, or lifestyle, these recommendations are frequently based on traditional views or what worked for them, rather than what might be best for you.

The reality is that the images and messages you see on social media are often not reflective of real life. Social media tends to amplify the highlight reel of people's lives while obscuring the everyday struggles they face. If you are constantly comparing yourself to these often-unrealistic standards, you risk undermining your own sense of satisfaction and happiness. True contentment comes from within and from living a life aligned with your own values and desires, not from adhering to a fabricated standard of success.

On matters of money, while saving and investing are important aspects of financial planning, they should be tailored to your unique needs and goals, not dictated by generic advice or aggressive marketing. The conventional wisdom pushed by financial institutions often fails to account for individual circumstances and personal satisfaction. It's essential to balance financial prudence with what genuinely makes you happy, rather than simply following a one-size-fits-all approach.

At the same time, while family and societal input can be valuable, it's important to remember that their experiences and advice may not perfectly align with your own life goals and desires. Following these suggestions without considering your personal happiness can lead to a life that feels unfulfilling or overly constrained by others' expectations.

Saying no to conformity is about embracing your unique path. It is about aligning your actions with your FUM© goals to ultimately lead a more fulfilling and contented life. True happiness is not found in following the crowd but in living authentically and according to what genuinely matters to you.

In the same way society has opinions about how you live your life, it also has opinions on how you do sales. These societal expectations and conventional wisdom can influence your strategies, often prioritizing metrics and numbers over genuine connections. However, reaching the FUM© state of independent contentment in sales requires a shift in focus from chasing numbers to building meaningful relationships.

Conventional wisdom often emphasizes quantifiable metrics such as sales targets, conversion rates, and performance statistics. Society and corporate cultures frequently value these numbers as the ultimate indicators of success. The focus is on achieving specific benchmarks, meeting quotas, and delivering results that can be measured and compared. But while numbers are important and provide useful benchmarks, they don't always capture the full picture. Sales figures and metrics can sometimes be misleading or fail to reflect the quality of customer interactions and relationships. In pursuit of these numbers, sales strategies can become overly transactional and less focused on the human element of the process.

To truly reach the FUM© state of contentment in sales, the emphasis must shift from merely achieving sales targets to cultivating genuine relationships with clients and prospects. FUM© is truly revolutionary.

You may ask, why exactly is FUM© revolutionary? To which I respond with a question of my own. What exactly has the capitalistic order and a status quo mindset done for us?

Ask John Wesley, 72 looking more like 92, living in a retirement home knitting bed socks to supplement his income, more than the need to pass the time and kill the boredom of long empty days. When John was in his thirties, he was promised an amazing retirement with regular vacations on exotic islands. He would have enough money to buy a house on the beach and eat meals in fancy restaurants. He could buy the car of his dreams and play golf three times a week. To date, John has knitted away several hundred miles of sheep's wool. He lives in a state-run retirement home with a bunch of grumpy old people, eating three meals a day, which he is sick of.

Who promised John the Life of Riley? The person who sold him the retirement dream he paid into religiously every month for 45 years. And the lyrics of the popular 1880s song.

Is that Mr. Reilly, can anyone tell?

Is that Mr. Reilly that owns the hotel?

Well, if that's Mr. Reilly they speak of so highly,

Well upon my soul, Reilly, you're doing quite well

John stopped working after a lifetime in a steady job and had to adjust to living with the reality of a room full of knitting when his monthly pension turned out to be half of his working wage. He doesn't smile much, and even less when his grandchildren help him check in on social media on his antiquated mobile phone. His school buddy Bob and his wife Sue on vacation on the French Riviera turn him green with envy. Not to mention the jealousy he feels towards Morgan, an ex-neighbor who lives in a lavish retirement home on a golf Estate regularly posting pics of himself on the golf course. John constantly wonders where he went wrong.

Let's bring it into your world on a Saturday afternoon. You're watching a news broadcast on TV. There's an ad break. A gray-haired couple is walking their handbag dog down a manicured path in a pristine retirement estate, smiling from ear to ear, glowingly healthy with calming background music and the words 'This could be you at 65' in colorful, happy-looking font. The contact numbers, email address, and website link replace the contrived scene as the music fades, and the ad is replaced by the next one, advertising a saving scheme to support your retirement dreams by the age of 65. If you continue watching the newscast, you will most likely have the same brainwashing ads thrown in your face several times.

When you've had enough of the news, you pick up your mobile phone to scroll through your Instagram feed. A friend has posted a pic of the great meal he enjoyed at a restaurant in Paris on vacation with his family. A twinge of envy pulls at your gut as you switch to search for info on travel to Spain. The following day, while you're scrolling Instagram, a sponsored ad from a bank pops up offering travel loans at zero interest. What a coincidence. You know you can't afford a holiday, but consider the possibility of taking a zero interest loan from the bank for the holiday you deserve to take. All of this in the space of a few minutes of the 18 hours you are awake in a day, still with many hours left for you to watch news, movies, scroll social media, and be bombarded with more of the same.

There's not much ancient wisdom in social media research. Marketing companies provide statistics to assist companies in optimizing their social media advertising, looking at the history of your scrolling from all angles, hence the offer of a bank loan for your trip to Spain a day after looking at Spanish holiday travel. Social media will come under more and more scrutiny in the future, but until it does, it will continue to condition our minds into conformity. Everything in me, including ancient wisdom, tells me to be cautious of the influence of this force de frappe that would like to sink my FUM© ship.

It would be an unrealistic surprise to read this message- only if you can afford it- in the final line of a social media ad offering you a low-interest loan covering a fly now-pay later travel deal including hotels and car hire. Rather than the standard bullsh$t- book now or regret it for the rest of your life. How cool would it be to get a call from a bank manager or see an ad from a financial institution inviting you to- please pay us a visit, we'd love to discuss your:

- Dreams for the future
- Financial planning
- Investment opportunities

And when you take up the offer, to be met by a warm-hearted person who looks you in the eye, offers you a seat, and begins with a personal 'how do you do', enquiring about you, your family, your job, your interests, your fears of the future and your dreams, before getting into the financial talk. Do banks even have managers anymore? I quickly terminate telephone contact from a call-center agent reading scripted questions like automated answering machines. I shudder to think what their response would be to a request for investment advice or anything not on the script. Other than hopefully helping you reset your security code, they will direct you to the frequently asked questions on the bank's website and terminate the call. This is a loud call to arms – do all you can to reject conformity.

The FUM© Way of Selling

When you sell from the FUM© mindset, you sell differently. The FUM© way is a way that accepts the fact that sales is not just about hitting targets; it's about forging a path that's uniquely yours. It is about creating a passive source of income that allows you to sell from a place of independent contentment. It is working yourself out of the rat race so that you can truly sell with the interests of the people you are selling to at heart.

And no, I am not arguing that you stop paying attention to your pipelines, leave behind your forecasts and hope for the best. That would be ridiculous; we need that hunger to succeed. I am saying that there is a different way to deal with people that does not place targets front and center. I am saying that you can crush your numbers without having them drive everything you do. Every deal does not have to be reduced to a dollar amount and every new prospect is not just another obstacle to hitting that target. There is a non-interruptive, non-pushy and helpful way to sell that de-prioritizes the very thing you measure each month but also guarantees that you meet it.

You see, spreading positive energy and acting ethically leads to lasting success. When people are honest, kind, and fair, they build trust and create a positive environment. Positive energy attracts good outcomes, creating a cycle of success. That's what this book is about. Along the journey I am about to take you on, I share my unconventional journey to success in the industry. With a combination of education, personal experience, and a determination to overcome adversity, I've discovered how to master the art of selling. Through my story, you'll learn your own path to get to the top and become a true sales maverick.

The FUM© way of selling will cause you to ask yourself; what is my intention of selling? Why do I do what I do? Is it just to make money? I make the case that the ultimate goal of sales should be happiness, and when the ultimate goal of sales is happiness, how you go about closing your deals has to change; it has to be all about relationships. If your sales techniques are sacrificing your relationships and ethics, you are cheating yourself out of the future you want and are shooting yourself in the foot. You are stealing your own happiness, and that will surely manifest in your life. Happiness is the end goal; this is the philosophy behind FUM©.

The key to mastering sales? It's a mix of real-world experience and ongoing learning. Salespeople need to adapt to their customers' changing needs and keep refining their approach. Building trust, understanding customer needs, and being empathetic are what create lasting customer relationships that stand the test of time. The journey I am about to take you on will hopefully create your individual success in both sales and life. The lessons that you will uncover throughout this book will be the natural laws of sales which I summarize as the sales commandments at the end of the book. The pathway will provide the ability to reach your FUM© goals and happiness.

In many ways, this book is a call for you to dare to do sales differently; to embrace the concept of FUM© and dare to make sales about human connection and building relationships. I have said it before and will reiterate: money doesn't buy happiness. It cannot. It may seem counterintuitive in a world where material wealth often equates to success and fulfillment, but the truth behind this statement lies in the fact that human nature is intricate, and happiness itself can be elusive.

At its core, happiness is a multifaceted and subjective concept, shaped by many internal and external factors. It encompasses not only material wealth but also emotional well-being, social connections, and a sense of purpose and fulfillment in life. While money can undoubtedly alleviate certain stressors and provide access to comfort and luxury, it falls short in addressing the deeper, more profound aspects of happiness.

One of the fundamental flaws in the belief that money buys happiness lies in its reliance on external validation and material possessions as sources of fulfillment. In a society driven by consumerism and the relentless pursuit of wealth, people often equate their self-worth with their net worth, measuring success in terms of monetary achievements rather than personal growth and contentment. Besides, the pursuit of wealth can often lead to a cycle of insatiable desire, where the acquisition of material possessions becomes an endless quest for more. This hedonic treadmill mentality perpetuates a never-ending cycle of craving and dissatisfaction, as you constantly seek the next big purchase or financial milestone in a futile attempt to fill the void within.

I have found that the pursuit of wealth, if not well contextualized, can come at the expense of other aspects of life that are crucial to overall happiness, such as meaningful relationships, personal development, and work-life balance. The relentless pursuit of financial success can lead to burnout, stress, and a sense of emptiness. Research in psychology and social science has consistently shown that beyond a certain threshold, increases in income have diminishing returns in terms of overall happiness and life satisfaction. Once basic needs are met, such as food, shelter, and security, additional wealth has a marginal impact on subjective well-being. Instead, factors such as social connections, personal growth, and a sense of purpose emerge as stronger predictors of happiness and life satisfaction.

So then, how do you make it all last? How do you reach that optimal output point and use the law of diminishing returns to your advantage? How do you harness your hunger for more to make a life that you will enjoy now and for as long as you are alive? The answer lies in the concept of FUM©, a cultural blend intertwining ancient wisdom and modern capitalism. Embracing this ideology allows for freedom from conditioned thinking, fostering happiness and openness to change.

FUM© harmonizes these principles with the capitalist system, acknowledging that the value of money is finite. It's a flexible discipline that demands monitoring, not micromanagement, acknowledging that change is the only constant, both in life and in setting FUM© goals. Adjustments are made as the goalposts shift, ensuring alignment with evolving circumstances. FUM© takes the Devil's Dealbook and makes those tools positive ones. It makes them sustainable, long-term and a force for good. My hope is to help you embrace a paradigm shift into this way of thinking about sales, money and success. And my question to you is: will you stand up and become FUM© in sales?

Key Takeaways

- Money and wealth are not the have-all and end-all for life. Happiness and contentment are.
- You can sell from a place of gratitude, contentment and positivity. You can sell the FUM© way.
- The FUM© way makes sales more sustainable and enduring. It allows you to create passive income and affords you the freedom to do the things you truly love.

CHAPTER 4

WILL THE REAL DEAL MAKER STAND UP?

If I have seen further, it is by standing on the shoulders of giants.
— **Isaac Newton.**

What do you know about yourself as a salesperson, or would-be salesperson, at the moment? What life experiences have you had that have contributed to your interests and to who you are? Do you believe that these can be shaped, sharpened and honed to make you a great salesperson? I know for a fact that you don't have to have your mentor next to you, even though it is pretty great when you do. My first mentor was Rambo. I learnt so much from a movie character. I was influenced so much by someone I will never meet. This is because a mentor's influence is about you accepting their input into your life and humbling yourself enough to be guided by their wisdom.

That's the call of this chapter (and this book). Will the real deal maker in you stand up? Will you dare to be trained by the principles I have learnt from my own experiences and from the people who have mentored me; from countless other influences, such as the books I have read and the stories I have told? Will you dare to stand on the shoulders of giants?

Isaac Newton (1643–1727) was one of the most influential scientists in history, making groundbreaking contributions to physics, mathematics, astronomy, and optics. His achievements include the development of calculus, the laws of motion, the theory of universal gravitation, and advancements in optics through his work with prisms. Pick someone at random and if they have been through formal education, they will recognize the name. And yet, Newton did not become who he was alone. He didn't achieve the great things that he did without Isaac Barrow, Nicholas Mercator and other influences. By his own admission, his inventions and innovations were not born out of a vacuum; they were as great because he stood on the shoulders of giants.

That's what this chapter is about- the importance of a good mentor cannot be overstated. A good mentor will inspire you to push and break barriers, they will develop you and expand your perception. They will chip away at your edges until you are perfect and will mold you into a better salesperson; all of this without judgment. Whether that's an experienced acquaintance who recognizes your potential or a businessperson who takes you under their wing, there is never a wrong place to get a mentor. There's never a wrong place to find the giant who will hone your hunter skills and hoist you to the heights of sales you couldn't have dreamt of. That's what you will see in this chapter.

Why Mentors Matter

Plutarch once said, 'the mind is not a vessel to be filled, but a fire to be kindled.' When it comes to sales, it is our mentors who kindle that fire. They inspire us, help us in difficult situations and guide our paths. When we are starting out, as much as we would like to know everything, we just don't. Having someone to call for guidance is a great way to help us deal with the unknown.

Imagine someone who is new in sales; a hunter – a relentless pursuer of new business opportunities. They are just beginning though, and their career is uncertain, all they know is the promise of high commissions and the reality of a modest salary. As such a person, you enter the field without a clear sense of identity, unsure whether you have the necessary skills to thrive.

This is where a mentor comes in. They guide you and impart the wisdom they have earned through years of experience. They teach you the nuances of the trade – the art of persuasion, the importance of persistence and the strategies to close deals. You see, hunting is not just about the kill; it is about understanding your prey, adapting to their movements, and seizing the opportunity when it presents itself.

In sales, success is not just making one sale. It is building relationships, solving problems and consistently delivering value. It is facing rejections and setbacks, and learning to refine your approach, sharpen your skills and cultivate your resilience. A great mentor helps you to discover your strengths and weaknesses, gradually molding your identity as a salesperson. They transform you from a novice to a seasoned hunter. To them, you are like Michelangelo's block of stone- they sculpt you into the true salesperson that you are.

Great People Who Were Shaped by Mentors

Sales is a rollercoaster ride of highs and lows. One moment, you're a hero; the next, you're contemplating career changes. During the inevitable dry spells, the pressure can feel suffocating. What keeps salespeople in the game is advice and moral support. Having someone to talk to— a confidant who can rationalize setbacks and guide you back on track— is invaluable in navigating the emotional ups and downs of sales.

Mentorship has been a cornerstone of many extraordinary achievements throughout history, and some of the most influential figures in modern times have benefited significantly from the guidance of their mentors. Their stories not only illustrate the impact of mentorship but also underscore the timeless nature of this invaluable relationship.

1. Mark Zuckerberg - Facebook

The relationship between Mark Zuckerberg, the co-founder of Facebook, and Steve Jobs, the iconic co-founder of Apple Inc., is a compelling example of a mentor-mentee dynamic that had a significant impact on both individuals and their respective ventures. Although their direct interactions were relatively limited, the influence Steve Jobs had on Zuckerberg's thinking and approach to business was profound.

Mark Zuckerberg and Steve Jobs' paths crossed in the early 2000s when Facebook was in its formative years and Apple was already a well-established tech giant. Jobs, known for his visionary leadership and innovative mindset, was a natural source of inspiration for Zuckerberg, who was focused on growing Facebook into a global phenomenon.

Their initial meeting took place in 2006, when Zuckerberg was invited to Apple's headquarters in Cupertino. The meeting was informal but impactful. At this time, Facebook was gaining traction but had yet to achieve the global dominance it would later attain. Zuckerberg, eager to learn from the successes of established tech leaders, saw in Jobs an opportunity to gain insights into product design, business strategy, and leadership.

Steve Jobs was renowned for his uncompromising vision and insistence on product excellence. He was a proponent of simplicity in design and a relentless focus on creating products that users loved. Jobs' approach was heavily influenced by his belief in the intersection of technology and liberal arts, which he considered essential for creating innovative products. Zuckerberg absorbed these principles, which became evident in how Facebook's interface evolved over the years. He adopted a design philosophy that prioritized user experience and intuitive navigation, reflecting Jobs' influence. Zuckerberg's emphasis on creating a seamless, user-centric platform can be traced back to the lessons he learned from Jobs.

Another influence of this relationship was about product focus. Steve Jobs was famous for his focus on creating products that were not only functional but also emotionally engaging. He believed that the best products combined form and function in a way that resonated deeply with users. Under Jobs' indirect mentorship, Zuckerberg adopted a similar focus on product design and user engagement. Facebook's evolution, from its early days as a college networking site to its status as a global social media powerhouse, reflects an ongoing commitment to enhancing user experience, a concept Jobs championed.

You can also see Job's influence on Zuckerberg when you look at his leadership and strategy. Jobs' leadership style was characterized by his passion, high standards, and the ability to inspire his team to achieve excellence. He was known for making bold decisions and staying true to his vision, even in the face of skepticism. Zuckerberg's leadership style has shown echoes of Jobs' approach. His willingness to make audacious decisions, such as acquiring companies like Instagram and WhatsApp, and his focus on long-term vision rather than short-term gains, align with Jobs' philosophy of maintaining a bold and visionary approach to leadership.

Steve Jobs was a pioneer of innovation, constantly pushing the boundaries of technology and design. His risk-taking attitude was instrumental in shaping Apple's trajectory and transforming it into one of the most valuable companies in the world. Zuckerberg embraced a similar risk-taking mentality in scaling Facebook and experimenting with new features and acquisitions. The bold move to rebrand Facebook as Meta and pivot towards the metaverse reflects a willingness to innovate and explore uncharted territories, reminiscent of Jobs' approach to groundbreaking technologies.

Although Steve Jobs did not serve as a formal mentor to Mark Zuckerberg, his influence was evident in Zuckerberg's approach to business and innovation. Jobs' emphasis on design, user experience, and visionary thinking left a lasting imprint on Zuckerberg, shaping his leadership style and strategic decisions. Zuckerberg has publicly acknowledged the impact of Jobs' work and philosophy on his own career, in various interviews he has spoken about how Jobs' focus on product excellence and his ability to inspire teams influenced his approach to building Facebook.

2. Ray Kroc - of McDonalds

Another great mentor-mentee relationship we can learn from is the relationship between Ray Kroc and Walt Disney. Whilst Disney did not mentor Kroc in a traditional sense, his principles and philosophies had a profound impact on Kroc's approach to business, particularly in transforming McDonald's into a global franchise powerhouse. Although Disney and Kroc's professional paths did not closely intersect, their connection began during World War I, when they both served as ambulance drivers in the American Red Cross. They reconnected later in life, and Disney's philosophies indirectly influenced Kroc's business practices.

Ray Kroc, a skilled salesman with a keen eye for business potential, saw the promise in a small, single-location burger restaurant owned by the McDonald brothers in San Bernardino, California. Kroc's vision and sales acumen were instrumental in turning McDonald's from a modest regional chain into a global franchise empire. His approach to scaling the business through a franchise model was innovative and transformative, setting new standards in the fast-food industry.

Walt Disney, a pioneering force in entertainment, was known for his emphasis on high standards, brand consistency, and creating immersive customer experiences.

He was renowned for his obsessive attention to detail and commitment to quality. He established a reputation for delivering exceptional entertainment experiences, from the meticulous design of his theme parks to the high standards of his animated films. Disney's focus on maintaining consistency and quality across all aspects of his brand was central to his success.

Inspired by Disney's dedication to quality, Ray Kroc applied similar principles to the McDonald's franchise model. Kroc was meticulous about ensuring that every McDonald's restaurant delivered the same high-quality food and service. He implemented rigorous standards and operational procedures to maintain consistency across the growing chain, mirroring Disney's approach to brand excellence.

Disney was a pioneer in brand building, using his name and creations to establish a powerful and recognizable brand. His focus on innovation in entertainment, from animation techniques to theme park design, set new standards in the industry. Ray Kroc drew inspiration from Disney's innovative approach to brand building. He revolutionized the fast-food industry with the franchise model, introducing innovative practices such as the Speedee Service System, which standardized food preparation and delivery. Kroc's efforts to innovate and expand McDonald's aligned with the principles of brand-building and innovation that Disney exemplified.

The influence of Walt Disney on Ray Kroc's business practices is evident in the success of McDonald's as a global franchise. Disney's emphasis on quality, consistency, and creating immersive customer experiences resonated with Kroc, shaping his approach to building the McDonald's brand. The alignment of these principles with Kroc's vision for McDonald's helped establish the company as a leading force in the fast-food industry.

3. Frank Lucas - Drug Lord

As you will see, the impact of mentors is everywhere, even in organized crime; after all, every tool a salesperson has is a tool that can be used for good or for bad. Think about the relationship between Frank Lucas and Ellsworth "Bumpy" Johnson. Bumpy Johnson was a well-known figure in Harlem's criminal underworld, revered for his influence and mastery in navigating the complexities of organized crime. Johnson's reputation was built on his ability to maintain control over his territory, manage illicit operations effectively, and maintain strong relationships with key figures in the criminal ecosystem. His expertise in these areas made him a valuable mentor to those looking to succeed in the drug trade.

Johnson understood that a strong network was essential for success in organized crime. He taught Lucas the importance of establishing and maintaining relationships with suppliers, distributors, and other influential figures. This network was critical for accessing resources, gaining intelligence, and ensuring operational security. He provided Lucas with insights into the operations of the drug trade, including how to handle conflicts, manage rivals, and navigate law enforcement scrutiny. His strategic guidance helped Lucas avoid common pitfalls and build a robust framework for his own operations.

Bumpy Johnson's experience in running a criminal empire included managing finances, overseeing distribution, and handling interpersonal dynamics within the organization. Lucas learned how to apply these operational principles to streamline his own drug trade, making his operations more efficient and profitable.

Frank Lucas rose to prominence in Harlem during the late 1960s and early 1970s by transforming the heroin trade. His innovative approach, which involved bypassing middlemen and sourcing heroin directly from Southeast Asia, allowed him to offer a purer product at a more competitive price. This strategy revolutionized the drug trade in Harlem and established Lucas as a formidable player. Lucas adopted Johnson's lessons on the importance of sourcing and distribution. By cutting out intermediaries and establishing direct connections with suppliers in Southeast Asia, Lucas was able to secure higher quality heroin and undercut his competitors. This approach significantly improved his profit margins and market share.

He applied Johnson's advice on managing operations and developed sophisticated distribution networks and a tight operational structure. This efficiency allowed him to scale his business rapidly and maintain control over his territory, despite increased competition and law enforcement pressure. Lucas leveraged the relationships and networks he had built under Johnson's mentorship. He understood the value of maintaining alliances with key figures in both the criminal world and legitimate legal sectors, which helped him to expand his reach and influence.

The mentor-mentee relationship between Bumpy Johnson and Frank Lucas was instrumental in shaping Lucas's approach to the drug trade. Johnson's mentorship provided Lucas with the foundational knowledge and strategic insights necessary to excel in a highly competitive and perilous environment. Lucas's ability to apply these lessons effectively allowed him to revolutionize the heroin trade and build a powerful empire.

You see the trend with other people like Oprah Winfrey. The global icon and advocate for mentorship has, throughout her career, acted as a mentor for thousands without even knowing; her philanthropic endeavors and open demeanor will have guided and inspired many who watch her, or follow her in the media. Oprah's success story is also deeply intertwined with the mentorship she received from various figures, including her early mentor- her grandmother- who played a significant role in her development.

The concept of mentorship is not a modern phenomenon but has roots in ancient history. As mentioned at the start of the chapter, Plato, a towering figure in Greek philosophy, was himself mentored by Socrates. This relationship profoundly influenced Plato's philosophical work, which he later passed on to Aristotle. The enduring legacy of Socratic mentorship has shaped Western philosophy and thought, illustrating the long-standing significance of mentorship in intellectual and personal development.

Notice how these examples are from diverse fields and all of them demonstrate that mentorship is a powerful force that can shape careers, foster growth, and drive innovation. From ancient Greece to the modern era, the mentor-mentee relationship remains a fundamental aspect of success. As Oprah Winfrey puts it, nobody makes it alone.'

What Makes a Good Mentor?

Not all mentors are created equal, and the most impactful mentors share certain essential qualities. When considering someone to enter a mentor-mentee relationship with, or when aiming to improve your own mentoring skills, it's crucial to recognize these key attributes.

1. Relevant expertise and experience

It's vital for a mentor to have relevant expertise. Ideally, they should be a few levels ahead of you in the sales hierarchy or possess substantial experience in your target industry. Their background should enable them to offer valuable insights and practical advice based on real-world experience. While experience is beneficial, it's also important that they aren't too far removed from your current situation, ideally, they should be within five to ten years of your level. This ensures that their advice remains applicable to the present-day sales environment.

2. Enthusiasm for sharing knowledge

A great mentor isn't just knowledgeable; they're also eager to share their wisdom. They should be enthusiastic about passing on their experiences and insights, without any hidden agendas or reluctance. The best mentors are genuinely motivated by the desire to help others succeed, rather than seeking personal gain or recognition.

3. Respectful conduct

Respect is a cornerstone of effective mentoring. A mentor should provide constructive feedback without being harsh or disrespectful. They should treat you and others with dignity and professionalism. When mentors do make mistakes, they should own up to them and offer sincere apologies, demonstrating their commitment to maintaining a respectful relationship.

4. Commitment to investing in others

Mentoring is a voluntary and often unpaid role, so a mentor should have a genuine interest in investing their time and energy into your growth. They should be patient, understanding that development takes time, and they should be committed to building and nurturing a meaningful professional relationship without expecting immediate rewards.

5. Ability to provide honest and constructive feedback

An effective mentor provides honest feedback that is both direct and constructive. They shouldn't shy away from giving you tough love when necessary. This kind of feedback, although sometimes uncomfortable, is crucial for personal and professional growth. A mentor who can candidly point out areas for improvement while supporting your development is invaluable.

6. Active listening and empathy

Good mentors excel at listening and empathizing with their mentees. They should ask questions to understand your perspective and be genuinely curious about your experiences and goals. An empathetic approach helps them tailor their advice to your specific needs rather than imposing their own solutions.

7. Willingness to act as a sponsor

While not all mentors are sponsors, having a mentor who can advocate for you in addition to offering guidance can be incredibly beneficial. A sponsor actively supports your career advancement, using their influence to open doors and create opportunities that you might not access on your own. They champion your skills and potential within their network, which can significantly boost your career prospects.

To determine if someone could be a good mentor, consider these questions:

- Do they have practical experience relevant to your career path?
- Are they genuinely interested in helping you succeed?
- Are they effective at giving and receiving constructive feedback?
- Do they communicate in a respectful and truthful manner?
- Are they committed to their own professional growth?
- Do they value the importance of investing in your development?
- Do you respect and get along well with them both professionally and personally?
- Are they well-regarded by others in their network?
- Do they have mentors themselves, indicating their understanding of mentorship's value?

Finding the right mentor takes time and effort. It's important to build relationships and learn from various people, which can naturally lead you to a mentor who aligns with your needs. Remember, having a mentor is about gaining valuable skills and knowledge rather than simply mirroring their career path. Focus on leveraging their guidance to enhance your own journey and success in sales.

Ineffective Mentors to Watch Out For

In the same way there are traits that make a great mentor, there are characteristics that make a mentor a 'bad' one. I highlight them to help you know what to look out for and what signs mean someone is not a great match. Not every mentor will be a boon to your career, some can actually hinder your progress. Here are some common types of ineffective mentors to watch out for:

1. The 'All Talk, No Action' Mentor

This mentor promises advice, support, and assistance but fails to deliver. Initially, their assurances might sound promising, especially when you're just starting out and craving guidance. However, you'll quickly realize that they provide little to no real help when you need it most. Their involvement is more about appearances than actual commitment. They may be stretched too thin to offer meaningful support, and their intentions often don't match their actions. To avoid falling into this trap, set clear expectations and a structured plan for mentorship. If they hesitate, it might be wise to reconsider whether they're the right fit for you.

2. The 'Sourpuss' Mentor

A mentor with a consistently negative outlook can be a drain on your motivation. Their perpetual dissatisfaction and cynicism can taint your view of the sales industry and your career path. Instead of inspiring you, they might make you second-guess your enthusiasm and potential. Engaging with a sourpuss mentor can lead to unnecessary stress and negativity. It's often best to limit interactions and focus on mentors who bring constructive positivity and practical guidance.

3. The 'MIA' Mentor

The Missing in Action (MIA) mentor is often absent or hard to reach, making it difficult to get timely advice and support. If you rarely connect with them and their engagement is minimal, their value as a mentor diminishes significantly. Even if they have a prestigious background, if they don't know you well enough to offer personalized advice, their input might not be as relevant. In such cases, rely on other mentors who are more accessible and invested in your growth.

4. The 'Too Nosey' Mentor

A mentor who digs too deeply into your personal life can be uncomfortable and intrusive. They might want to know about your weekend plans, relationships, or personal beliefs, all details that are irrelevant to your professional development. While curiosity can be a sign of engagement, excessive probing can indicate a lack of professional boundaries. Be cautious about sharing personal information and ensure that your mentor respects your privacy.

5. The 'Always Busy' Mentor

This mentor constantly gives you tasks and projects that seem to take up excessive time and effort. Often, they may not fully understand how long certain tasks take or may have unrealistic expectations about your availability. They might treat you more like an assistant than a mentee. Learning to assertively manage these demands is crucial. Seek advice on setting boundaries and negotiating realistic expectations with your mentor.

5. The 'Bully' Mentor

A mentor who uses criticism to demean rather than to help is a bully. This type of mentor will focus on tearing you down rather than building you up, offering no constructive support to help you improve. If you feel persistently belittled and powerless, it's essential to reassess the mentorship and to seek out alternative mentors who provide feedback constructively and supportively.

While some mentors might exhibit these problematic traits, it's essential to remember that no mentor is perfect. You can navigate certain issues, such as setting boundaries with a 'friendship-focused' mentor, or manage occasional absence with an MIA mentor by seeking additional support elsewhere. However, mentors who fall into the 'bully' or 'overly forward' categories should be avoided entirely. To ensure a fruitful mentoring relationship, establish clear goals and expectations from the start. Keep open lines of communication and be proactive in addressing any issues that arise.

The Negatives of Not Having a Mentor

In the high-stakes world of sales, the presence of a mentor can be the key to a thriving career. Without one, you risk becoming stagnant and veering off course. Without a mentor, you may struggle to advance and develop your skills. Sales is a field where continuous learning and adaptation are crucial, without someone to guide you, you might find yourself stuck in outdated methods and unable to refine your strategies. This stagnation can hinder your growth, leaving you in a constant state of underperformance and missed opportunities.

A mentor helps steer you in the right direction, providing insights and advice that prevent you from making costly mistakes. Without this guidance, you risk heading down the wrong path, making decisions based on trial and error rather than informed strategies. This lack of direction can lead to misguided efforts, ineffective approaches, and ultimately, failure to achieve your sales goals.

The absence of mentorship means missing out on valuable feedback and strategic advice. A mentor offers a roadmap through the complexities of sales, helping you navigate challenges and seize opportunities. Without this guidance, you might find yourself navigating the sales landscape alone, making it difficult to find your footing and achieve success.

The thing with mentorship is that not all mentorship is good. A wrong mentor can cause a lot of harm. If they lack the relevant experience or if their strategies are outdated, it can lead you in the wrong direction. Sales methodologies evolve rapidly, and a mentor with outdated approaches may inadvertently steer you away from effective modern techniques. This misalignment can lead to poor performance and frustration.

They may offer conflicting advice. If a mentor's approach doesn't align with your personal style or the specific needs of your sales role, their advice might be counterproductive. Conflicting advice can create confusion and prevent you from developing a cohesive strategy, ultimately impacting your sales performance and confidence.

Their support may be inadequate. The wrong mentor might provide inadequate support or fail to address your specific challenges. This lack of personalized guidance can leave you feeling unsupported and unsure of how to tackle obstacles effectively, impeding your progress and success in sales.

Now imagine if their influence is also toxic; it becomes doubly harmful. A mentor who is negative, overly critical, or manipulative can have a detrimental impact on your morale and confidence. Their toxic influence can undermine your motivation, affect your decision-making, and create a hostile work environment, leading to reduced job satisfaction and performance.

Effective mentorship involves aligning with your career goals and aspirations. The wrong mentor may have different priorities or expectations that do not match your own, which can hinder your ability to achieve your career objectives and may result in frustration and disillusionment.

In sales, having the right mentor— or any mentor at all— can make a substantial difference in your success and satisfaction. Without mentorship, you face the risk of slower growth, increased stress, and missed opportunities. With the wrong mentor, you might encounter misguided strategies, conflicting advice, and even toxic influence. You have to look for mentors who not only have relevant experience and a supportive attitude but also align with your personal and professional goals. A well-chosen mentor can be a game-changer, providing the guidance and support needed to excel in the dynamic world of sales.

Key Takeaways

- You may be born a salesperson, but it is a good mentor who brings it out.
- A mentor teaches you the nuances of the trade. Without a mentor, you risk getting stagnant in your sales career.
- A great mentor will bring you home to yourself and will touch every aspect of your life.

CHAPTER 5

THE LAW OF ATTRACTION

When you are joyful, when you say yes to life and have fun and project positivity all around you, you become a sun in the center of every constellation, and people want to be near you.
— **Shannon L. Alder.**

*I*n sales, as in many aspects of life, the central thread connecting successful traits is positivity. I'll introduce this concept as a fundamental law in this chapter because it underpins the effectiveness of all other strategies and approaches. At its core, positivity is not just an attitude but a powerful force that shapes our interactions and outcomes.

I firmly believe in the concept of the universe and the idea that we are all made of energy. Our energy, particularly the positivity we exude, plays a crucial role in our professional success. As salespeople, we have the unique ability to harness this energy to attract opportunities and build meaningful relationships. My own success in sales can be largely attributed to the positivity I bring to my interactions. This isn't merely about maintaining a cheerful disposition; it's about embodying an optimistic mindset that influences every conversation and transaction.

Shannon L. Adler encapsulates this idea beautifully: "When you are joyful and positive, you become the sun around which everyone and everything wants to rotate." This metaphor speaks to the magnetic power of positivity. In sales, when you radiate genuine joy and enthusiasm, you draw people to you. Clients and prospects are naturally inclined to engage with someone who brings a sense of optimism and excitement to the table. This positivity not only makes you more approachable but also inspires trust and confidence in your abilities.

This is true in all of life and most emphatically in sales, that positive people draw people to themselves. At the same time, negativity repels. When you approach sales with negative energy, it affects how you utilize the tools in the Devil's Dealbook. Negative energy can lead to pessimism and self-doubt. This mindset can cause you to use your sales tools ineffectively, as you may lack the motivation or confidence needed to deploy them successfully. When you are negative, challenges and setbacks in sales can feel more overwhelming, which can cloud your judgment and cause you to make poor decisions or abandon strategies prematurely. Negative energy often repels potential clients and partners. People are generally drawn to positive, enthusiastic salespeople. This chapter will discuss the science and the laws behind this to help you understand why positivity plays a big role in sales success.

What the Law of Attraction is About

The law of attraction is a powerful law that governs all of life. According to this law, what we think about and how we feel can influence what happens in our lives. If we focus on positive thoughts and believe in our goals, we're more likely to attract good things, but, if we dwell on negative thoughts or doubts, we might bring more negativity into our lives. It's not just about wishing for things, it's about actively shaping our thoughts and feelings to match what we want. By staying positive, visualizing success, and setting clear goals, we can align ourselves with positive outcomes. Based on the law of attraction, our mindset and attitudes play a big role in creating our reality.

Some people argue about whether the law of attraction is scientifically proven, but whether or not you question it, the chances are that you've seen the effects of it in your life. The law of attraction is about taking control of your thoughts and actions to make things happen the way you want. At its core, it is the truth that what we focus on grows, whether it's success, happiness, or other positive outcomes. Practically, it means practicing positive thinking, using techniques like visualizing our goals, repeating affirmations, and staying focused on what we want to achieve. That way, we can feel more confident, motivated, and ready to pursue our dreams.

One of my favorite quotes by Jim Rohn goes like this: "Success isn't something you chase after, it's something you attract." When you look at successful entrepreneurs around the world, this seems obvious. Successful entrepreneurs aren't out there cold calling hundreds of people to beg them to buy their products or services. They aren't using high-pressure sales tactics or interruptive advertising either. Yet, they have hundreds, thousands, even millions of customers eager to use what they offer. Just think of people like Mark Zuckerberg, Steve Jobs, Richard Branson, and Bill Gates, to name a few.

You might think these people just got lucky, being in the right place at the right time. But how do you position yourself to be in that right place at the right time? It's through the law of attraction. In simple terms, the law of attraction means you attract what you focus on.

This law suggests that your thoughts, whether positive or negative, bring corresponding experiences into your life. People with an optimistic outlook, who focus on abundance and future possibilities, tend to see their lives and the world around them in a positive light. Those with a negative, pessimistic mindset often find their reality reflects their negative beliefs. The law of attraction works in three simple steps: asking, believing, and receiving.

First, **asking** means clearly stating what you want or desire. It's about setting your intention and being specific about what you hope to achieve or attract into your life. This step involves being clear and focused on your goals.

Believing is about having faith and confidence that what you've asked for is possible and already on its way to you. It's about maintaining a positive mindset and trusting that you deserve what you're seeking. This step requires you to let go of doubts and negative thoughts that might block your desires.

Finally, **receiving** is about being open and ready to accept what you've asked for into your life. It involves being aware of opportunities and signs that align with your desires. This step requires gratitude and a sense of readiness to embrace the positive outcomes that are coming your way. These three steps— asking, believing, and receiving— allow you to harness the power of the law of attraction to manifest your dreams and goals into reality. It's about aligning your thoughts and actions with what you want to attract and staying open to the possibilities that the universe presents to you.

In practice, they might look like this:

Asking - For instance, you might set a specific goal to acquire a new client in the tech industry who needs your company's services.

You write down your goal, detailing the type of client you're targeting, the services you'll offer, and the expected outcome (e.g., a signed contract for a service package worth $50,000). This step involves crafting a clear, detailed vision of what success looks like and setting your intention.

Believing - This involves having faith that you have the skills and resources necessary to land this client. You might visualize successful meetings, anticipate positive outcomes, and remind yourself of past successes that reinforce your ability to close deals. To maintain a positive mindset, you might read inspiring sales stories or affirmations, and work on overcoming any doubts or negative thoughts about your capabilities or the feasibility of the deal.

Receiving - Finally, you prepare to accept the opportunities that arise. This means staying alert to any signs or opportunities that could lead you to your target client. For example, you might attend industry events where you can network with potential leads, follow up on introductions made by colleagues, or recognize the right moment to pitch your services. You express gratitude for every small step that brings you closer to your goal, such as a positive response from a prospect or a valuable referral. By being open and receptive, you're in a better position to seize the opportunities that align with your goal and ultimately close the deal.

By practicing asking, believing, and receiving, you align your actions with your desired outcome and remain open to the possibilities that will help you achieve your sales goals.

But simply having beliefs isn't enough to attract success into your life. The key to attraction is action; you must match your beliefs with actions to attract anything valuable. Doing nothing won't attract success, hope alone won't produce results, nor will believing you can get what you want just by wishing for it. Your beliefs form the foundation of your results, but it's your actions that build upon that foundation.

Actions are the real catalyst for attraction. The law of attraction only works if you take action. People with positive mindsets are proactive and believe in their ability to shape their own success. They act in accordance with these beliefs. On the other hand, people with negative mindsets see the world as controlling them, so they act out of fear. They might feel powerless to change their circumstances, leading them to avoid taking action.

Positivity Draws People to You

Everywhere you look in the world, you will see people whose positive outlook and visionary approach attracted people to them and built strong, supportive networks. Their ability to inspire and motivate others through positivity plays a crucial role in their success and influence. Whether through leadership, innovation, or personal charisma, these figures demonstrate that a positive attitude can be a powerful magnet for attracting people and achieving great things. Think men like Barack Obama, Henry Ford or Mahatma Gandhi.

Barack Obama, the 44th President of the United States, is a prime example of someone whose positivity attracted people. Known for his calm, hopeful demeanor and his ability to inspire, Obama's presidential campaigns were marked by themes of hope and change. His 2008 campaign slogan, "Yes We Can," resonated with many and attracted a diverse coalition of supporters precisely because of its positivity. His optimism about the future, combined with his message of unity, helped him build a broad base of support and foster a sense of collective purpose.

For Mahatma Gandhi, the leader of India's non-violent independence movement, positivity was not about leading a nation, but it still drew people to him. His philosophy of non-violence (ahimsa) and his commitment to peaceful resistance attracted millions to his cause. Gandhi's positive vision of a free and just India, coupled with his personal example of humility and dedication, drew people from various walks of life to join his movement. His ability to remain positive and focus on his goals, even in the face of adversity, inspired widespread support and mobilized a nation.

The Law of Attraction at Work in Sales

In sales, the law of attraction is at work too, I can think of a number of scenarios. For starters, if you truly believe in your product and its value, you can make others believe too. Customers won't buy from someone who doesn't love and showcase their product. Whether you're selling to businesses or consumers, knowing and believing in your product's greatness is essential. Before each interaction, clear your mind and believe in your ability to make a sale or secure a crucial meeting. Show how your product improves lives, because you genuinely believe it does. As the saying goes, "whether you believe you will fail or succeed, you are right!" Keep this in mind as you approach your next call or meeting. Go out there with belief, and the universe will work in your favor.

In a sales meeting, maintaining a positive attitude is necessary. Your mindset can significantly impact the energy and outcome of the meeting. If you're having a bad day or feeling negative, it's important to recognize how that might affect the atmosphere and productivity. Take the rest of the day off when you're not in a positive frame of mind if you need to. It allows you to reset and come back with renewed energy and a better attitude. That way, you maintain professionalism and ensure that you contribute positively to the meeting.

I know for a fact that in sales meetings, positivity is contagious. When you exude confidence and enthusiasm, it not only boosts your own performance but also inspires your colleagues and impresses clients. It creates a conducive environment for productive discussions and effective decision-making. Remember, your presence and energy impact the overall dynamics of the meeting. Taking care of your mental state ensures that you bring your best self to every interaction, maximizing your chances of success and leaving a lasting positive impression.

Live In the Present

I am sure that Richard Carlson's 1997 book is for entrepreneurs. Outside of my formal education, I educated myself in life lessons by reading books like this. He taught me the valuable lesson of avoiding the worries of little things that used to drive me crazy. His thoughtful and insightful language introduced me to ways to calm down amid a hurried, stress-filled life. It changed my thinking, putting things in perspective by making small daily changes and importantly, thinking of problems as potential teachers. He gives the simple advice of remembering that when you die, your inbox will not be empty and to do only one thing at a time. Carlson puts a lot of emphasis on something I have always tried to do too: Live in the present moment.

It is much easier to be positive when you are in the present moment. Positivity thrives on clarity and focus, which are best achieved when you are immersed in the present. When you're fully engaged in the here and now, you're less likely to be bogged down by regrets about the past or anxieties about the future. This presence allows you to experience life more fully and appreciate the positive aspects that might otherwise go unnoticed.

Research supports the power of positivity in various contexts, including professional settings.

- Studies have shown that a positive outlook can significantly impact job performance and interpersonal relationships. For instance, a meta-analysis conducted by Luthans, Youssef, and Avolio (2007) found that positive psychological capital, including optimism and resilience, is a predictor of job performance and satisfaction.
- Research by the Harvard Business Review found that teams with a positive atmosphere are 31% more productive and 37% more successful in achieving their goals than those with a negative atmosphere.
- A study by Barsade (2002) demonstrated that emotional contagion, including positivity, significantly affects group dynamics and performance. When a leader exhibits positivity, it can enhance team morale and cooperation, leading to better overall outcomes.
- A study by the University of Pennsylvania's Positive Psychology Center revealed that positive communication leads to better problem-solving and more effective team collaboration. When you bring positivity to your sales dealings, you're fulfilling a deep human need for connection and teamwork.

When we are positive, people want to work with us. People are drawn to positivity because it speaks to our basic human instincts. Throughout history, we've thrived in groups like tribes and clans, where working together was crucial for survival. This instinct still influences us today. When you're positive in business, several things happen. First, which is reiteration, positivity is contagious. Your upbeat attitude can lift others' spirits and make the atmosphere more enjoyable and productive. It builds trust and makes people feel good about working with you.

From the perspective of quantum physics, every interaction involves the exchange of energy and information at a fundamental level. Quantum entanglement suggests that particles can be connected regardless of distance, implying a subtle interconnectedness in our interactions with others. This essentially means that your interactions with people are exchanges of energy. What kind of energy do you want to be emitting?

Secondly, being positive shows confidence and resilience. It tells others that you believe in what you're doing and can deliver on your promises. This confidence makes people more likely to trust you and want to work together. Positivity also shows that you're focused on solutions, not problems. Instead of getting stuck on setbacks, positive people look for ways to move forward. This proactive approach impresses others and shows them you're committed to finding answers.

Plus, positivity improves communication. People listen more when someone is positive and open. It encourages collaboration and helps everyone understand each other better. When you bring positivity to your sales dealings, you're fulfilling a deep human need for connection and teamwork. It makes others want to engage with you because they feel valued and hopeful about what you can achieve together.

There are a number of ways you can harness the power of positivity in your sales career, including, but not limited to:

Start each day with a positive mindset

The way you start your day can have a profound impact on your performance. Embracing a positive mindset each morning sets a productive tone and prepares you to tackle the day's challenges with confidence. Begin your day with a structured routine that energizes and centers you. This could include a short workout, a healthy breakfast, or reviewing your goals for the day. A consistent morning routine helps you start the day on a positive note and creates a sense of normalcy and control.

Before diving into your tasks, take a few minutes to outline your daily objectives. Prioritize your key sales activities, such as client calls, follow-ups, and meetings. Having a clear plan not only helps you stay organized but also sets a focused and optimistic tone for your day. If you need it, start your day with positive affirmations or motivational statements. Remind yourself of your strengths, achievements, and capabilities. Positive self-talk can reinforce your confidence and readiness to face the day's challenges.

Despite your best efforts, some days may not go as planned. Sales can be unpredictable, and it's not uncommon to encounter obstacles. If you find that your day isn't going as smoothly as anticipated, don't be afraid to take a short break. Step away from your tasks, clear your mind, and recharge. A brief pause can help you regain perspective and reduce stress, allowing you to approach your work with renewed energy.

After the break, reassess your situation and adjust your strategy if needed. Identify any issues that may be causing problems and make necessary changes. Whether it's modifying your sales approach or addressing client concerns, a fresh perspective can help you course-correct. If you're unable to resolve certain issues by the end of the day, plan to tackle them the next day. Ensure that you outline a clear action plan and set priorities for the following morning. By doing so, you can start the next day with a sense of purpose and readiness to address any outstanding challenges.

Cultivate gratitude

Regularly acknowledge and appreciate the good aspects of your work and interactions. Create a habit of noting down three things you're grateful for each day. This could include positive client interactions, successful meetings, or personal achievements. A daily gratitude journal helps you stay focused on what's going well and reinforces a positive mindset. Dedicate 5 minutes at the end of each workday to write in your journal. Reflect on moments or achievements that made you feel good about your work. This simple practice can shift your focus from challenges to successes.

Whenever possible, take time to send thank-you notes or messages to clients and colleagues who have positively impacted your workday. Whether it's a follow-up email thanking a client for their time or a quick message thanking a colleague for their support, expressing gratitude strengthens relationships and builds goodwill.

Key Takeaways

- Action is the catalyst for the law of attraction.
- Positivity is contagious. It builds confidence and inspires loyalty. You become like the sun, drawing everyone and everything to yourself.
- Begin your day with a positive mindset.

PART II

LIVE AND LET DIE - MY JOURNEY THROUGH SALES

"The best way to predict the future is to invent it." – **Alan Kay.**

*I*n the first part of this book, you have read about the different tools inside the Devil's Dealbook and how they can be used for good or for evil. You have seen why positivity matters for the salesperson and the role mentors play in the life of a salesperson. In this second part of the book, I hope to illustrate it all through my life story. Here, you will see how I arrived at some of those lessons and how sales changed my life. You will see my struggles to survive and my success stories and how each of the tools in the Devil's Dealbook served me. I aim to bring these concepts to life through the lens of my own experiences.

You will witness how these lessons are not just theoretical concepts but practical realities that transformed my life and can transform yours. You'll see how I navigated the complexities of the sales world, faced personal and professional challenges, and ultimately crafted a future that aligns with my values and aspirations– my FUM©. My struggles for survival and the successes I've achieved are not just milestones; they are the results of actively shaping my path rather than waiting for it to unfold.

I love Alan Kay's quote because it captures the power of taking initiative and creating your own destiny. By sharing my journey, I hope to illustrate that predicting the future isn't about foreseeing what will happen but about actively designing and influencing it. You'll see how I applied these principles in my sales career and personal life, and how you too can harness the tools and lessons discussed to shape your own future.

CHAPTER 1

WHERE IT ALL BEGUN - THE ENVIRONMENT THAT SHAPED ME

"Hope is important because it can make the present moment less difficult to bear. If we believe that tomorrow will be better, we can bear hardship today." – **Thich Nhat Hahn.**

*L*et me take you back to the beginning; to the moment when my story truly began. I was born in Germany, in a quaint maternity home nestled within a vibrant community. The world outside was a landscape of contrasts, shaped by the deep divisions of the Cold War.

In the West, Germany was buzzing with the energy of economic prosperity and cultural revival. I can almost picture my arrival being met with a sense of optimism and excitement. The maternity home, though modest, was a reflection of the broader economic boom known as the Wirtschaftswunder. The walls of that small establishment likely resonated with the quiet hum of progress as the country reveled in its newfound affluence. My parents, like many others, were caught up in this wave of advancement, which, in part, fueled my father's ambitious drive.

Just across the border, in East Germany, life was a stark contrast. The state-run maternity homes there were under strict socialist policies, with an emphasis on collective welfare and state control. Had I been born on that side, my early days would have been shaped by a very different rhythm— one marked by meticulous organization and the constraints of life under a socialist regime. The air there was heavy with the weight of state oversight and the challenges of a tightly controlled existence.

Family lore has it that I was the largest baby ever delivered in that maternity home; my demand for milk was so insatiable that it kept the caregivers on their toes. It seems fitting, considering my lifelong passion for food. I'm also told that my presence created quite a stir. Germans would often stop my mother on the street, intrigued by this unusual brown baby with a broad, infectious smile. I like to think this early fascination with people sparked my lifelong love for human connection. Maybe it is the reason why I find networking so easy even now.

Before I was born, my parents had made the significant decision to leave India. My father, driven by ambition and a thirst for knowledge, sought to further his career and studies in Europe. This move was more than just a change of scenery; it was a deliberate step towards achieving his professional goals. It meant leaving behind the familiar comforts of home in India for the challenges and opportunities of the West.

My mother, Asha, came from a world of luxury and privilege. As the only child of affluent parents in Calcutta, she grew up in a life of opulence and exclusivity. Calcutta, during her upbringing, was a city teeming with cultural, political, and social dynamism. It was a place where significant historical events unfolded, from its role as the capital of British India to its pivotal role in the independence movement. By the time my mother was born, Calcutta had transitioned into West Bengal, a region known for its cultural richness and intellectual vibrancy.

Roots in Motion – A Nomadic Childhood

My mother's father was a renowned doctor, and her upbringing was steeped in the privileges of education, healthcare, and cultural exposure. Leaving all of that behind to follow my father's ambitions must have been daunting. And it wasn't just a one-time move. By the time I was four, we had lived in Finland, the UK, and then Chicago, as my father pursued various opportunities. Each move brought its own set of challenges— adapting to new cultures, languages, and social norms while raising a family.

By the time we settled in Toronto, Canada, I was five years old and ready to start school. Looking back, I can only imagine the resilience and adaptability my mother demonstrated through all these transitions. Each relocation required her to balance the demands of a growing family with the responsibilities of supporting my father's career. Her strength and commitment speak volumes about her character and the dedication she had to our family.

Even though we moved around a lot in those early days, I was well loved. I was nurtured. We were living well. Through every move and transition, my mother worked hard to create a nurturing environment. She made sure that I was surrounded by love, no matter how many times our address changed. In those early days, we were like our nomadic ancestors, always moving and looking for a new food supply. We stayed in Toronto for four years until my father got another offer in Halifax.

While in Canada, I found myself yearning for connection. During the 60s and 70s, the country had become a magnet for immigrants seeking new opportunities and a fresh start. It was a place where many families, including ours, sought to build a better future away from the familiar comforts of their homeland thanks to the incentives the government offered. Toronto in particular was bustling with a diverse array of people from all corners of the globe. The city's neighborhoods were a mosaic of cultures, each bringing its own flavor and traditions. As a child, I was surrounded by a vibrant tapestry of backgrounds and stories, which was both exciting and overwhelming. Despite this rich diversity, I felt a strong desire to connect with others. The constant moves from one country to another had given me a unique perspective but had also left me craving deeper relationships and a sense of belonging.

When we moved to Halifax, things changed a bit as well. I remember that while there, I got my first taste of entrepreneurship shoveling snow off driveways to earn some pocket money and supplement the housekeeping for reasons better left unwritten here. When it wasn't snowing, I expanded my entrepreneurial endeavors by landscaping and just selling whatever I could, like cookies and oranges. For sure, I was born to sell. I didn't know it then, but when I think about it now, it amazes me that a 9-year-old had the fortitude to do all that.

Two years later, when I was eleven, we packed up and moved to Montreal, Quebec. This shift marked a significant turning point in my life and was the first major inflection for my mother. Prior to this, I had been thriving. I was attending a private school where I excelled academically and athletically, and I was surrounded by a close-knit group of friends. My ambitions were clear; I wanted to follow the stereotypical path and become a doctor, a goal that seemed both practical and prestigious in the eyes of my family.

The move to Montreal was a jarring transition. I went from a private school where I was flourishing to a public school in a new city, where everything felt unfamiliar. Montreal, with its predominantly French-speaking population, presented a whole new set of challenges. The cultural and linguistic shift was substantial, and I found myself grappling with not only the academic adjustment but also the social isolation that came with being in a new environment without the support of my previous friends. I ran to sports as a way to process my emotions and make friends and found that I excelled in basketball and football, and I enjoyed them very much.

This move was particularly traumatic for me. I had left behind a school where I was thriving, a circle of friends who supported me, and a life that felt stable and fulfilling. The change was not just physical but emotional and social. My father's decision to relocate us, coupled with his subsequent detachment from family life, left us in a difficult position. In Montreal, he became increasingly absent, his focus shifted away from being a present husband and father, which left my mother and me to fend for ourselves in this new, challenging environment. With no friends and an absent father, I was thrust into a situation where I had to adapt quickly.

My loving and wealthy grandparents, who had always been a source of comfort and support, suggested that my mother and I return to Calcutta. They offered us the chance to enjoy the luxuries and stability of their home, but my mother had different plans. She was determined that I should receive a Western education, believing it would offer me the best opportunities for the future. She was really dedicated and committed to providing me with an international education.

So, my mother and I formed a team and faced the challenges head-on. We set about making the best of our new circumstances. I threw myself into my new school environment with determination. Despite the difficult racial and cultural adjustments, I worked hard to excel academically and socially, and within a short time I had made new friends and found my footing. I quickly made it back to the top of the honor roll.

Let Your Ambition Drive You

What came out of this period of my life was the desire to win. I became competitive. This wasn't just a fleeting feeling, it became a core part of who I am. My drive to be the best was so intense that I couldn't stand being number two. This relentless ambition has remained with me, influencing every aspect of my life and work. At the time, it meant that I did well in class and in sports. Today, it means that I do everything I can to excel in everything I set my hands to. It means I am constantly driven by my ambition.

To escape a really terrible environment or to rise above challenging circumstances, you need more than just basic motivation. You need a deep-seated drive, an almost indescribable inner force. This drive often comes from within, but it can also be sparked by the environment around you. The tougher the situation, the stronger your drive can become.

In sales, you also need that *'je ne sais quoi'*. You need to harness that competitive edge to push through obstacles and setbacks. If you're dealing with a difficult market or challenging targets, let those difficulties fuel your ambition. Use the environment to your advantage, transforming pressure and adversity into motivation and energy. Let your ambition be the driving force behind your success. Strive for excellence, not just to outdo others, but to surpass your own expectations.

Je ne sais quoi is that special quality, something intangible that makes certain salespeople stand out. It's not just about skill or technique; it's an innate charisma, a blend of passion, confidence, and authenticity that draws people in.

Other Early Influences

Growing up, sports were everything to me, and Magic Johnson was my absolute hero. I was completely captivated by his charisma and his incredible skills on the court as a Los Angeles Lakers star. He wasn't just a basketball player; he was a symbol of success and a glimpse into a world that seemed almost unreal. Magic had it all— the championships, the flashy cars, and that undeniable charm. He represented everything I wanted to be.

In the 80s, TV was our main window to the world, and we were glued to it. The commercials were filled with images of wealth and luxury that felt both mesmerizing and distant. One program that really stuck with me for a while was "Rich and Famous". It showed a glamorous lifestyle that seemed almost like a fantasy. Magic Johnson was living that dream and watching him made me yearn for a similar kind of success.

Then there were shows like *Different Strokes* and movies like *The Wolf of Wall Street*. *Different Strokes* featured a young boy who went from a tough upbringing to living in a mansion with all the trimmings of wealth. It painted this amazing picture of transformation and possibility. *The Wolf of Wall Street* presented a much darker view of ambition and success, illustrating the seductive nature of wealth and the moral compromises that often come with it. Both were like a window into a world of success that felt both exciting and achievable.

The TV shows, movies and Magic Johnson's real-life success story became more than just entertainment, they became the blueprints for what I wanted to achieve. They sparked a deep drive in me to excel. It wasn't just about getting good grades; it was about striving for a level of success that felt extraordinary.

Seeing Magic Johnson's wins and his glamorous life depicted on mainstream entertainment made me dream bigger. They pushed me to aim higher and work harder. They turned ambition into a tangible goal, showing me that with dedication and perseverance, reaching for the stars wasn't just a pipe dream, it was something within my grasp.

I Wanted to Make as Much Money as Possible

I have made the case that our environments shape us. These early influences, coupled with our situation in Montreal shaped me. Imagine being in a foreign city, with no money and no father figure. What would you do? Many kids resort to drugs and destructive coping mechanisms. For many, the absence of a support system and the pressures of a new environment can lead them down dubious paths. I have seen this firsthand.

I am sure that the city's underbelly offered easy access to these distractions. I could have gone down that route; it's a dark, alluring path, promising temporary relief from the overwhelming pressures of poverty. But thankfully, I chose something different.

It was in Montreal while I was at senior school that my working career began at the Holiday Inn. It helped that my mother worked there as a supervisor in the housekeeping crew. I was driven by my ambition to make as much money as I could; I wanted to maximize my sport, my academics and now, my money-making ventures.

Imagine the upheaval we went through with each move, being uprooted from everything familiar and thrown into a whirlwind of uncertainty. For my mother, it was an unimaginable challenge. She was grappling with the changes of that season of our lives and trying to find a way forward for us both. For me, the transition was tough too. I was young, but I could feel the gravity of our situation and how it was affecting us both.

In that period, I tried to be a pillar of strength for my mother. I would often find myself going to her, doing my best to lift her spirits. I remember standing there, trying to reassure her despite the chaos around us. "I'm gonna be a millionaire," I would say, not just as a promise to myself but as a surety that it was going to happen. I just knew it.

Again, my ambition was being fueled by my environment. My chief goal in life was to make as much money as possible and make my mother proud. So, when my mother found the job at the Holiday Inn and I found mine as a result, I gave it everything I had. We managed to make a comfortable life for ourselves. We didn't have millions of dollars, but we had the things we needed. We were happy. The cherry on top is that my entrepreneurship was sparked.

While there, the food and beverage manager at the Holiday Inn always called on me for any work they had because of my work ethic and my ability to do an excellent job for him. I would never say no and I was willing to work all hours. This supported my goal of earning as much as I could. I bought my first car, a Toyota Camry, for cash when I was 17 and graduating high school. Believe it or not, I was already planning my retirement. I wanted to make as much money as possible to get out of this situation that my mother and I were in. I wanted to be big.

Be an Entrepreneur at Heart

Those early work experiences— from my roles at the Holiday Inn to the various other jobs— taught me invaluable lessons about financial stability and entrepreneurial spirit. One of the most crucial lessons I learned was the importance of being an entrepreneur at heart, particularly through maintaining multiple sources of revenue. This principle is not just about diversifying income but about cultivating a mindset that embraces opportunity, innovation, and financial resilience.

Starting my career at the Holiday Inn while balancing school and sports, I quickly realized that relying on a single source of income could be risky. I began to understand the benefits of having multiple revenue streams. Here's why this approach proved to be so impactful:

- Having multiple sources of revenue provides a safety net in times of economic uncertainty or job instability. Research by the Federal Reserve Bank of St. Louis shows that people with diversified income sources are better positioned to withstand financial shocks. In my own experience, the variety of jobs I held and the income they generated helped me build a financial cushion. This early lesson in financial resilience highlighted the importance of not relying solely on a single source of income, especially in uncertain times.
- Embracing an entrepreneurial mindset involves seeking out new opportunities and being open to innovation. This was evident in my approach to work and finance. For instance,

during my time at the Holiday Inn, I was always on the lookout for ways to increase my income and gain new skills. This proactive approach mirrors the entrepreneurial principle of diversifying revenue streams.

According to a report by the Kauffman Foundation, entrepreneurs who actively seek out multiple revenue opportunities tend to experience faster growth and greater business success. This principle applies not only to starting new ventures but also to enhancing existing ones through innovative strategies and diversified income sources.

Have a Hobby

I learned the profound importance of having a hobby. Balancing my responsibilities between work, school, and sports taught me a valuable lesson that remains crucial for salespeople today: having a hobby is not just a pastime, but a vital component of personal and professional success.

Sports were my escape and a crucial outlet for managing emotions. Research from the American Psychological Association indicates that engaging in physical activities like sports can significantly reduce stress, improve mood, and enhance overall mental health. Sports provided me with a structured way to work through emotions, reduce stress, and maintain focus amid the demands of work and academics.

According to a study published in the *Journal of Sport & Exercise Psychology*, regular participation in sports can lead to lower levels of anxiety and depression, and better overall psychological well-being. This aligns with my experience, where the physical exertion and camaraderie of sports helped me manage the pressures of a busy schedule and maintain a positive mindset. These benefits translate into improved work performance and efficiency.

For salespeople, having a hobby can be especially beneficial. Engaging in activities outside of work can provide a mental break, allowing for greater creativity and problem-solving abilities when back on the job.

My involvement in sports also contributed to the development of key skills such as teamwork, leadership, and resilience. I know from research that sports can foster these essential skills, which are transferable to professional environments. For salespeople, the ability to work well in teams, demonstrate leadership, and bounce back from setbacks is invaluable. Participation in team sports like football taught me about collaboration and strategic thinking, while basketball enhanced my ability to handle pressure and stay focused under challenging circumstances. These skills proved to be beneficial in my career, enabling me to navigate complex sales scenarios and build strong relationships with clients.

Do you have a hobby? How do you spend your downtime?

Key Takeaways

- Your environment will change and that will shape you. See that it changes you in your favor. Let it drive you.
- Look for opportunity whenever it may be found. When you find it, don't waste it.
- Role models come in all shapes and sizes.

CHAPTER 2

A TIME TO KILL

'Survival was my only hope, success my only revenge.'
– **Patricia Cornwell.**

I have already mentioned that I wanted to be big. But something happened along the way while working at the Holiday Inn, which made this longing even stronger. To understand my choices, it's important to consider the things I had come to believe.

The Philosophy I Embraced

I would say that in Montreal, I found clarity in a singular, driving philosophy: the pursuit of financial success as the means to transcend the limitations of my situation. I wanted to make as much money as possible and elevate myself beyond the constraints of my current circumstances. I wanted to be big not just in terms of wealth, but in influence and impact.

I embraced the idea that financial independence was not merely about wealth but about liberation from dependency and vulnerability. Financial stability would grant me control over my life, a sense of security, and the freedom to make choices without being hindered by financial constraints. The desire to "be big" was fueled by a blend of ambition and necessity.

According to a report from Pew Research Center in 2024, income inequality has been a growing issue globally, with the wealthiest 10% of households holding a disproportionately large share of wealth. In 2023, the top 10% in developed economies owned around 52% of total wealth, underscoring the significant disparities in financial resources and the opportunities they afford. Not only that, but research by the Brookings Institution highlights that economic mobility— the ability to improve one's economic status relative to one's parents— is a key factor in achieving financial success. In the U.S., for instance, only 7% of children born into the bottom quintile of income reach the top quintile as adults. This statistic emphasizes the challenge of overcoming socioeconomic barriers. Like the many people in the world who find themselves in a less-than-ideal financial situation, I was going to transcend my circumstances, no matter what it took.

Bear in mind that I grew up in the 1980s. This decade was marked by significant shifts that shaped attitudes toward wealth and success, and these influences played a crucial role in driving my determination to escape poverty through financial achievement.

I was influenced by Magic Johnson, with his charismatic presence and unparalleled skills on the basketball court. He was more than just a sports icon; he was a symbol of excellence. I admired Joe Montana, known for his remarkable performance as the quarterback for the San Francisco 49ers, he epitomized athletic excellence and strategic thinking in sports. His ability to lead his team to four Super Bowl victories and his reputation for maintaining composure under pressure were great examples for me.

Then there were other voices like Michael Jackson, the "King of Pop," who redefined the music industry with his groundbreaking albums and performances, and Madonna, known as the "Queen of Pop," who both gave a certain vision of success. This was the 'glamorous' version that the media favored however, and they often failed to show the other side of these stories, or less exciting roads to success, the determination, grit and hard work that went on behind the scenes. I was determined to make a truckload of money on my own terms; maybe differently to others in my generation, but I knew I would achieve it. That's the hope that kept me moving.

At that point, for me, things were looking up in a surprising way. I was raking in tips which were more than what my mom was making from her salary. It felt incredible to be pulling in that kind of cash at such a young age, and it gave me a glimpse of the kind of success I was chasing. I was 16, I was making decent money, and it felt like I was on the right track toward achieving my dreams.

But then, something shifted. I started to get a bit careless, letting my ambition cloud my judgment. My ambition became greed. I was so focused on making as much money as possible that I began to slip in my work. The quality of my service deteriorated, and it didn't take long before I was let go from my job at the Holiday Inn. It was a wake-up call I didn't see coming.

I had always been driven by a vision of greatness. I wanted to be like Magic Johnson, living the high life with championship glory and success. I envisioned myself enjoying the kind of lifestyles I'd seen on *Different Strokes,* the luxurious, almost otherworldly success that seemed so out of reach. I was determined to be a millionaire, and I knew that excelling in my academics was the key to getting there.

But working at the Holiday Inn had introduced a new element into my life— greed. The more I earned, the more I wanted, and my focus started to shift from achieving success through hard work and academic excellence to just chasing immediate gains. My ambition became clouded by this growing sense of greed and as a result, I lost my job.

A Great Salesperson Knows How to Recover

Losing my job at the Holiday Inn was a significant blow, and the reality of it hit me hard. I had to quickly recalibrate and find a way to move forward.

In sales, much like in life, you have to be myopic at times, focusing intensely on the present and being able to let go of past setbacks to maintain forward momentum. When things go wrong, it's crucial to take a step back, deal with the disappointment, and then start fresh the next day with renewed energy. That's what I had to do.

The sting of losing my job was compounded by the knowledge that if my mother found out, she would be deeply disappointed. Remember that one of my primary goals was always to make her proud, and I didn't want to add to her worries. She was already facing her own challenges, working hard alongside me at the Holiday Inn, and I couldn't bear to be the source of her additional stress. So, I made the tough decision to keep the truth from her, telling her instead that I was looking for work elsewhere.

In the immediate aftermath of losing my job, I found myself with zero money, so I needed to quickly find a new path to regain my footing. The next day, I embraced a new beginning. Remarkably, I found a teaching job in Montreal. Imagine that. In one day, I was able to find employment in one of the most unlikely places in the world.

At the time, Montreal was grappling with one of the highest unemployment rates in Canada. In fact, during the early 1990s, Montreal's unemployment rate soared above 15%, one of the highest among major cities globally. The city faced economic challenges that made job hunting particularly difficult, but this also made the teaching position an unexpected source of joy.

I think I was able to do this because of my ability to persuade. This was a great thing. I was using another tool in the Devil's Dealbook to advance myself, way before I ever thought I would be writing this book.

Anyway, teaching sports in Montreal wasn't just a job, it was a fresh start. The role allowed me to leverage my background and passion for sports, and it provided a new direction and a chance to do better.

Things Happen for a Reason

Landing the teaching job turned out to be a transformative experience. The role gave me a new perspective on life and work and made a significant impact on how I viewed my own journey.

Teaching sports to kids in a city with such a challenging job market brought unexpected rewards. It wasn't just about the paycheck— though it helped, even if it wasn't much— it was about the connection I formed with the students. Seeing their enthusiasm, their struggles, and their growth gave me a profound sense of empathy. I realized how much impact a positive adult presence could have on young lives. This job was more than just a job; it was a chance to contribute meaningfully to something bigger than myself.

The role also provided me with a newfound sense of belonging. Despite the economic difficulties, the sense of community and purpose I found in the classroom was invaluable. I was able to help my family financially, and while the salary wasn't large, it was a significant improvement from having zero income. It also provided me with stability and a reason to keep pushing forward.

The teaching job also made me reflect on my broader goals. I began to see that simply working to make ends meet and dreaming of retirement was not enough. The job gave me a sense of fulfillment, but it also made me realize that retirement wasn't my ultimate calling. The job wasn't the dream I had envisioned when I was chasing the success of figures like Magic Johnson or the glamorous lives depicted in TV shows. Instead, it was a steppingstone that helped me understand that my true passion lay elsewhere.

This newfound clarity led me to refocus on my academic goals. I realized that while work was important, it couldn't be the sole measure of my success. In that realization, I was recommitting to knowledge- yet another tool in the Devil's Dealbook. The teaching job brought into sharp focus the value of education and personal growth. The experience taught me that sometimes, things happen for a reason. The detour into teaching, though not part of my original plan, helped me gain insight and realign my goals. It provided me with empathy, a sense of purpose, and a deeper understanding of what I truly wanted in life. Sometimes, the unexpected turns and setbacks are precisely what we need to find our true direction.

Getting A Higher Education

Recalibrating my focus and dedicating myself to my studies had a major impact on my academic performance. I quickly rose back to the top of my class, and by the time I graduated high school and left college, I was back on the academic honor roll. After this I went to McGill University, excited about the new chapter in my life. McGill was a big step up, and I was eager to dive into my studies and make the most of this opportunity. While I was balancing classes and hitting the books, I landed a job at a pharmaceutical company. The work was tough, but it was also a great fit for me at that time.

I was in fantastic shape, standing 6 feet tall and all muscle. The job had me hauling 200-pound barrels of Neutrogena around, which was no small feat, every day was a workout. I'd load these heavy barrels onto pallets and move them around the warehouse, and let me tell you, it wasn't easy. But the physical demands of the job were just what I needed. It wasn't just about getting stronger physically; it also gave me a serious boost in mental toughness.

Dealing with the physical strain taught me how to push through challenges, both mentally and physically. Every time I thought I couldn't lift another barrel or tackle another task, I had to dig deep and keep going. It built a kind of resilience in me that extended beyond the warehouse. I learned how to handle pressure, stay focused, and keep grinding even when things got tough.

This job wasn't just about the money, it was a crucial part of my personal development. It gave me a sense of discipline and a strong work ethic that I carried with me through my studies and beyond.

My boss was particularly difficult, often bitchy and never shy about showing it. "No, you will not be like your age mates," she'd say, "you will make as much money as possible, and this will pay for your university." She made it clear that if I wanted to keep my job, I had to put in the work, no matter what. That meant working through the summer, a time when my friends were out having fun, soaking up the sun, and enjoying their vacations. While they were living it up, I was stuck getting up at 5 a.m., hauling Neutrogena, and pulling double shifts.

Even though it was a tough gig, it was a steady source of income and kept me afloat while balancing university life. The work was physically demanding, but it kept me focused and provided for my university needs. The long hours and hard labor were a far cry from the carefree summer my friends were enjoying, but they were a necessary part of my journey.

At this time, I was in Med School. I was on track to study medicine, a path that seemed like a natural choice given the expectations of my family and the prestige associated with being a doctor. One day, my uncle— who was a renowned brain surgeon— came up to me with a serious look on his face. When he spoke, it wasn't what I expected. He told me to seriously reconsider my career choice.

"Medicine is a tough field," he said. "You get tied to the government, and the financial rewards aren't as great as you might think. You spend countless hours reading and studying, and the stress can be overwhelming. If you want to make it big, medicine might not be your game."

His words hit me hard. Here was someone whose success I admired and that I had always looked up to, telling me that the path I was on might not lead to the kind of success I was aiming for. I had always seen medicine as a guaranteed route to achievement and respect, but my uncle's perspective opened my eyes to a different reality. He painted a picture of a career filled with long hours, immense pressure, and a salary that- while respectable- might not match the financial heights I was aspiring to. The thought of being tied down by government regulations and the constant grind of medical studies made me question whether this was truly the path I wanted to follow.

The Influence of Garrick Killbery

The conversation with my uncle was a pivotal moment. It forced me to reevaluate my goals and consider whether my ambition was aligned with my chosen field. I changed from Med School to Business. During that summer, just as I was making this transition, an incredible opportunity came my way; I landed a job with Garrick Killberry at Abbott Laboratories. This was a major break for me, as Abbott Laboratories was, and still is, a leader in the pharmaceutical industry. Founded in 1888, Abbott is renowned for its innovative healthcare products and has established itself as a global powerhouse in the field. The company is known for its cutting-edge research and development, and it operates in over 160 countries.

Pharmaceuticals, as an industry, are among the best-paid sectors in the world. According to the U.S. Bureau of Labor Statistics, the median annual wage for pharmaceutical sales representatives, for instance, was around $87,000 in 2023, with some positions earning well over $120,000. The sector consistently ranks high in terms of salary and job growth prospects, making it an attractive field for ambitious professionals.

Working in the finance department at Abbott Laboratories was an excellent opportunity for me. The company's reputation for excellence and innovation provided me with a unique platform to grow and develop my skills. Abbott is known for its strong commitment to employee development and its supportive work environment, which was evident in my day-to-day experiences. The job not only offered competitive compensation but also allowed me to immerse myself in a field that was both dynamic and financially rewarding.

The shift to business and the opportunity to work at Abbott Laboratories marked a turning point in my career. It aligned perfectly with my ambition to achieve significant financial success and to have a meaningful impact in my chosen field.

Garrick was the first man I met outside of my family that took a sincere interest in me as a person. He was willing to share his time, knowledge, and wisdom with me. He put a lot of trust in me at the tender age of 23, which boosted my self-confidence and stretched me at the same time.

I could have easily settled into a lucrative career at Abbott Laboratories. The offer on the table was compelling— a permanent position in the marketing department with a starting salary of $100,000. It was a substantial amount of money, especially for someone fresh from graduation, and it promised financial stability and growth. It was a tempting prospect, one that seemed to align perfectly with the career success I had been aiming for.

However, Garrick Killberry, who had become more than just a mentor to me, saw something beyond the immediate benefits of that offer. He knew me well and understood my true potential. One day, he pulled me aside and said, "that's not who you are. I know you. You can be so much better. You are good at finance, you are ambitious, and you don't want to stay in Montreal. Everyone is leaving Montreal."

His words struck a chord. Garrick was right; I was ambitious and had a strong inclination towards finance, which was becoming increasingly clear. Montreal, at that time, was embroiled in political and social tension due to the ongoing separatist movement. The Quebec sovereignty movement was a significant issue, with discussions about Quebec's potential independence from Canada creating a sense of instability and uncertainty in the region. Many people were looking to leave Montreal, seeking opportunities in more stable environments.

Garrick's insight into my situation pushed me to reconsider my plans. He believed that my talents and aspirations were better suited for a different path, one that could leverage my skills in finance and take me beyond the confines of Montreal's current climate. He advised me to do a Chartered Financial Analyst (CFA) degree.

At that time, the CFA had not become as popular as it is today. Still, if you had a CFA, you had a leg up. It is a rigorous 3-year program that focuses on investment management and financial analysis. It's known for its depth and complexity, covering a broad range of topics from ethics and professional standards to quantitative methods and portfolio management. The CFA credential is highly respected in the finance industry and is often seen as a hallmark of excellence in financial analysis and investment management. It's designed for professionals who want to advance their careers in finance, investment banking, asset management, and related fields. The program includes three levels of exams, each progressively more challenging, and requires a combination of coursework and practical experience to earn the designation.

The best advice Garrick gave me was when I was deciding to further my studies, when he said:

"Bobby, go to Wall Street. Do an MBA. You should get away from the family and be on your own for this. It will be the best for you. It will make you a superstar."

He saw potential in me that I hadn't fully recognized yet and knew that an MBA could be the key to unlocking even greater opportunities. By then, I had successfully completed the CFA program. I graduated with honors and got into Canada's Wall Street - Bay Street.

Working in Canada's Wall Street - Bay Street

For a bit of context, my work experience at Abbott Laboratories and my education set me up for exceptional opportunities. By the time I was wrapping up my MBA, I had accumulated a wealth of experience that made me highly desirable in the job market. Imagine a young professional with a solid background in finance, having tackled the rigorous demands of a major pharmaceutical company like Abbott, combined with hands-on experience as an Investment Specialist at CIBC— one of Canada's largest and most respected banks. This blend of experience and education created a compelling profile.

At Abbott Laboratories, I gained practical experience in a high-stakes, fast-paced environment, which provided me with a deep understanding of the pharmaceutical industry and its financial intricacies. Working as an Investment Specialist at CIBC honed my skills in investment strategies and financial planning, allowing me to work closely with clients to manage their portfolios and offer tailored investment advice. Entering into the CFA program, with its comprehensive and challenging curriculum, further solidified my finance credentials and demonstrated my commitment to the field.

Given this impressive background, it was no surprise when I received a job offer from Deloitte & Touche. The firm, known for its global reach and prestigious client base, recognized the value of my unique combination of skills and experience. Deloitte & Touche was keen to leverage my finance background, analytical prowess, and the practical insights I had gained from both Abbott and CIBC. I was offered a position as an investment analyst specializing in Mergers & Acquisitions (M&A). This role was not just a job; it was a significant milestone in my professional journey, marking my entry into one of the most prestigious financial sectors in the world.

Located on Bay Street in Toronto, this address is often referred to as the Canadian equivalent of Wall Street, a hub of financial activity and influence. To have the opportunity to work in such a high-profile area was both thrilling and validating. It represented the pinnacle of financial career aspirations, where the best in the industry converge to shape the economic landscape.

Relocating to Toronto was, in many ways, a return to my roots. I found myself back in the city of my childhood, where my journey had begun and where my early experiences had shaped me. The familiarity of the city was grounding, even as I embarked on this new and challenging role. The return to Toronto was both a homecoming and a step forward, blending the comfort of the familiar with the excitement of new professional opportunities.

The role of an investment analyst in M&A was a dream job for someone with my ambitions. It was a position that not only carried an impressive title but also offered a platform to build a serious and impactful CV. Working in M&A meant engaging with complex financial transactions, evaluating company valuations, and advising on strategic business decisions. I was smack in the heart of Canada's financial district. The energy of the area was palpable, with a constant buzz of activity and a network of influential professionals. The prestige of working at such a prominent address added a layer of credibility and status to my career.

In this role, I experienced what can only be described as job heaven. The combination of a prestigious job title, a prime business location, and the dynamic nature of the work created an environment where I felt truly fulfilled. Each day brought new challenges and opportunities to grow, and my passion for finance was fueled by the excitement of being at the forefront of significant financial deals and transactions.

This period marked a significant turning point in my career. It was a time when my professional dreams and personal aspirations converged, allowing me to thrive in an environment that matched my ambitions and capabilities. I was on my way to being a millionaire with the vision of a comfortable retirement in my sights. I no longer believe in retirement, but at the time, it was my ultimate goal; after all, the media said it was the thing to aspire to.

Success as Revenge

The quote *"Survival was my only hope, success my only revenge"* at the beginning of this chapter in a lot of ways resonates with my personal journey. For me, survival was not merely about enduring; it was about overcoming the odds that life had stacked against me. It was a primal drive to move beyond mere existence, to rise above the challenges and create a life of meaning and accomplishment. Success was the ultimate form of vindication, a way to prove my resilience and ability to transform struggles into triumphs.

Survival, in my context, was more than just physical endurance; it was a mental and emotional battle against the backdrop of a challenging environment. Working at the Holiday Inn, facing the absence of a father figure, and navigating a foreign city without a safety net; all these factors created a harsh reality where the primary objective was to secure a stable foundation for myself and my mother. Each day was a fight to maintain hope, to find ways to navigate the systemic barriers and personal hardships that threatened to undermine our aspirations.

Survival meant more than just making ends meet, it involved a relentless pursuit of self-sufficiency and stability. Every challenge faced was an opportunity to learn and adapt. It was about finding ways to secure not just immediate needs but also to create a pathway toward long-term security.

So, imagine what it must have felt like when I was doing well in Canada's Wall Street. Success was not merely an individual achievement, it was a powerful statement against the circumstances that had once held me back. It represented a form of revenge against the adversity and limitations I had faced. The desire for success was fueled by a need to demonstrate that the struggles and setbacks had not defined me but rather had shaped my drive to achieve greatness.

The idea of success as revenge is deeply rooted in the concept of turning challenges into opportunities. It was about proving to myself that I could rise above the conditions that once seemed insurmountable. Success became a form of redemption, a way to validate my efforts and to show that despite the hardships, I had triumphed and created a life of significance and impact. Achieving success was not just about personal satisfaction but also about making a statement to those who doubted or underestimated my potential. It was a way to assert that my background and the challenges I faced did not define my limits. Success was the ultimate form of payback, demonstrating that I could overcome and excel despite the difficulties.

As far as I was concerned, and at this stage of my life, I was transforming adversity into an asset. I was persistent. Each challenge faced was a steppingstone toward achieving my goals. I was using the tools in the Devil's Dealbook well, and I was succeeding more than I thought possible.

Key Takeaways

- When things go wrong- and they sometimes will- learn to recover. Take the next day as a fresh start.
- Build upon your skills, gain experience - you never know when you will need them.
- Allow the people who know you and have walked the path you are on, to influence your life.

CHAPTER 3

THE MISTAKE

'Have no fear of perfection – you'll never reach it.' – **Salvador Dali.**

When I watched the 'Wolf of Wall Street,' I knew I wanted to make money like that. It played into my already established philosophy that I would make plenty of money and get influence. That was the way to live. What I didn't know was that I was making a mistake - similar to what happened at the Holiday Inn leading me to be fired, but not quite the same. Something with my philosophy was not right, this I would learn through a series of events that I will detail in this chapter and as I tell the rest of my story. Unbeknownst to me, I would live the law of marginal returns to a T. I would optimize every input and get more and more output until there was no more reward to be gained. Let me not get ahead of myself.

Climbing the Ladder of Success

While working at Deloitte & Touche, a consultant from Morgan Stanley noticed me during a joint project between our two firms. He saw something in my work and put my name forward as a candidate for a position with one of the biggest players in the market— a firm with a reputation for hiring top talent from Harvard, MIT, and Stanford.

This was an opportunity I had only ever dreamed about. To think that a twenty-five-year-old like me, with my background and experience, could land a job at such a prestigious firm in an even better address than Deloitte's seemed almost too good to be true.

The interview process was intense. I flew to New York and spent three days undergoing a grueling series of interviews— 22 in total. The interviews covered everything from technical skills to industry knowledge and were designed to test not only my expertise but also my ability to handle pressure. The firm was known for its cutting-edge work in equity research, especially in technology and the internet, with the likes of Mary Meeker and Richard Bilotti. They had a reputation for only hiring the best.

Despite my strong performance, I didn't get the job immediately. Instead, I was given a set of five books and one week to read them. These weren't just any books— they were dense with advanced tech concepts and industry jargon. The task was daunting, but I was determined to show them that I could rise to the challenge. That week, I barely slept. I devoured the books, highlighting passages and taking notes, immersing myself in the world of technology that I needed to master on the fly.

Two days after submitting my summary and reflections, I received a job offer from the firm. The hiring director was upfront about the salary; since I wasn't from MIT, they would reduce my starting pay compared to what they might offer a candidate from one of those top institutions. Still, even with the reduced salary, the offer was ten times more than what I was making before. It was a massive leap, and the opportunity was incredible.

The offer was a bittersweet victory. On the one hand, it was a clear acknowledgment of my skills and potential, a testament to how far I had come in my career. This was me using knowledge as a tool to advance my career. It was also a reminder of the steep competition and the high standards that come with working at such a prestigious firm. Joining the firm was a step up into the upper echelons of Wall Street, working alongside some of the brightest minds in the industry. It was a role that required not just financial acumen but also the ability to understand and navigate the rapidly evolving tech landscape. It was a rollercoaster ride of excitement, surprises, learning, stress, rewards, and everything I had seen in the movie that initially triggered my interest. If I had doubted it before, I was certain now that I would achieve my dreams of becoming a millionaire.

Suddenly, the possibilities seemed endless. The salary was substantial, and with it, I could finally achieve some of the goals I had long dreamed about. One of the first things I did was buy my mum a house. After everything we had been through, the years of struggle and the hard work she had put in, it was a deeply fulfilling moment to be able to provide her with a place she could call her own.

Buying that house for my mum was one of the most fulfilling financial transactions of my life.

Beyond the house, the financial security also opened doors to other dreams I had held onto. I could travel (not that I did, but I could afford it), invest in experiences, and explore opportunities that had seemed out of reach before. Just imagine where I had come from; working at 16, juggling school and a demanding job. My days were spent hauling heavy barrels and working double shifts while my friends enjoyed their summers. It was a tough time, but it built the foundation of my work ethic. From those early days of hustling at odds and ends jobs, to the long hours and occasional setbacks, it had all led to this point. I had worked my way up from the bottom, and now I was in a position to enjoy some of the rewards of that hard work. It was a surreal transition from those days at the Holiday Inn to the bright lights of Wall Street and the sense of accomplishment that came with it.

It was there that I met another person who mentored me – Richard Bilotti. Richard, a seasoned veteran in the industry, took me under his wing. His deep knowledge and experience were evident in every conversation and lesson. He had a way of breaking down intricate financial concepts into manageable pieces, making them accessible even to someone new to the advanced aspects of the field.

Richard's mentorship introduced me to the core principles of finance and taught me how to be an amazing analyst. I learnt how to analyze market trends, evaluate investment opportunities, and assess financial risks. We spent countless hours poring over data and analyzing companies. Looking back, meeting Richard Bilotti was a turning point for me. His mentorship enriched my understanding of finance, research and investment banking and provided me with the guidance needed to excel in a competitive industry.

I later co-authored a book with him - *Digital Decade Metamorphosis 3*. The book became the bible for analyzing the cable and satellite industry in the US. It also helped trigger several huge IPOs like Insight Communications and triggered one of the largest M&A deals ever in the history of technology. On January 10, 2000, America Online Inc. announced plans to acquire Time Warner Inc. for around $182 billion in stock and debt. This merger resulted in the formation of a $350 billion mega-corporation, AOL Time Warner, which held dominant positions across various media sectors including music, publishing, news, entertainment, cable, and the internet. The merger occurred at the peak of the so-called "internet bubble," when the allure of dot-com companies was at an all-time high. The vision was to meld Time Warner's extensive resources in traditional media with AOL's 30 million internet subscribers to create an unmatched media powerhouse.

Under the merger's terms, AOL shareholders gained 55% ownership of the new company, while Time Warner shareholders held 45%. Steve Case, AOL's co-founder and CEO, became the chairman of the new entity, with Time Warner's Gerald Levin stepping in as CEO. However, the anticipated synergies never materialized, and when the internet bubble burst in 2001, AOL Time Warner faced staggering losses, reaching a record $54 billion in a single quarter.

Working at US Bancorp

When the time came for a new chapter in my career, I made a pivotal decision to leave Morgan Stanley and join US Bancorp in Minnesota. This came at a great time - opportunities were booming in technology especially with smaller investment banks. These banks paid more money and had more upside opportunities. The decision also meant that I moved to San Francisco, California, the heart of the tech boom and success of internet/Tech companies. It was like living in a fantasy world; big money, big lifestyle and countless opportunities to succeed.

In many ways, this move marked a significant shift in my professional journey, with the journey to Piper Jaffray. This decision was not merely a change of location but a strategic step that propelled me to new heights in the high-stakes arena of equity research. I was their first bulge bracket hire.

Bulge bracket firms are the largest and most prestigious investment banks in the world, known for their comprehensive range of financial services. Their global reach and extensive resources enable them to facilitate complex financial transactions and offer sophisticated financial products across various markets.

The opportunity to join US Bancorp came at a crucial moment in my career and I was using my knowledge to my advantage. With Morgan Stanley's prestigious credentials and my track record in equity research, I was well-positioned to leverage my experience, reputation and passion.

According to a report by *Financial Times*, moving to a new firm within the bulge bracket banking sector often offers significant career advantages, including higher compensation, increased responsibilities, and enhanced professional networks. This move allowed me to enter a top-tier banking environment, where the stakes were higher and the opportunities for advancement were substantial.

At US Bancorp, I found myself at the pinnacle of my game in the highly competitive field of equity research. The transition from Morgan Stanley to Piper Jaffray provided me with an elevated platform to showcase my skills and make a significant impact. The demand for equity research expertise from a bulge bracket firm is invaluable. It made me a valuable asset.

At this point, I was still approaching any change in my career as a strategic move to make more money, still clinging to the hope of retirement. Of course, I had no way of knowing that I would come to debunk the whole idea of retirement altogether.

The Burst of the Internet Bubble

As I was settling into my role at US Bancorp, the internet bubble burst, and it felt like everything was turning upside down. The dot-com bubble, which had been growing since the mid-90s, had reached a point where tech companies were valued based on their potential rather than their actual earnings. With the internet booming, investors poured money into any company with a ".com" in its name, even if they were still in their infancy and lacking solid business plans.

But then, in late 2000, things started to go south. The Federal Reserve increased interest rates several times, making it more expensive to borrow money. This shift caused investors to pull their funds out of risky tech stocks and move them into safer investments, like bonds. At the same time, Japan's economy slid into a recession, which triggered a global financial panic.

The Nasdaq Composite Index, which had been a symbol of the tech boom, began its steep decline. By October 2002, it had lost nearly 80% of its value from its peak. The impact was widespread, and many tech companies went under or had to scale back drastically. The stock market entered a bear phase, and the tech sector in particular, was hit hard.

For those of us working in finance, this was a tough period. Jobs were lost, hiring freezes were implemented, and the excitement of the previous years was replaced by a harsh reality. I saw firsthand how quickly fortunes could change in the financial world. It was a stark lesson in the risks of speculative investing and the importance of having a solid, sustainable business model. Of course, all of this affected me. For starters, I lost all my accumulated wealth!

I have always believed that maintaining a positive mindset and focusing on what you want can influence the outcomes in your life, and this belief proved crucial during this turbulent time. With the market in disarray, it was a period of reevaluation and recalibration. As the dust began to settle, I reminded myself to keep my energy focused on my goals. The law of attraction— believing that focusing on positive outcomes would bring about those outcomes— played a significant role in how I navigated this phase. I knew that dwelling on the negativity of the situation would only hold me back, so I chose to channel my energy into optimism and determination.

Just when I needed it most, the stars seemed to align once again. A friend from London reached out and suggested that I come over to stay with him for a few days and explore job opportunities there. The timing couldn't have been better. While the US was experiencing its own set of challenges, it was still more stable compared to other parts of the world struggling with economic turmoil.

I took his advice and headed to London. While I was there, I had the opportunity to interview for several positions, which opened up new possibilities for my career. The energy of being in a different city, coupled with the positivity I carried with me, played a crucial role in the new opportunities that began to unfold.

It was not long until I found myself in a promising position with HSBC, one of the largest and most prestigious investment banks in the world at the time. It was a significant step up, and I felt a deep sense of accomplishment. The combination of my background, which included stints at Morgan Stanley, Piper Jaffray, and my CFA credentials, made me a standout candidate. HSBC was looking to expand its team with experienced professionals who could bring a wealth of knowledge and a proven track record, and they saw potential in me.

The bank was a powerhouse, known for its global reach and robust financial services. I worked there for a short while when the internet bubble caught up with us there too. The same speculative fervor that had driven the tech boom in San Francisco was now seeping into the UK market. The internet bubble was expanding across the Atlantic, creating an environment of unchecked optimism and inflated valuations.

In the early 2000s, the UK market began to experience the same kind of speculative frenzy that had previously led to the collapse of numerous tech firms in the US. Companies were being overvalued, and the market was awash with excessive enthusiasm for internet-based businesses. It felt like history was repeating itself, and the signs of a potential downturn were becoming increasingly evident. The parallels between the two situations were striking. Just as I had seen in the US, the rapid rise in valuations and the speculative investments were creating a bubble that seemed destined to burst. The energy in the financial markets was reminiscent of the days leading up to the dot-com crash, and it was clear that the UK was not immune to these broader economic forces. The same issues that had plagued the US market were now affecting the UK, and I found myself facing similar challenges in a different context.

London, this time around, was the beginning of a very interesting adventure, transition, adaptation, and evolution into full-blown entrepreneurship and the conception of constructing my thinking into the eventual culture of FUM©. It took time for my ingrained retirement thinking to deconstruct, preparing me for the mind shift.

The Hero's Journey

Think of the hero's journey. The hero's journey is a narrative archetype famously articulated by Joseph Campbell in *The Hero with a Thousand Faces*. This journey begins with the hero heeding the call to adventure— a pivotal moment that marks the transition from the ordinary world into a realm of challenge, transformation, and profound change. It typically looks like this:

1. Understanding the call

The call to adventure represents a critical juncture where the hero is beckoned to leave their familiar, comfortable world and embark on a quest that promises both peril and reward. This call is often unexpected and disruptive, challenging the hero to confront the unknown. In real life, this can manifest as an opportunity, a challenge, or a profound realization that prompts significant change. For instance, consider a professional who, after years in a stable job, receives an offer to lead a groundbreaking project or start a new venture. This offer may feel daunting but represents the call to adventure that could lead to transformative personal and professional growth. For me, London was a call to adventure.

2. Overcoming reluctance

The hero's initial reaction to the call is often one of reluctance or fear. This hesitance stems from the uncertainty and risks associated with leaving the known world behind. The journey to embrace the call involves overcoming internal doubts and fears. For example, the entrepreneur considering a major business venture may initially feel apprehensive about the risks and potential failures. But overcoming this reluctance and taking action can lead to significant personal and professional growth.

3. Commitment to the journey

Heeding the call to adventure requires a commitment to embark on the journey, despite the uncertainties. This commitment involves preparing for the challenges ahead and embracing the unknown with courage and determination.

In literature and mythology, heroes who commit to their quest often receive guidance or support from mentors, allies, or supernatural forces. Similarly, in real life, people who commit to their goals and seek support or mentorship are better equipped to navigate challenges and achieve their objectives.

4. Facing trials and challenges

The hero's journey is often characterized by trials and challenges that test their resolve and abilities. These trials are not merely obstacles but opportunities for growth and learning. The hero emerges from these experiences with new skills, insights, and strengths.

5. Achieving transformation

By the end of the journey, the hero undergoes a significant transformation, having gained new wisdom, skills, or understanding. This transformation often leads to a return to the ordinary world with a renewed sense of purpose and capability. In professional terms, this transformation can manifest as a significant career advancement, a new skill set, or a deeper understanding of one's strengths and potential.

6. Returning with the elixir

The final stage of the hero's journey involves returning to the ordinary world with the "elixir" of newfound knowledge, skills, or insights. This return represents the hero's ability to apply their experiences and contribute positively to their original world.

I didn't know it, but my decision to move to the UK was to begin me on a journey similar to the hero's journey. All the seeds had been planted to set me up for success, but it was going to take some time for me to figure things out in my head. I will reveal more of my path between these covers, beginning with the key lesson I learned which initiated the shift in my thinking. It happened when I got really serious about what I wanted my future to look like. Sometimes a paradigm cannot be shifted unless it is blown apart and reconstructed. Mine was.

It's all in the Mind

But before that, here is what was happening in my head as I worked hard in all of those jobs. It is the mistake I made.

For most people, being rich or being poor starts with a mindset. Where you begin in life is possibly defined by fate, where you eventually end up is primarily based on providence, your thoughts, beliefs, and mindset. How your circumstances, relationships, and finances trend are due to your actions and the root of most actions are based on how you think. To see this, let's look into the different mindsets of growing wealth and struggling with personal finances, by starting with the mindset of the wealthy.

- According to a 2023 report, approximately 72% of those who receive a significant inheritance fail to maintain their wealth for more than 10 years due to poor financial planning and mismanagement.
- A 2022 survey by *Charles Schwab* found that 41% of Americans who received an inheritance reported spending it within a year, with a significant portion not investing it wisely.
- A 2023 study by *The National Endowment for Financial Education* revealed that 77% of lottery winners, regardless of the amount, end up broke or in financial trouble within five years.

Imagine that! Consequently, there are many people born into humble situations that go on to build wealth and conversely, wealthy children that squander their opportunities and end up broke. But it is also true that regardless of where you find yourself, you can redirect your thinking into a new path and create a healthy, wealthy money mindset.

The healthy, wealthy mindset thinks about creating, building, and compounding assets. Wealthy people create more than they consume and love their work more than their vacations and buying stuff. They build wealth by managing their finances, investment portfolios, real estate holdings, business, or cash-producing assets. The wealthy mindset incorporates the calculated risk mentality, concerning the return on capital risk versus reward. It is typically an entrepreneurial mindset of creating products, services, investments, businesses, and jobs for others. They are creative and turn their ideas into reality to produce value.

On the other hand, the person with the unhealthy money mindset is surrounded by opportunities but they will ignore them because they have a poverty mindset. Their negative energy stems from victimhood, jealousy, and blaming fate for dealing them a low blow. Closed-mindedness is the primary sign of an unhealthy money mindset. Conversion of this mindset takes the effort of seeing abundance instead of scarcity - to stop going with the flow that poverty is your lot in life.

Chasing Only Money – The Mistake

From the get-go, my mindset was on acquiring money, amassing as much as I could for myself. And yet, there is wisdom about money that I was coming to understand/learn, that money is a means to an end, not the meaning of life. At Deloitte, Morgan Stanely, US Bancorp and every other place I worked, my life was about making money. I dedicated nearly every waking hour, outside of sleep, to working tirelessly to amass wealth. Money was the axis around which my daily existence revolved. The pursuit of financial success can be all-consuming.

My experiences in various entrepreneurial ventures taught me that generating income is not particularly challenging when one is determined and resourceful. The real difficulty lies in defining when enough is truly enough. The constant drive to earn more can become a never-ending cycle, where the focus on financial gain overshadows other aspects of life.

Research by *Psychology Today* emphasizes that the pursuit of money can lead to a cycle of perpetual dissatisfaction. In their 2022 report, they found that people who chase wealth without satisfaction or a clear purpose often experience diminishing returns in terms of happiness and life satisfaction. This aligns with the idea that while making money can be straightforward, knowing when to stop and finding balance is where the real challenge lies.

I was in the rat race. The concept of the rat race refers to the relentless, competitive pursuit of financial success and material gain, often leading to burnout and a sense of unfulfillment. The challenge of "checking out" of this race is about more than just financial stability, it's about finding contentment and purpose beyond the daily grind. Other research has highlighted that many high-achieving people struggle with the concept of "enough," leading to a perpetual state of striving for more, stressing the importance of defining personal success and finding a balance that allows for fulfillment and well-being, rather than just chasing after more wealth.

I have learnt over the years that the question of how much is enough is deeply personal and often requires introspection. I will tell you more about this later.

Money is undoubtedly a powerful tool, but it is not the ultimate measure of a meaningful life. My journey through relentless work and financial achievement taught me that while making money is relatively straightforward, understanding when enough is enough and how to exit the rat race is more complex. True fulfillment comes from finding a balance between financial success and personal purpose. Money is truly a terrible master. But these lessons didn't come easy.

Key Takeaways

- Sometimes changes in your environment will affect you. How you deal with them depends on your attitude and energy.
- Whether you're poor or rich is influenced by your mindset.
- Money is a good servant but a terrible master. It is a means to an end, not the meaning of life.

CHAPTER 4

STEPPING INTO MY FUTURE

"A mentor is someone who sees more talent and ability within you, than you see in yourself, and helps bring it out of you." - **Bob Proctor.**

*I*n the recounting of my story, I have mentioned people who were pivotal to the different stages and changes I went through. I learnt from Magic Johnson what I desired out of life. My boss while in college helped me save up for university and taught me how to be diligent at work. Garrick Killberry gave me direction; he shaped my vision. Richard Bilotti gave me skills and confidence in my ability to execute that industry specific knowledge. Each of these people came into my life and changed its course.

Besides the influence of these people, other events shaped the person I would turn out to be. In this chapter, you will find the stories that ushered me into my life now, as a business owner, entrepreneur and FUM© architect.

The Events Leading to My Sabbatical

When my friend called me to go to London to interview for different positions– including HSBC- I did not get the job immediately. To work in the UK, I needed a work visa, and the only way I could be granted that is if HSBC was sure I was the best man for the job.

A week passed, and then another, dragging me into a whirlpool of anxiety. My hope flickered with each passing day, and by the end of the third week I was on edge, refreshing my email more times than I care to admit. The longer I waited, the more I questioned if I was making a monumental mistake in moving across the globe for this opportunity.

With bills piling up and my savings dwindling, I took a telemarketing job to keep myself afloat. It was far from ideal— long hours spent on the phone trying to convince uninterested customers to consider products they didn't want. But I did the job anyway because it allowed me to scrape by. I had lost all my money, so this was a lifeline.

Just as I was beginning to lose hope, the email came. The subject line read "Job Offer – HSBC," and my heart raced as I opened it. They had approved my work visa! I was officially hired as a Vice President. Elation surged through me, drowning out the noise of my telemarketing days. I felt like I was standing on a precipice, ready to dive into a new chapter.

The pay was excellent, and I reveled in the possibilities that lay ahead. I was eager to throw myself into my work in this prestigious position at a renowned bank. But, as I already described earlier, a shadow hung over my excitement: the looming uncertainty of the economic climate in the UK. Rumors of the downturn started swirling around the office. On the sell side, positions were often the first to be cut during financial struggles. The non-compete clause in my contract gnawed at me; if I were let go, I would be unable to explore new opportunities for a couple of months. I was a bit like a bird trapped in a gilded cage, and despite the comfort of my salary, the fear of the unknown kept me up at night.

That is where David Sheridan, the man who had hired me into HSBC stepped in. He was then the head of our division (my boss's boss) and the first person in all of London to wear a gold-threaded suit— yes, you read that right, a gold-threaded suit. David was a character, known for his flamboyant style and larger-than-life presence in the banking world.

He approached me and explained that because of my non-compete, I would not be able to find another job immediately if I left HSBC. He suggested that since there was not much going on (thanks to the burst of the internet bubble), I could take three months to travel Europe.

"Bobby, you're still very young. I know you were born in Germany, but you've never really seen Europe. How about this: we'll give you a three-month sabbatical with pay. When you come back, you can either resume your job here or explore other opportunities. It's up to you." He said.

The offer was unexpected and rather generous. A three-month paid sabbatical was a rare luxury in the banking world, and it felt like a golden opportunity. There was no business happening due to the market slowdown, so sticking around without the chance for bonuses seemed pointless. Instead, I saw the sabbatical as a chance to take a step back, explore Europe, and recharge.

David's offer was a kind of bonus in itself, a chance to gain new experiences and perspectives without worrying about my finances. I was thrilled at the thought of finally seeing more of Europe. So, I accepted the sabbatical with enthusiasm. It was an opportunity to travel, reflect, and perhaps even reconsider my next steps, a rare chance to step away from the grind of investment banking, savor new experiences, and come back with a fresh perspective, whether I chose to stay at HSBC or pursue new opportunities.

Traveling Through Europe

During those three months in Europe, I immersed myself in experiences that felt as refreshing as they were transformative. After the relentless pace I'd maintained from 1997 up to that point, this sabbatical was like hitting the reset button on my life. I used the time to truly soak up Europe's rich historical culture, savor street cuisine, and bask in the warm hospitality of locals. It was a far cry from the high-flying lifestyle I had become accustomed to.

Most of my previous travels had been business-related; flying first class, staying in five-star hotels, and dining at Michelin-star restaurants. My sabbatical funding, however, turned my journey into a far more grounded adventure. I found myself flying on budget airlines, crashing at backpacker lodges, and sampling local street food. The change in pace was invigorating. Instead of high-end dining, I enjoyed hearty meals in parks and sidewalk cafes. I wandered through small, out-of-the-way villages, connecting with the people who lived in them. It was in these unassuming corners of Europe that I discovered a different kind of richness, one that money couldn't buy– the FUM© mindset.

This slower pace allowed me to reconnect with something I had lost sight of amid the whirlwind of my career. Without the relentless drive pushing me forward, I had space to reflect and get to know myself better. The time away from the constant grind was revelatory. I found joy in the simple pleasures of life, such as sharing stories with locals or exploring cobblestone streets that seemed untouched by time. Each new experience was like a piece of a puzzle, helping me understand what truly made me tick and what living life meant for me.

The Bobby who set off for Turkey at the beginning of this journey was not the same person who returned to London. The transformation was profound. Just as Rambo's (yes, the movie starring) evolution from an average joe to a full-blooded Green Beret combat soldier was marked by intense, deliberate changes, my own journey through Europe felt like a series of deliberate, soul-searching moments that chipped away at my previous self.

By the end of the trip, I had encountered so many wonderful people, each with their own stories and ways of seeing the world. The genuine connections I made and the experiences I had were invaluable. The fast-paced, high-stakes life I had known before was replaced with a sense of clarity and purpose. I was no longer just chasing after money; I was learning to appreciate life and live in the moment. It was an unexpected but amazing journey of self-discovery. I returned to London with a new perspective, having peeled back the layers of my former self to reveal something more authentic and meaningful.

Meeting Colin Rodgers

As I wandered through the vibrant streets of Paris, the serene canals of Amsterdam, and the historic ruins of Rome, I had begun to realize that the sell side- with the long hours, constant stress, and job insecurity- no longer suited me. The grueling 17-to-18-hour days were exhausting, leaving little room for life outside the office.

I wanted a different path for myself on the buy side. Asset management felt like a sanctuary, offering not just stability but a genuine work-life balance. While the pay might not match the dizzying heights of the sell side, the thought of enjoying my work, finding fulfillment, and having time for my passions became increasingly appealing. With this newfound clarity, I decided to explore job opportunities throughout Europe while I traveled.

During my trip, I connected with several firms, and by the time I returned home, I had three promising job offers on the table. But as fate would have it, the markets had gotten worse. When I followed up with the companies, I received disheartening news, they had stalled their hiring processes. "We no longer have the mandate to bring you on," they said. I was left feeling as if the ground had shifted beneath my feet once again.

I was in the same place I had been before, with no money and no job. I needed to reset my mind. Thankfully, the trip to Europe had really changed me, and I had embraced the idea that you can enjoy life without that much money. I spent some of my time visiting museums and trying to squeeze as much joy out of life that I could with my limited resources. I had learned in Europe that joy could be found in the simplest of moments, like sipping coffee at a quaint café or enjoying the quiet beauty of a park. There was nothing stopping me from living out this newfound perspective.

Then, out of the blue, something unexpected happened. One afternoon, while I was sketching in a café or something like that, my phone buzzed. It was Colin Rodgers, a name I did not recognize at the time. He introduced himself with an air of enthusiasm, saying he'd heard of me through media coverage and from mutual acquaintances. "I've received glowing reviews about your work," he said. "I'd like to invite you for an interview. I'm looking to grow my firm, and I believe you could be a key player in that vision."

If this opportunity materialized, I would not have to return to Canada. I could stay in London.

Fate would have it that Colin would be the sculptor to take up the hammer and chisel and craft me into what he perceived me to be, his Director of Research and his UK sales director. He played the role in my life that Colonel Tautman played for Rambo.

Colonel Tautman understood Rambo's complex nature. He saw not just a soldier hardened by war, but a man capable of greatness if only given the right guidance and support. Similarly, Colin sensed the drive within me; the tenacity I had honed during my years on the sell side and the insights I gained while traveling. He could see that I was ready to shift gears and embrace a role that demanded creativity, analytical thinking, and a genuine passion for asset management.

When I think back on all the interviews I had attended before, the one with him was the first one where the real Bobby Rakhit showed up. I could not see myself as Colin did, but there was most definitely a salesperson in me waiting to be discovered.

While meeting Colin, I was clueless about the job on offer, or the domain that Colin operated in until a very strange feeling swept over me as we chatted. For the first time in my life, I didn't feel the usual fear of poverty that had been dominant in all my previous job interviews. It was weird, unfamiliar, peaceful, and a feeling I wanted to hold on to forever. I knew I still wanted to make a ton of money, but now it was for a different reason. I was hungry to succeed in the job, but it was not simply to assuage my fear of poverty with a big salary. I knew about being hungry to be successful from my early days of shoveling snow and selling my bike. I thrived on the gratitude of my satisfied customers with clean driveways and the look on my mother's face when I handed her the cash from the proceeds of the bike sale.

I drew a parallel for my life from Rambo's; his hunger for succeeding on a mission, rather than being paralyzed by the fear of failure. The interview was more like a friendly chat than an intense interrogation. I felt comfortable enough to be vulnerable and share parts of my past and future ambitious aspirations and fears. Colin couldn't believe that I began my university studies in the medical faculty before switching to financial studies and setting myself up for a dream career in investment banking on New York's famous Wall Street. He laughed when I told him about my telemarketing job in London while I was waiting for the job with HSBC, selling faceless people a financial product. He smiled and nodded when I told him about my entrepreneurial endeavors as a kid in Canada. He looked doubtful about my brief attempts at landscaping and home improvements with a mate from the Holiday Inn. Selling my bike must have sealed it for him. He went quiet for a while before cocking his head to one side, nodding slowly and saying with a smile,

"*You know, Bobby, I see in you something I have not seen in anyone I've interviewed for this job. You have an entrepreneurial wick waiting to be lit. You would have been bored to tears in the medical profession, and I have a hunch that investment banking will not hold your attention forever. You are neglecting that desire in you. You need to unleash it on the world. You will do a great job in Sales.*"

It was my turn to be silent for a minute, digesting his comment and enjoying the adrenaline rush set off by my childhood memories shared with him. I still wasn't sure what sales was about, so I asked him what he needed from me if I took the job. He told me he was looking for someone to crank up sales. I would be his sales director and should forget any reservations I had about having no sales experience. When he fleshed out the job in detail, these are the things that made me perfect for the job:

- My technology knowledge – I knew the industry well thanks to my experience.
- My confidence and ambition – These were clear from my recounting of my life experiences.
- My networks – I had worked for banks so I could be useful to a firm that sells data and technology to financial institutions and banks.

He wasn't concerned about the specific skills related to data because he saw traits in me that convinced him I was a good fit for the job at JCF. This is exactly what I mean when I say that a good mentor sees things in you that you may not see yourself and helps to bring them out. Notice also how the tools inside the Devil's Dealbook were again commending me for an opportunity.

According to Colin, given the opportunity, I could do exceptionally well at the job, far beyond my wildest expectations. My equity research background was an unusual asset for a person in the position he was offering me. My easy manner, social skills, and high level of EQ attracted him too. Besides opening up the market for him, Colin wanted me to infiltrate the London financial and media circles. I would form connections and gain exposure for the JCF brand, building credibility in the marketplace. He was sure I could establish a network and do whatever it took to convince a client to sign a deal. It sounded so simple; I still wasn't sure though. He noticed my reluctance and put me at ease, saying that I had nothing to lose and everything to gain from the challenge if I pulled it off.

This opportunity would be perfect for me, I figured. For starters, I wanted to work on the buy-side and everything in my new job description would fall smack on the buy-side. I would get to work directly with their hedge-fund. Secondly, I would get a chance to be a bit of an entrepreneur. How fitting for me!

The deal was clinched when he said, *"You're a likable guy, Bobby. If you take all the attributes I've mentioned and apply yourself, you will make a killing."*

I don't know how, but Colin, the genius, saw who I was and what I wanted from life, although FUM© was a very young part of me then. Just to assure me that he wasn't sugar-coating a bitter pill, he frowned, shook his index finger at me, and said, *"I won't lie to you Bobby; Sales is not for sissies. But in you, I see the heart of a lion. You will do well!"*

I made a killing in sales exactly as I set out to do. It wasn't just a haphazard arrival at a destination. The plan, albeit unknown to me, had been triggered subconsciously years before in a hotel room staring into the face of a rat who wanted my bowl of cereal as much as I did. He was totally comfortable and at home in his environment, being the rat he was. I was totally uncomfortable being the person I was and resolved to never ever share a room or my food with a rat again in my life. I had no choice, and neither did my mother, but that sh$tty predicament flipped a switch that would not have flipped if I lived in a comfortable, privileged, environment where I felt entitled to everything I had.

My mother and I had two options in that hotel room. To blame my father for everything and become two victims looking for something the world owed us, or to get the hell out of there as soon as possible and pull ourselves up by our bootstraps to prosper. Notice,

I say prosper, not survive. That was not an option as far as we were concerned.

And here I was, prospering.

Reflecting on My Journey

Changing lanes in my career sparked an interest in the stories of how people's careers take unexpected turns that lead to success. It interests me to see how some deviations are born out of necessity rather than following the planned path. I began by studying medicine and ended up as an entrepreneur breathing life into my FUM© vision. Working in sales did it for me, and I would never have known it if it wasn't for Colin Rodgers.

Who knows what will do it for you? Perhaps you are in the ideal job to get you there, in which case, the decision will be to simply change your mindset about how you plan your future.

Unlike the walks we take with a planned destination, a career walk takes some twists and turns; planned or unplanned, they ultimately make up the walk. Mine began when I taught the investment team in the Canadian Imperial Bank of Commerce a course on Canadian Securities. They offered me a permanent job, which I turned down because I set my sights on bigger things. The first full-time job in my chosen career was with Deloitte Touche in Canada as an Investment Analyst in the Mergers & Acquisitions Division; this job set me up for my dream job on Wall Street with Morgan Stanley for the best Equity Research (ER) team in the world. Equity research became my forte, and I worked in several firms, always ambitious, looking to make more money.

From Morgan Stanley, I moved on to join Bancorp Piper Jaffray on their newly formed ER team. From that job, I changed countries and moved to the UK, where I landed a job with HSBC in London, still in ER. London introduced me to the international banking world and expanded the knowledge I had gained in the insular Canadian and US markets. I put this experience to good use when I changed lanes into my new job as a sales director with JCF, which later became FactSet. The Bobby Rakhit Brand emerged through printed as well as televised media. Colin Rogers set me off and then nurtured me through this phase to draw attention to JCF's products. He allowed me the freedom to test many of my untapped skills, particularly entrepreneurship.

I will never forget when Colin told me he saw vibrant entrepreneurial energy in me. The drip-feeding I'd received as a child selling my bicycle and subsequent input from the surrogate fathers in our friendship circle at the time, was pertinent. They shared their daily business experience freely with me and cathected my spirit when I needed it.

Circling back to my childhood, it occurs to me that instead of running around with my friends, I'd chosen to sit in men's company with both ears open. The seeds that grew into Rambo's career grew from playing war games with his young buddies and watching movies like *The Bridge on the River Kwai*, *The Longest Day*, or my favorite, *The Great Escape*. His will to survive kept him going when his life balanced on a knife edge, hanging by his fingertips on the side of a cliff face, gritting his teeth while a crazy cop fired shots at him from a hovering helicopter. That drive came from somewhere in his life. We both began preparing for our eventual careers as young boys.

My connection with entrepreneurship at this level was not immediate because of the misperception that I needed to be the next Richard Branson to succeed. It was only natural considering my crude make-as-much-money-as-possible-to-avoid-poverty-and-retire-one-day mentality. Branson owned a magazine at 16 and went on to create record labels and airlines; I worked in the Holiday Inn at 16, and I never even had my own business.

Then I got to thinking and saw this scene in my mind from *Honey I Shrunk the Kids,* the dad shrunk his kids with the machine he invented. The kids stood eye to eye with a mouse. It changed my perspective and brough entrepreneurship into a relative focus of possibility in my life. I didn't have to be as big as Richard Branson. It's all relative, looking at the thousands of small business entrepreneurs in informal markets, the gadget shop owner in the local shopping mall, my internet provider who started as a computer technician straight out of school and millions more. They all took risks creating their businesses and continue taking them daily to succeed and make a enough of a living to enjoy the fruits of their labor.

They are all Richard Branson, creating something out of nothing.

Perhaps the lesson here is to take risks. If you don't take risks, you don't get luck. If I had not risked more rejection when interviewing with Colin Rodgers, I wouldn't have gotten the job. Many people make the mistake of only asking God for things and then waiting for them. My life experience has taught me that God (or the universe, or the divine), doesn't just give you things. The universe rewards calculated risks. It rewards effort. What looks like luck to the outsider is in fact your hard work and risk receiving due reward.

It also occurs to me that the title of entrepreneur is not only for people with businesses. I have met hundreds of entrepreneurs that don't own their own companies. I was in a new pond where I would tread water for a while, gathering confidence and momentum before confidently swimming freestyle. I walked until I could run. It was my first real excursion into serious entrepreneurship before eventually establishing businesses of my own.

If you do a good job of selling yourself and forming relationships, you are doing a good job! The next big deal could come from a lost sale referral. Word of mouth is the most effective marketing you will ever achieve. The stars had aligned, bringing Colin and me together at the precise time I needed to meet him. The JCF job had seemed like a long shot, far from the job I was after. I took Colin's challenge with guns blazing and my hunting knife tucked into my combat boot. Adapting a little more every day as the environment needed me to.

The ancient wisdom that iron sharpens iron described the fit between Colin and me. He continually sharpened my skills, taking nicks and scratches out, honing me to perfection. I responded by stretching myself into the role and responding to the trust that he had in me to do a great job with minimum supervision. I'm not shy to tell you- and he would agree- that managing my energy and enthusiasm was a new experience that made me a handful for him to control. He never complained though, because I made it worth his while by delivering sales as he had never seen before.

Creativity and empathy, synchronized with my enthusiasm for the JCF job, stirred the dormant skills I relied on to make a name for myself with my literary prowess in junior school. I could not have reached the level of sales greatness without it. Rambo's creativity kicked in whenever he needed it in tight situations, regularly saving his bacon. There was no time in the height of combat to park off in a comfort zone, lest he lost the battle or his life. I never took my foot off the pedal either, lest I lose a deal, or worse still, my job. We both used our creativity and empathy to the max to succeed.

I was continuously looking for new challenges that required every bit of my creativity to pull off, and every ounce of empathy I had to connect to the people involved. Improvising was the name of the sales director's game, because it felt like I was suddenly in a pro football game, fumbling with an oval ball that often bounced opposite from my expectations. I found it an exciting challenge compared to my colleagues, who complained about the volatility of client decisions. I never dodged the bullets; I simply asked probing questions to understand my client's needs so I could provide solutions. My deep knowledge of the product I was selling and the dynamics of using financial research made my job easy.

Opportunity Strikes

One evening having a few drinks with a man who shared my passion for QR, he offered to introduce me to his colleague at the Financial Times. When the door opened a crack, I got my foot in quickly, and we got together. We shared interests, stories, and our research insights. It was a meeting of minds; and it led to me writing articles for the Financial Times. The readers liked me, turning it into a regular Bobby Rakhit column. The writing gig got me invitations to appear on Financial TVs programs like Bloomberg, CNBC and BBC sharing my insights, and lead to regular speaking appearances in conferences. I built my Brand– Bobby Rakhit, Market Expert. I was a product, I was in demand. Mission accomplished: JCF got exposure, and I expanded my already substantial network.

It's a fact that you become like the people you hang out with. I am drawn to like-minded people and love socializing with them as often as possible. It is no small wonder that my mates and I raise the eyebrows of people within earshot with our passionate conversations around financial research methodologies in restaurants and pubs; the intensity of our discussion rises in proportion to our passion for the subject. I am always the loudest and am continually apologizing to the surrounding patrons. It is a platform for sharing ideas on our business life in a relaxed setting, educating each other to go out and do a better job in the marketplace.

Rambo's influence is the inspiration for my b@lls to the wall approach to life, sustaining my passion for life, the universe, and everything wrapped up in and beyond my everyday existence. I soon perfected my craft, closing deals with some heavyweight clients. My meticulous approach to the job garnered Colin's confidence in my ability enough to trust me and give me the freedom to run my own show and deliver the goods for him. I have always lived by my maxim: There is no room for shoddiness in my life. In one of our debriefing sessions, Colin commented on a trait I never knew I owned until then. Without it, I would not have been successful. The words rang in my mind for a long time after the discussion. Cocking his head to one side and waving his index finger at me, he said,

"Bobby, my boy, you have a ruthless killer instinct. You don't take no for an answer. I love it son, it's your biggest asset."

To which I responded, *"I don't like losing!"*

To this he sternly replied- narrowing his gaze and nodding his head, still waving his index finger at me- *"That attitude, Bobby, is what will put you at the top of the leaderboard!"*

JCF made me come alive, just like my sporting days when I was so in tune with my body and my ability to do well. It came back to me as if I was on the basketball court, or on the soccer field scoring goals again. On the basketball court, I timed my passes to perfection, swerving, dodging, and regularly adding points to the scoreboard. I was equally impressive on the soccer field and football stadium too. Sales required accurate information and predictions for my clients' defined needs, timing the passes precisely, (asking questions) waiting for a response, and scoring the goal (getting a signature on a contract).

So with this in mind, I focused my planning on the Bobby Rakhit brand too. I ensured each client remembered our meetings because of my unique approach to presenting myself and the brand. I became synonymous with JCF and the media. When people heard the name Bobby Rakhit, they automatically thought of JCF. When they heard JCF, they thought of Bobby Rakhit; fun, relaxed meetings, plus knowing that we (JCF and I) could solve their problems.

Working at FactSet

FactSet, a global player in the field of finance, bought JCF in 2003; I was now thirty years old and ready to test more of my entrepreneurial prowess in a much bigger market. When FactSet acquired JCF, they realized the utility of keeping me around and created a role specifically for me. I was now the head of the division called New Business Sales (NBS) and I took the new challenge on with both hands, upped my energy levels, infiltrated the top management structures, and made a name for myself very quickly. I have used the term 'taking it to a new level' possibly too many times now to keep it credible, but I must use it again when it comes to the level of my innate leadership skills, nurtured from my childhood when my peers followed me as a leader of my friendship groups.

In the classrooms at school, Bobby always stood out from the crowd and was never afraid to take the lead. From my first and every subsequent job, I took on leadership roles. I volunteered to teach the young staff in FactSet to prepare them for their Chartered Financial Analyst (CFA) exams. Teaching and leadership are two of my passions. FactSet opened opportunities for me to grow my empire across continents. Between 2003 and 2012, I opened offices in Dubai, India, and Hong Kong, and expanded the Middle East, Africa, and Asian markets. My FactSet walk was more of a climb up the corporate ladder. My division grew year on year every year and produced unmatched sales across the company. It was a difficult task for management to keep my salary confidential and it led to much disgruntled discussion between the directors who earned less than me.

Leadership was never a conscious decision at a fixed point in time; it was a gradual process of easing into my purpose on planet earth. I was meant to lead and have an influence on the world. When I taught my staff in the national offices how I wanted them to do their jobs, I showed them by example the excellence that I expected from them and revealed their potential to do the same. As before, the FactSet staff respected me, not only my staff, but globally. People requested to come and work for me as I continued the work hard, play harder ethos, which elicited outstanding performance and was appropriately rewarded. My staff were all highly motivated. When I left FactSet, there was a string of unhappy staff all asking me not to leave. Several of them left FactSet shortly after I did, and some now work for me across various businesses.

My life was still action-packed and somewhat fast-paced at FactSet. I got things done. By providing relevant solutions through detailed research as quickly as possible, I moved into the fast pace of NBS. All that was left for me to do was merge my research experience into newfound selling skills to make it a success. I was fortunate that my career evolved from a firm foundation in the finance industry to a broader skill-set which matched my enthusiasm for making a lot of money.

Rambo's drive and energy drove my hunger for success and encouraged me to take on the challenge on offer in my new career. I was up for the challenge. Bobby Rakhit, young buck, oozing testosterone, psyched up and ready for the first big deal to make my mark. NBS turned out to be a perfect fit for the new Bobby, who brought some ready-made skills needed to cook up the perfect dish for FactSet.

Again, my experience there had a lot of parallels with Rambo.

Think Colonel Trautman preparing Rambo for combat, sending him onto the battlefield and nurturing him until he finally leaves the service. We both did a great job for our boss. Rambo's first assignment in combat with live enemies, real bullets, and a big knife after his specialized training was the same as my first client meeting. We were anxious about the unknown and soon settled confidently into our respective roles. The only difference was that my business suit had replaced the makeshift combat gear.

(Please allow me a quick diversion to share a funny story about my transition from a Canadian country bumpkin to a fashionably dressed Wall Street Equity Analyst at Morgan Stanley. It is about the outfit I wore on the first day of my New York job. The suit that was fashionably acceptable at Deloitte's back home looked like a potato sack compared to the tailored threads my colleagues were wearing. It hit me like a hammer looking at myself in the men's room mirror. I noticed the guy next to me looking at my reflection, with a smile curling his lips as he straightened his tie and jacket, smoothing his neatly groomed hair to perfection. Needless to say, my first salary was spent on suitable threads.) My FactSet armory, except for an expensive tailored suit, consisted of a laptop, my product knowledge, good social skills, and loads of enthusiasm.

I was as alert as Rambo, ready for action, challenged, excited, and hungry for success. I was aware of everything going on in my surroundings, picking up cues, reading body language, and listening to the tone of my client's voice. I saw Rambo in the desert waiting for the enemy helicopters, predicting the direction they would come from so he could find the best vantage point from which to shoot the arrows that blew them out of the sky. I was looking for the most opportune moment to fire my arrows and close the deal. If I were to sum it all up, I would say that a few things helped me succeed at first JCF, and then multiply that success at FactSet's NBS:

- Ambition and persistence

I possessed ambition and persistence as naturally as Rambo's predisposition for adventure and achievement. We were both often finding ourselves in sticky situations that we never expected. Afterall, how do you predict situations when you run your life at a pace which would make most mortals lose traction and fly off the planet? Like Rambo, when I set my hand or mind to something, I focused all of my attention on the task, there was no pulling out until the job is done and dusted. No matter the mission, it was not a haphazard plunge into the unknown, hoping for the best. I saw this attribute lacking in my peers, which put me ahead of the pack. I never lost my mojo when I didn't close a deal, I just went after the next one.

- Adapting to the environment

The first few weeks of my sales career were like when I had seen Rambo in the unfamiliar forest above Hope with a bunch of barking sniffers closing in on him. He had never set foot in the place until then, but used his skills to expertly adapt and orientate himself. I acquainted myself with the unfamiliar sales environment, got to know the lay of the land, and stayed the course.

Remember how I had to unlearn my country bumpkin Canadian dress sense and adapt to the Wall Street fashion code? That set me up for when I expanded my FactSet empire to include India (you'll read about this later), to teach my uneducated staff about the unfamiliar corporate environment they had joined. The only difference was that I sponsored my recruits because they were not in a financial position to purchase the expensive tailored suits.

- Relationships and networking

Relationships have always been easy for me, but the requirement of getting out from behind a desk was the significant change needed to make it happen. It was a welcome change to get out and about and find a marketplace where I felt so at home. The second minor change was an easy one, using my very well exercised social skill of forming friendships and casual acquaintances to create connections with business clients. It is still a skill I exploit to transform business meetings from tense situations into less formal, relaxed experiences. I took to the role as gracefully as an eagle on its first flight and kept flying from there.

Networking with the purpose of lead generation was no different to socializing with colleagues, or like I had done with school friends, and like I still do in my everyday life even now. For FactSet, I contacted colleagues and friends to get going and then dug into the extensive list on my Rolodex, which was full of equity research contacts from my time with HSBC. I was fortunate to have friends and contacts on both sides of the pond, many colleagues had moved from the US to the UK fr the same reasons as I had, so networking was easy for me. I always spend time finding out about my contacts' partners, significant others, and broader family, showing interest in life beyond the individual connection. I also made special note of specific business requirements for the clients I met; it gave me an immediate edge over my competition because I could extract research data and construct financial models relevant to their business in the current climate. It was fresh, cutting edge, and unique to the proprietary software they had acquired from JCF.

If you remember, selling myself began early for me, complimenting my 11-year-old entrepreneurial spirit when I ran my snow shoveling enterprise. Adults did not intimidate me when I knocked on their door to introduce myself and my services to them. I carried that same boldness into my work at FactSet as if I was back there knocking on doors for business. From the first call setting up a meeting to the actual event of signing the deal, forming solid relationships was easy for me. My new colleagues were confused. After years of making calls trying to drum up sales, they were still in the starting blocks compared to me (even Colin, who believed in me, was surprised at how quickly I turned things around for him and even more so when he saw me developing into an expert salesperson).

- Knowledge and passion

These were the final pieces of the Bobby Rakhit New Business Sales job. They completed the requirements needed to increase FactSet's sales and exposure in London's financial marketplace. My expert knowledge in Quantitative Research (QR) came from my intention to learn as much as possible to support my energetic performance. It was an aspect of my life that came naturally to me, beginning with my first exposure to formal tuition when I aced the entrance exam and was accepted into the Halifax Grammar School- a school my mother chose for me because she wanted only the best for me. I ended the year at the top of the honor roll and repeated the achievement every year until I went to college.

Since that entrance exam, I have never stopped educating myself and passing my knowledge on to others. Applying my passion for success in the job with my expert QR knowledge, I set to work getting myself into a situation that presented the perfect opportunity to fulfill my tasks at FactSet.

Working Hard, Playing Hard

Here I was, living in my new paradigm, making tons of money and having fun. Imagine that. I have always enjoyed a good party since I was a kid, having a lot of fun. I even clowned for kids' parties to make some dough. Briefly tasting the excitement of entrepreneurship as a kid supplemented my allowance and helped my mother with some housekeeping costs. But I made sure there was always some fun money in the kitty.

My college and university days weren't short of the usual student shenanigans, and Wall Street took things to another level- Watch The Wolf of Wall Street, and you will see what I mean. My winning streak took off like a rocket when I signed a deal with one of the largest financial institutions in the UK early in the walk. The undisputed Heavyweight Champion of the World, Muhammad Ali, summed up a winning attitude when he said to an opponent one day, *"How tall are you? So I can know in advance how far to step back when you fall down!"*

I never wanted to see the NBS cookie cutter, and Colin never showed it to me. I not only aimed to be super successful, but I planned to have loads of fun doing it. I was soon traveling all over the United Kingdom, recruiting new clients. I was away from home for twenty days a month, staying in the best hotels, dining in the finest restaurants, and signing record-setting business deals.

I celebrated my success by drinking premium brand champagne and smoking hand-rolled Cuban cigars. I met film stars, sports legends, and rock stars. I was mistaken for and treated like a Bollywood film star more than once. Living Dean Winters' saying, "I work hard, so I play harder." Playing hard was part of the Bobby Rakhit NBS culture. Working hard wasn't restricted to the job, I must add. Late nights, long lunches, and being the first one in the office in the morning doesn't just happen because you say it must. I worked out in a gym before work every morning, rising early has always been the norm for me. Late night or not, I was in the gym for a workout and a detox in the steam room the next morning.

At one stage when I was living in London, the gym was right below my building, and I joined the spinning class with an instructor who attempted to break world records. You can imagine the intensity he expected from us. It always surprised my colleagues and friends that I could be up and at it after a night out with minimal sleep. I am blessed with the superpower to function on little sleep. I also believe that without my workout regime, I would not have done as well in sustaining my long-term stamina doing NBS so efficiently. I was often asked what I was 'on' to keep me going, to which I could respond with a wry smile in all honesty, "nothing, mate. Just a good gym workout and 30 minutes in the steam room every morning." I never succumbed to the temptation of experimenting with drugs or any chemical substances, for which I am eternally grateful. I hate to think what would have happened to me knowing that I don't do anything in half measures.

Go Big or Go Home

Making friends and nurturing friendships went up a notch at this time because I met so many new people. Okay, so this is excessive- and it's not always about quantity over quality- but there were days when I had up to eight back-to-back meetings. Most of those short meetings resulted in follow-up appointments and extended lunches. The lunches weren't a waste of time either, because amongst the business talk was a lot of not so small talk, getting to know each other and connecting at a deeper level. I was not afraid to let people see who I was, so the real Bobby Rakhit showed up at meetings and drew out the 'real client' sitting opposite him as we got to know each other.

The trust created formed the glue of solid relationships. I had some good laughs with my wingman when he complained about a client's dreary demeanor, to which I responded with a list of stuff I had learned about them or found interesting because we had connected on a deeper level. I never let an opportunity to get to know someone a little better pass, and it paid off more than I could have imagined.

I took Cindy Lauper's song title, Girls Just Wanna Have Fun, as an indictment on men being boring. Men also wanna have fun, so I deliberately planned meetings at venues out of the client's office. If possible, I made it close to their office to make it easier for them to get there and be more relaxed; my modus operandi created a relaxed, friendly atmosphere. I had a few favorite spots where I knew the staff well, and they complimented my intentions with excellent service.

The focus was on entertaining the client rather than mind-numbing them to death. No topics were barred, and fun was on the agenda.

This is what a typical day in my NBS life looked like:

Venue - Gaucho Grill, Liverpool Road, the best steak restaurant in London. Their biggest serving portion - 1.2kg of prime cut steak; bonus – they allow cigar smoking!

The Client - Top management from a prominent bank

My crew - Me, two salesmen, and my Head of Consulting

Hors d'oeuvres - Assorted main course - mainly steaks between 800g and 1.2kg

Dessert - Assorted Cognac, port, and cigars

More drinks, chatting about the product and a lot of 'small talk'.

Dinner – More steak (two clients from another bank who have become friends, join us for dinner)

After dinner and dessert, we have more wine and cigars.

My phone rings (on silent) - A call from the boss to find out where we were – he declines the invitation to join us

Midnight – We transfer to a members-only nightclub

The evening ends as we sign a sales contract with the bank worth £500 000 (with some handwritten notations to sweeten the deal).

The next morning, I am the first one in the office after my gym session as usual, and I place the signed contract on the boss's desk. Consistently signing huge sales deals resulted in healthy profits for the company and a great annual bonus for me. The job satisfaction and lifestyle I enjoyed were awesome, this wasn't a required attribute for success in New Business Sales, but it made life there a hell of a lot sweeter in the long run.

Key Takeaways

- When the door opens a crack, get your foot in quickly. Grab every opportunity that comes your way and give it your best. Show up authentically and bring that out in the people you meet.
- Greed for money is a good thing, as long as it is not the primary thing running your life.
- Whenever possible, choose an option that allows you to balance your work and your life.
- If you don't take risks, you don't get luck.
- Work hard, play hard.

CHAPTER 5

THE FINAL CHAPTER

'I'm selfish, impatient and a little insecure. I make mistakes, I am out of control and at times hard to handle. But if you can't handle me at my worst, you sure as hell don't deserve me at my best.'
— **Marilyn Monroe.**

After countless good single malt whiskeys and hand-rolled Havanas celebrating big deals worth mega dollars, my ten-year walk with JCF/FactSet ended. The job with Colin had come wrapped up in a big red bow; I loved it, had tons of fun doing it, and made a giant success of it. But what goes up must come down; all good things end. NBS was a good thing for me, which set me up in the confident position to step out and do business for myself, relying on my entrepreneurial skills to make a success. My tenure with FactSet drew to a natural end as my strong desire to branch outgrew in tandem with my skills.

There were possibilities of other jobs with good prospects, but that would mean working for a boss and stunting my growth as an entrepreneur, a person, and an FUM© thinker. I had outgrown the corporate world, with its fickle promise of taking care of me. Despite creating a substantial business for FactSet and injecting significant impact into their growth, I was still just an employee, and all employees are dispensable.

Everything begins with a thought. I have an active mind, and thoughts run through it like London underground trains. I am not consciously aware of all of them, but my non-conscious mind, as I have learned from neuroscientists, never sleeps. It knows every thought and stores the significant ones in memory for later recall. FUM© was one such thought that ran through the station fifteen years before it was ever named, without stopping long enough to be labeled. But it was stored in my memory to be recalled several times in the decisions I made from that first brief notion.

Business Person, Entrepreneur & FUM© Architect

I believe that my positive energy continually combines with my thoughts. Energy is transferred, never lost, so by the time I left FactSet, I had built a contact base of over one thousand 'C' level contacts covering Africa, Asia, and the Middle East. Constructed with the future in mind, my network was a building block in the solid foundation I could rely on when I established my own enterprise. It was something I steadily maintained by keeping regular contact with these people. Because of the strong entrepreneurial passion running through my veins, I spent my years in corporate employment making a point of creating the Bobby Rakhit brand.

Consequently, my thoughts subconsciously always included entrepreneurial vision, just like FUM©. My close involvement in each deal created a following and laid down a solid track record that I could leverage in any future career, including going solo. My passion for learning was something that stood with me from the day my uncle gave me a set of encyclopedias for my tenth birthday in Halifax. It launched me into a world of information that I wanted to turn into knowledge, and inspired me to pursue more throughout my school career, college, and university. I accumulated several degrees and certificates with several academic accolades. I never restricted my appetite for knowledge to formal education either. I was a sponge soaking up experience and skills, then teaching others. The personal, well-maintained library of information I had to draw from put me in the perfect position to do two important things now that I was on my own.

First, I could confidently take calculated risks by applying my knowledge across various business disciplines. I also had the ability, as my peers put it, of being able to sell ice to an Eskimo. My FUM© mindset originally began, as you've read, when I invested money at the age of sixteen and my mother couldn't believe it. Here's an excerpt from my autobiography with a little more detail:

Not only was I going to be rich, but I also have the savvy to work out that the money I made could be increased without taking on more jobs or working harder. The hard work paid off without a doubt, but the money had to be invested to attract interest and grow my savings. The Royal Bank of Canada opened its doors and a savings account for me to take my first steps on my journey to feed my curiosity in the world of investments. I even took out a retirement plan with my first pay cheque at the tender teenage time when other kids were oblivious to the fact that they were getting older, or even thinking about their retirement.

The mindset was evolving when I purchased our family home, settling the mortgage for my mother with the first real cash I earned. Then the mindset of planning my retirement as a kid eventually deconstructed and reconstructed into FUM©. I was always looking for ways to make more money, I worked multiple jobs simultaneously, twice as hard as necessary, until I learned to let money work for me.

The transformation began when I was still at university and continued throughout my career to where I am today. Needless to say, I am not the same person today as I was standing in front of a group of bankers in a classroom during my first formal job in the finance industry. Each job I had changed me in some way, but fundamentally I was always focused on amassing as much wealth as possible. FUM© only came into the picture once I was a business owner and included my entrepreneurial skills into the equation, planning the growth of my wealth.

Entrepreneurship would become a piece of the puzzle that fitted perfectly into the culture. It helped me flesh out my thinking about creating passive income streams and has evolved, keeping me consistently on the lookout for new investment opportunities. All the subsequent investing and creating passive income streams became the basis of my eventual FUM© strategy, which turbo-boosted during my time at JCF/FactSet.

Before an offer of a great job, I could not say "F$CK YOU MONEY", but it was just what I needed to nudge me into finally transforming into a full-blown entrepreneur. The new mindset embraced the well-being of myself and my family and removed the insatiable greed and obsolete security of my retirement schemes. My time with JCF and eventually FactSet put me in a financial position with a secure enough buffer to allow me to resign and go on my own. I was on my way.

My Walk Continues

It is 2024, and I am 51 years old with a wonderful wife and a couple of great kids. I was wrong about my life slowing down after my sabbatical. I long ago saddled up my entrepreneurial steed to go solo into full-on independence for the Rakhit family, taking on the responsibility without a hint of compromise. I was able to leverage my media exposure and network to build the business. Doing it for myself took me to another level of accountability compared to having the backing of a large corporate company where I operated as an internal entrepreneur.

My passion for doing business, taking on a new challenge, making a success and having fun doing it- although different from the Wolf of Wall Street world I lived in in New York- has taken on a completely new identity as the intensity grows. I have matured. When I started, my family's security was paramount, all our futures were at stake, so the steps I would take from the beginning were critical. I immediately constructed a solid foundation by securing permanent residency in Dubai for my family and all the factors needed to ensure a seamless transition from perceived 'corporate security'.

Having peace of mind knowing that my family's future was secure, I moved on to set up a company. I created a credible advisory board made up of people I knew and trusted, most of whom are still with me today, and launched a website to facilitate online client communication and expose my brand in a manner that matched my credibility in the marketplace. The company profile uses the Golden Triangle of Asia on top, Africa on the bottom left, and the Middle East at the bottom right as its base. I set up a family office to oversee all of my investment operations and ensure the continuity of my legacy. I made the definite decision that all of my future business dealings would be on a contractual or partner agreement basis; I was never going to be employed by a company again. I was my own boss. With the Free Zone Enterprise (FZE) company registered, I would decide what the business activities would be.

I decided from the onset that I:

- Would be the conduit for FUM©.
- Would have more than one income stream, to ensure a consistent flow of revenue to provide the security I prioritized for my family and my future.
- Would have a sustainable company and provide a family legacy.

FACT: Roughly 80% of new businesses survive past their first year of operation. However, only around half of all new businesses exist after five years, and only one-third make it past their tenth anniversary. These statistics have been remarkably consistent through the years, even during major economic downturns. The good news is that survival rates begin to flatten out after several years of operation. The longer a business lasts, the more likely it is to last even longer.

I have always considered my options based on my skills, my track record, my network and the opportunities in the marketplace. My mindset is ring-fenced with the modus operandi of taking a calculated risk, every decision I make will pass through that filter. The business or businesses I choose need to have the three requisites of being unique, profitable and sustainable. Ultimately, these active sources of income need to convert into my sustainable FUM©.

Over the years, I came across the difficulties that individuals and companies faced when trying to raise capital. When I worked at Deloitte in Mergers and Acquisitions, I gained in-depth knowledge of the process, more than simply raising capital. I assessed a company's investment viability. As a result, I have a global network putting me in a great position to match capital requirements with several providers. I have become a conduit for companies trying to raise capital from abroad. I put my feelers out in the local Middle East market and got some quick bites.

One such opportunity, among the earliest I got, was funding Rare Earth projects that provide significant economic value for particular countries. This was perfect because many Middle Eastern countries' long-term vision was to become less dependent on oil exports. It was an opportunity with the potential to create a gravy train that rapidly set up as a serious player in the capital markets. The substantial monthly retainer helped to meet my immediate financial needs.

Unfortunately, it turned out to be a well that ran dry. However, it taught me a good life lesson- nothing is as easy as it seems. It did, however, set up the infrastructure for better vetting of future deals. Deals that turned into substantial rewards and contributed significantly to building up my passive income. The first pillar of the business was decided. Closing deals is my forte, especially in the Fintech business. The years spent in investment banking and technology companies, where I rubbed shoulders with numerous CTOs and COOs of these financial firms, put me in a privileged position. These people make purchasing decisions. My intimate knowledge of solving complex problems and understanding their technology gaps still gives me an unprecedented advantage.

One time, I connected with some contacts in the field. One of them put me in touch with a Dutch-based fintech firm that addresses some of these gaps. To my benefit, they also hit my 'Goldilocks' area. A growing firm with a well-established client base in several European banks, but no presence in the East or African markets. It was perfect! They offered me a partnership agreement - the start of my fintech business. The second pillar was decided.

I always knew I could find a way of making money by feeding my passion for sharing knowledge through formally educating young people who wanted to get into the finance industry. I approached several high-level educational institutions in Dubai, leveraging my previous experience as a guest lecturer in several universities in the UK. I got a call from SP Jain School of Global Management's Executive MBA (EMBA) program. They offered me a slot to teach portfolio management in Dubai. It was an opportunity to work with the World's Top 100 (81st) and Asia-Pacific's Top 10 (7th) by Ivy Exec (USA) EMBA Rankings, making it one of the world's best EMBA programs. The third pillar was decided.

I remember how it felt - like an unnecessary suit of heavy armor was removed from my shoulders. I could breathe my own air, not filtered through a corporate mask. I still feel that way many years down the line. I am Muhammad Ali, as light as a butterfly dancing around the ring, ready to sting like a bee. I am well prepared with all the attributes and skills to make every punch count. My eyes are open, and my naivety is safely locked away to avoid any nasty surprises. All the years of sparring are behind me as the bell rings for yet another professional bout. This is what my typical day today looks like:

5:00 am – Get up. Take 1.5 liters of water with lemon, turmeric, flaxseed and gut formula

5:30 am – Meditation

6:00 am – Catch up on news

7:00 am – Exercise. Go for a walk, do a HIIT workout or lift weights while listening to podcasts, news or audiobooks

9:00 to Noon – Calls/ emails/ e-meetings

12 onwards – Interactions. Meetings, lunches etc.

5 pm onwards – Family

11 pm - Bed

Key Takeaways

- Take the risks necessary to create the life you desire for yourself.
- If you cultivate your networks, your relationships will always help you no matter what change you make to your life and sales journey.
- Try to create your own brand.

PART III

TRIAL BY FIRE – THE DEAL

'It's never too late to be what you might have been.' – **George Eliott.**

*I*n sales, every deal has a story, and every story is as unique as the person who has lived it. From the thrill of a recent graduate stepping into the sales arena to the seasoned retiree dusting off old connections, each journey is different.

The young person gets freshly out of school and enters the sales world, and they have to learn to listen and hone their skills. They have to figure out how to harness their passion to grow into a great salesperson. The old retiree has the knowledge and the networks, but they have to figure out how to use them in new contexts to make sales. Whatever the situation, the sales tools remain the same, but they have to be applied differently.

That is what this section is about. Here, you will meet Henry, the young enthusiast eager to break into sales, armed with passion and hoping to learn the tools of the trade. You'll read about Mark, a seasoned executive ready to pivot his career after years in research and development in a pharmaceutical company, into the sales department, hoping to harness his experience in a new arena. We'll also hear from

Lisa, whose unexpected layoff became a catalyst for reinvention, and Josh, a determined guy fresh out of prison, eager to rebuild his life and make his mark. We'll finish the section with the story of Grace, a retiree who- inspired by a newfound passion- decides it's never too late to start anew.

As you follow their journeys from incubation to designation, and watch their ideas and inspirations take root and their efforts turn into tangible success, notice the way the tools in the Devil's Dealbook help them. You will see how these tools are not just strategies; they are lifelines, empowering our protagonists to navigate the challenges they face, embrace their unique circumstances, and ultimately, secure their place in the competitive world of sales.

Let that inspire you to make the same journey. Let their stories shape yours. Let the differences in their circumstances help you reflect on your own and figure out the ways in which you too can utilize these tools in your own sales journey. It does not matter where you are starting from, only how you commit to get to your FUM© goals.

CHAPTER 1

INTO THE SPOTLIGHT - GETTING INTO SALES AS A YOUNG BUCK

"Your network is your net worth." – **Porter Gale.**

Young people have never been as uniquely positioned to go into sales as they are today. From technological proficiency to shifting consumer behaviors, the landscape of sales has evolved in ways that favor the younger generation. Growing up with smartphones and social media, they have an innate understanding of digital platforms and online communication. The Pew Research Center calls them the "true digital natives". These are people who spend more than seven hours a day on social media. Way before they come to themselves, they have already been exposed to many sales techniques, thanks to big data.

So, what is one such young person to do when they want to get into sales? What are you to do if you feel in you the passion, if you notice your killer instinct and know that you could succeed, but have no idea where to start? What do you do if your specific industry skills are limited and yet you need to sell?

Picture this scenario: Henry is an 18-year-old early university grad. His life almost looks like a scene out of a movie. The outside world is background noise to him, or a distant soundtrack, because he spends most of his life indoors.

He has worked a few odd jobs before but none of them quite captured his imagination. While working at a local coffee shop, helping out at a tech store, and even in his brief stint as a barista, each day felt like a blur, filled with the monotony of tasks that paid the bills but left his soul feeling restless. He spent hours scrolling through social media, getting lost in endless memes, videos, and posts that entertained him far more than the reality of his life.

He lives in his parents' house, and there, he is the self-proclaimed king of the couch, a master in the art of lounging. The sunlight that bathes California in golden warmth is more of a nuisance to him, especially when his mother drags him out for "family bonding" days at the beach. He sits there, half-listening to her chatter about ocean waves and sunshine, while his mind wanders to his gaming setup back home. When his mom tries to coax him outside, he rolls his eyes and shoots back, "Mom, I'm building my empire here! This is how the future works!"

Henry truly believes he knows everything. His parents often exchange glances of bewilderment as he confidently explains the latest gaming trends or drops knowledge about YouTube algorithms like he is the oracle of online culture. "Trust me, Dad, if you don't have TikTok, you're basically living in the Stone Age," he'll often declare, reveling in the way their eyebrows shoot up in disbelief.

For Henry, an ideal day consists of sinking into his gaming chair, headphones clamped on like a second skin, fingers dancing across the keyboard as he ventures into fantastical realms where he can be anyone. Online, he can be a fearless hero battling dragons or a cunning strategist outsmarting opponents in epic showdowns. In that world, he thrives, trading quips and banter with friends who understand him better than anyone else. They share inside jokes that only make sense in the confines of their digital universe, bonding over late-night chats filled with laughter and the occasional existential musing about life.

Recently, a friend introduced him to PewDiePie, and Henry dove headfirst into the colorful chaos of the YouTuber's content. He found that he loves the way PewDiePie navigates through hilarious gameplay. Each video is a whirlwind of energy and humor, interspersed with heartfelt moments that humanize him. Henry finds himself cracking up, often erupting into laughter alone in his room. The way PewDiePie embraces imperfection, finds joy in life's quirks, and shares his ups and downs strikes a chord with Henry, who is grappling with his own uncertainties about what comes next after graduation.

The Crisis

The only problem in an otherwise perfect existence for Henry is that he has grand dreams, he is *passionate* about something that could potentially help him achieve those dreams, but he has no idea how to begin to get there. Time is passing and he needs to figure out what to do with his life in order to get out of his parent's basement.

Henry dreams of living like Mr. Beast, who is currently creating waves in the YouTube community. With around 200 million subscribers, Mr. Beast is known for his extravagant challenges and philanthropic efforts. Henry is captivated by how he gives away millions of dollars, funding surgeries, and even planting trees to combat climate change. Mr. Beast's estimated annual earnings are between $54 million and $120 million, largely coming from ad revenue, merchandise sales, and sponsorships. The sheer scale of his influence makes Henry feel inspired. He dreams about being able to make a difference in the world like that, using success not just for himself but to help others.

He dreams of making such an impact, but in a niche market – video games. He knows it is possible because one of the people he admires is PewDiePie, and he has done it. PewDiePie has over 110 million subscribers and Henry fancies himself to be the best one. He loves PewDiePie's videos so much that he feels like PewDiePie is his virtual best friend. With estimated earnings ranging from $20 million to $40 million annually, PewDiePie has built a brand that resonates with millions. He is famous for being real and relatable and showing that it's okay to embrace imperfection. Henry appreciates how PewDiePie shares both his gaming experiences and his life's ups and downs, and wished he could do something like this.

Among others, these influencers shape the way Henry sees the world. Like them, he is ambitious. He shares some of their passions. He wants to build an empire the way they have built theirs and he longs to make an impact in meaningful ways. He imagines a future where he can tap into that same kind of power and make his own mark in the gaming world. In his mind, these YouTubers are not just successful; they are trailblazers. Each of them is carving out a unique path, showing Henry that with passion and dedication, anything is possible.

Henry longs to figure out how to turn his *passion* for video games into something real. He is knowledgeable about them, he can talk for hours about the latest releases, the mechanics that make a game great, and the stories that captivate players. But that knowledge alone can't pay the bills.

Henry envisions himself in a sleek game store, surrounded by colorful displays and enthusiastic customers. He could be the one sharing his knowledge, recommending the perfect game to a fellow gamer, and helping them discover the joy he feels every time he powers on his console. He decides. He wants to go into sales.

For Henry, sales is a means to an end. It is the way to get to the life he envisions for himself. Through sales, he could be as influential as Mr. Beast. He can have financial freedom to allow him to do as much as he desires in life.

You are a lot like Henry if:

- You often feel stuck or restless in your current situation, unsure of your next steps, but need to make a choice soon.
- You have a strong passion for a specific niche or industry, such as video games, technology, or online content creation.
- You dream of making a meaningful impact on the world, similar to the influencers you admire.
- You yearn for financial independence and the ability to pursue your passions without constraints.
- You are eager to learn new skills but don't know where to start or which skills to focus on. You have an interest in sales as a potential path to achieving your goals and aspirations.

Hopefully watching how he resolves his problem can provide inspiration for you as a possible template for a way forward.

Using the Devil's Dealbook

The thing is, Henry doesn't know the first thing about sales.

Whenever he imagines walking into a game store, trying to engage customers with his charm, the thought of it makes his palms sweaty. Could he really talk to people face-to-face? Most of his relationships are built online, where the stakes feel lower and the conversations flow easily. Online, he is a hero. In the real world, he is just Henry, the guy who talks back to his parents and lives in sweatpants.

He admires PewDiePie's charisma and Mr. Beast's larger-than-life challenges and realizes that each of them had built a brand by connecting with people. But how could Henry do that? He needs to learn the ropes of sales, understand what makes a great video game not just a personal favorite but a bestseller. What games are trending? Which ones are flying off the shelves? More importantly, how can he overcome the anxiety he feels washing over him each time he imagines himself standing in front of customers? He fears he could just end up stammering through a sales pitch while they look at him with confusion.

Henry has passion and ambition, but without skills or knowledge of the market, it does not matter much. What if he recommends the wrong game and his customers walk away disappointed?

Determined to bridge this gap, Henry decided to attend local gaming and entrepreneurship conferences. He booked a ticket to an expo because he knew he would find some familiar faces there. The thought of stepping out from behind his computer screen still terrified him though. He still preferred spending his days indoors, but in this case, he needed to get out of his comfort zone for the sake of his dreams for the future. He felt a surge of nervous energy as he registered for the gaming expo.

The day before the expo, he rummaged through his belongings, searching for the essentials. He found an old Dealbook and realized he needed to book a cheap hotel nearby. After a few searches online, he stumbled across a small, budget-friendly hotel not far from the expo center. The photos showed a modest room with faded wallpaper, but it was affordable, and that was what mattered most. He grinned as he clicked "book," feeling a wave of accomplishment wash over him. "This is happening," he told himself.

The next day, Henry woke up early, his heart racing with anticipation. He wore his favorite gaming-themed T-shirt, emblazoned with a classic character from one of his all-time favorite games, and a pair of comfortable sneakers. As he stood in front of the mirror, he attempted to muster a half-confident smile, whispering affirmations to himself. "You got this, Henry."

He arrived at the expo center, and the energy in the air was electric. The chatter of fellow gamers, the sound of controllers clicking, and the vibrant displays created an atmosphere he could only describe as magical. But as he stepped inside, that initial excitement gave way to a wave of self-doubt. He felt small in a sea of experienced professionals and enthusiastic gamers. "What am I even doing here?" he thought, panic beginning to creep in.

Henry made his way to the registration booth, clutching his ticket tightly. When he received his name badge, he couldn't help but feel a rush of pride. It read, "Henry – Attendee." He hung it around his neck, trying to embody the role of a confident participant.

As he wandered through the halls, he observed the different booths showcasing the latest games and innovations. There were panels featuring industry experts discussing everything from game design to marketing strategies. He was hooked. A well-dressed man with a confident demeanor was passionately discussing his journey in the gaming industry. Henry felt drawn to the energy surrounding the booth; he was curious.

Taking a deep breath, he approached the group and to his surprise, the well-dressed man is Mike, his neighbor. It turned out Mike was a successful sales manager for a well-known game publisher. As Henry listened, he couldn't help but be captivated by Mike's tales of challenges he had faced, the mistakes he had made, and the triumphs that followed. There was something genuine about the way Mike spoke, and Henry felt a spark of hope ignite within him.

After the presentation, Henry went to speak with Mike. "Hi, Mike. I'm really interested in sales, especially in the gaming industry. I didn't know this is also what you do," he said, trying to sound confident despite his nerves.

Mike smiled warmly. "Yeah, it's strange that it never came up, we'd have known we shared that interest sooner. It's always refreshing to see young people eager to learn. What brings you to the expo?"

Henry explained his passion for video games and his desire to transition into sales. He mentioned his struggles with stepping out of his comfort zone, the challenges he faced in building relationships, and his hope of finding a mentor to guide him through the process.

Mike nodded thoughtfully. "I get it. The first steps can be the hardest, but they're also the most rewarding. I'd be happy to chat more and share some tips on breaking into the industry."

They spent the next half hour discussing everything from essential sales techniques to the importance of networking. Mike offered practical advice on how to approach potential customers, emphasizing the value of building genuine relationships.

"Sales isn't just about making a sale; it's about understanding people and their needs," Mike explained. "You have to listen, ask questions, and show them you care about their experience."

Henry scribbled down notes furiously, eager to absorb every piece of information. He felt a sense of connection with Mike, who seemed genuinely invested in his growth.

As their conversation wrapped up, Mike looked at Henry seriously. "If you're serious about pursuing a career in sales, I'd love to help you. Why don't we meet up more frequently? I can offer guidance and maybe even help you find some internship opportunities."

Henry's face lit up with excitement. "That would be amazing! Thank you so much!" They exchanged numbers, and Mike promised to follow up with some resources to help him on his journey. Together, Mark and Henry drew up an action plan for Henry. Here's what it looked like:

Step 1: Gain industry knowledge

- Action - Research the latest trends and popular games in the industry.
- Resources - Subscribe to gaming newsletters, follow influential gaming blogs, and listen to podcasts about gaming and sales.
- Timeline - Ongoing, aim for at least 1 hour per week.

Step 2: Develop sales skills

- Action - Shadow Mike for a month to learn essential techniques and strategies.
- Timeline – One month

Step 3: Build a network

- Action - Attend at least two local gaming meetups or conferences in addition to the events attended with Mike.
- Resources - Use platforms like Meetup.com to find events and connect with other attendees.

- Goal - Aim to engage with at least five new people at each event and exchange contact information.

Step 4: Create a personal brand
- Action - Start a blog or YouTube channel discussing gaming trends, reviews, and sales techniques.
- Goal - Establish authority in the gaming space while practicing communication skills.
- Timeline - Launch the platform as soon as possible.

Henry Becomes a Salesperson

With a solid action plan in hand, Henry jumped into his new journey with enthusiasm. He started by researching the latest trends in the gaming industry, dedicating at least an hour each week to staying updated. He subscribed to gaming newsletters, followed influential blogs, and listened to podcasts that merged gaming with sales strategies. Each piece of knowledge he gained felt like a step closer to his dream.

In between his research and school, he shadowed Mike for a month, soaking up every bit of wisdom the seasoned salesperson shared. Watching Mike interact with clients was eye-opening. Henry learned how to read people, ask the right questions, and engage in meaningful conversations. Each day spent learning under Mike's guidance made Henry feel more *confident* about entering the sales world.

Everywhere he went, Henry focused on building his network. He attended local gaming meetups and conferences, using platforms like Meetup.com to find events. Using these contacts, Henry created personalized emails to follow up with everyone he met, recalling specific conversations to make each message memorable.

"Hi Corie," he wrote one day. "I loved our conversation at the indie game panel! I'm about to launch my online store, and I'd love to feature your game. I think it would resonate well with my audience. Let's set up a time to chat more about it!"

To his delight, the responses came quickly. Corie replied almost immediately, excited to collaborate. Linus, an influencer he had met at another event, responded with equal enthusiasm, saying, "Absolutely! I'd love to promote your store to my followers. Let's create something fun together!"

With these collaborations in place, Henry felt increasingly confident. He finalized the details for his online store, dedicating countless hours to writing engaging product descriptions and creating user-friendly prompts. His hard work began to materialize into a cohesive launch plan, and he was ready to showcase his passion for gaming to the world.

When launch day arrived, Henry could hardly contain his excitement. He had scheduled social media posts, crafted email announcements, and coordinated collaborations to spread the word. He was using *technology and media* to his advantage. It was a whirlwind of activity, but every moment was worth it. He felt like he was finally stepping into the role he had always envisioned for himself.

To make the launch even more special, Henry organized a virtual launch event. He invited all the contacts he had made, including the developers, influencers, and friends from the expo. During the event, he showcased featured games, shared stories behind each product, and highlighted the collaborative efforts that brought everything to life.

As the store went live, the response was overwhelmingly positive. Visitors flooded the site, eager to explore the curated selection of games and accessories. Thanks to Linus' promotion, Henry saw a significant spike in traffic, and within hours, sales began rolling in.

He couldn't believe it. His dream was starting to come true, and it was happening faster than he had ever imagined. Messages from excited customers poured in, expressing their love for the unique offerings and the stories behind each game. While he still had a long way to go to reach the heights of someone like PewDiePie, he felt the momentum building, and it was exhilarating.

If you fall in the same category as Henry, the important things to note are that you need a mentor. You need a Mike to help point you in the right direction. You also need a plan to harness your energy and passions. With a little luck on your side, you will become the kind of salesperson you envision.

Key Takeaways

- Building genuine relationships is crucial for success in sales and this needs to be done in person. Social media and technology are a tool to fortify and maintain those relationships.
- Confidence is a skill that develops over time. The more you apply the tools in the Devil's Dealbook, the more confident you become.
- Start where you are. Chances are you have some of the tools in the Devil's Dealbook already. Figure out how to develop the rest and you are on your way to succeeding as a salesperson.
- Be open to learning from each experience, and don't be afraid to seek feedback and adapt your strategies as you grow.

CHAPTER 2

EMBRACING CHANGE – ENTERING SALES IN YOUR INDUSTRY

"Opportunities don't happen. You create them." – **Chris Grosser.**

There are times when the problem is not that you are new to sales, but that you have been in sales for a while or have been doing a certain kind of work for a while. You have mastered everything there is to it and you are at the top of your game. Then suddenly, a certain je nais se quoi hits and you want a change. You want to go into sales for your own self. You realize that you could reach your FUM© goals sooner if you did this on your own. This is the case for our second protagonist, Mark.

Mark sits at his desk in the bustling offices of a well-known pharmaceutical company. There's sunlight streaming through the large windows, illuminating the space filled with activity. On this day, he is reviewing his sales reports, analyzing the data from the past month. Mark has been working in this industry for fifteen years, and he is currently one of the top salesmen in the company. He knows every detail about the products he sells, and he is constantly learning about the latest developments in the pharmaceutical world.

Every morning, Mark arrives at the office early, he enjoys the quiet moments before the day gets hectic. As he sips his coffee, he plans his agenda. Today, he is focusing on a few key clients who have shown interest in a new medication. Mark understands the importance of building relationships, so he is prioritizing his time with them.

He reaches out to Sarah, a pharmacy manager at a large retail chain. Mark has been working with her for years. They have developed a strong rapport, and he always makes a point to remember details about her personal life, like her recent vacation to Hawaii. On his call with her, he asks about her trip, genuinely interested in her experience. Sarah appreciates his effort, and they seamlessly transition to discuss the new medication Mark is selling. Mark provides her with all the necessary information and makes sure she feels confident recommending the product to her customers.

Throughout the day, Mark meets with his colleagues and they share insights and strategies. They brainstorm ways to approach potential clients and discuss what has worked for them in the past. To his team, Mark is known for his collaborative spirit; he believes that sharing knowledge leads to better outcomes for everyone. His colleagues appreciate his willingness to help and mentor them, as he often shares tips about building relationships and closing deals. They think of him as an empathetic salesperson.

In the afternoon, Mark heads out for a sales call with Dr. Thompson, a physician he has known for years. They have a friendly relationship, built on trust and mutual respect. Mark is prepared for this meeting, having reviewed Dr. Thompson's patient demographics and noted the recent changes in his practice. He arrives at the doctor's office, where he is greeted warmly. They catch up on personal matters before Mark shifts the conversation to the new drug. He presents data that shows how it can improve treatment outcomes for patients suffering from chronic conditions.

As he speaks, Mark watches Dr. Thompson's body language. He picks up on signs of interest and concern and adjusts his approach, emphasizing the support and resources the company offers to help doctors implement the new medication effectively. He answers questions thoughtfully and addresses any hesitations the doctor raises. This adaptability is one of Mark's strengths; he is always tuning in to his clients' needs and concerns.

This is what a typical day looks like for Mark. He always leaves his meetings feeling energized and happy to have helped change someone's life. Like clockwork, he drives back to the office and schedules follow ups with his clients. Sometimes it is in the form of a personalized email as he navigates through traffic, and other times it is a call. He decides which methods suit which client best after the meeting. In the email, he will often summarize their discussion and offer additional resources that might help. He believes in maintaining open lines of communication, and this follow-up is a crucial part of his strategy.

Before he leaves his office, Mark checks in with his team. They discuss their sales targets and celebrate small victories. Mark has always encouraged his colleagues to share their successes and challenges. For him, every call and meeting is an opportunity to learn and grow. He knows that success in sales isn't just about numbers; it's also about teamwork and relationship building.

Most of the time, Mark gets home satisfied with his work. But recently, something else has been gnawing at him - his changing family situation.

The Environment Changes

The thing with sales is that it is not always constant. You will be at the top of your game and then a change in the environment can create a chain reaction, necessitating something about the way you do sales changes. This could be anything; it could be that you lose a loved one and need to take time off, or that you have a newborn and that changes your needs as a family person. It could be that a global market collapses and your company has to change the way they do things and that affects you. Whatever it is, what do you do?

For Mark, the change in his environment had to do with his family. One late evening, Mark sat in his living room reflecting on the changes in his life recently; he was preparing for the arrival of his twins. Just a few weeks ago, he noticed something unsettling, he was starting to lose his hair. At 35 years old, this realization hit him hard. Each time he catches sight of his reflection in the hallway mirror and runs his fingers through his thinning hair, he feels the stress of the past few years weighing on him.

Mark attributes his hair loss to the mounting work-related stress that has crept into his life. While he has always been a top salesman, the pressure to maintain his performance had become increasingly intense. He was not just working for himself anymore; he was working for his growing family. He loved them, but he was acutely aware that the demands of his job were starting to take a toll on him, both physically and emotionally.

Mark crunched some numbers in his head. With twins on the way, he knows that his family's expenses are going to skyrocket. He and his wife, Jessica, are currently living comfortably, but they are starting to realize that the financial cushion they once felt secure in is becoming thinner. Right now, their monthly expenses hover around $4,500. This includes their mortgage, utilities, groceries, and other necessities. They are managing well, but he now has to factor in how much more they will need with two new babies.

The costs of raising a child are significant, and he was going to be raising two. The average monthly cost for diapers alone can range between $150 and $300, depending on the brand and whether you choose disposable or cloth options. If you go with disposables, that's around $200 for the first year. Feeding two infants will also add substantial costs, Mark estimates about $100 a week for formula if they decide to go that route, which totals around $400 a month. That alone adds nearly $1,600 a year to their budget.

Mark also considers the cost of childcare. With Jessica planning to return to work after her maternity leave, they will need full-time daycare for the twins. In their area, the average cost of daycare can be around $1,200 per child, which means they could be facing nearly $2,400 monthly. This hefty sum nearly doubles their current expenses and leaves little room for savings.

Mark knows that this financial pressure is going to require him to step up his game. He is currently earning a solid salary of about $85,000 a year, plus bonuses that usually add another $20,000. However, with the rising costs of living and the added responsibilities of parenthood, he realizes he needs to increase his earnings to sustain this new lifestyle. He starts thinking about what it will take to make that happen.

The pressure he feels at work is mounting as well. With the recent changes in their family dynamic, he knows he can't keep leaving the office at nine pm. While he has been dedicated to his job, working those long hours is becoming less feasible. He needs to be present at home, especially as Jessica prepares for the challenges of new motherhood. She is supportive and understands the demands of his job, but she also needs his help and presence during this transition.

Mark thinks about how he can balance his work life and home life. He starts thinking about what adjustments he can make to his schedule. Maybe he can aim to leave the office by six pm instead, but this means he must be more productive during the day. He brainstorms strategies to maximize his efficiency; he knows that this will require him to prioritize tasks and perhaps delegate more responsibilities to his team.

As he continues to think about his situation, Mark feels a sense of urgency. It dawns on him that no amount of increasing efficiency would get him where he wanted to be. To provide for his growing family, Mark needed to make at least $150,000 a year. He calculates that to meet the anticipated expenses of raising twins, he needs an additional $45,000 annually to cover the rising costs and keep saving for his family's future.

Breaking it down further, Mark knows he needs to make this increase over the next year, and if he were to meet this goal solely through commissions and bonuses, he would need to sell significantly more than he currently does. Last year, his bonuses averaged around $20,000, so he calculates that he needs to ramp that up to at least $65,000 in bonuses to hit the $150,000 mark. This would require not just maintaining his current sales but potentially increasing them three times over. It seemed impossible when it suddenly hit him- he was giving all this money to his company when it was his relationships and his hard work that he was using. He thinks to himself 'I have done this for the last 15 years to help this company. I can do this for myself and my family.'

You are likely reading Mark's story and find it deeply compelling if:

- You have been successful in your current sales role but feel a desire for change, or to pursue something more personal.
- You have years of experience in your industry and feel confident in your skills and knowledge.
- You want to take control of your career and work for yourself rather than for a company.
- You are experiencing changes in your personal life, such as starting a family or facing financial pressures, and are acutely aware of the financial responsibilities and costs associated with significant life changes.
- You have a specific income goal in mind to support your changing lifestyle or family needs and you need to achieve this with a better work-life balance.

For someone like you, taking actions similar to Marks will be beneficial.

The Pivot

At this point, the idea of becoming a sales consultant was taking shape in Mark's mind. It hit him that he had *ambition*. He had the *passion*. He had the *knowledge* and the *networks* to be able to succeed on his own. What would he need to get to his goal? For Mark, sales is a way to reach FUM© faster and to provide for his family and allow himself the freedom and time he needs to spend with them.

As he continued to think about shifting into sales consultancy, Mark realized that he was a little afraid. He knew he had the skills, *networks*, and *knowledge* to succeed; he had been successfully navigating the pharmaceutical sales landscape for 15 years after all. But what if he went at it and ended up failing? What if he dug his family into a financial hole instead of giving them a better cushion?

He needed to bolster his *confidence.* He needed to find a way to get himself to a place where he could make the transition without hurting his family. He needed to cultivate other tools inside the Devil's Dealbook.

To make this transition, Mark created a solid action plan, one that outlined how he would not only meet, but would exceed his sales targets; he decided to begin executing his plan while still working. That way, he could reduce risk and build his confidence while he still had a cushion. His goal was clear, he needed to generate $150,000 a year. This is what Mark had to do:

Step 1: Assess the market

Even though Mark has been in pharmaceutical sales for 15 years, he still needs to do a market analysis to understand the different dynamics that would affect him as a consultant; this is him growing his *knowledge*. He has to understand the demand for his services as a sales consultant within the pharmaceutical industry, this involves identifying potential clients— pharmacies, hospitals, and healthcare providers— that may benefit from his expertise. He has to leverage his existing relationships by reaching out to former clients and colleagues to gauge their needs and pain points.

Mark set a timeline for this research, aiming to complete it within the next month. By gathering information on competitors and their offerings, he could position himself effectively.

Step 2: Build a brand

The next thing Mark has to focus on is establishing his personal brand as a sales consultant and differentiating himself from others in the field. For this, he has to create a compelling value proposition that highlights his extensive experience, proven sales record, and the strong networks he has built over the years.

He has to create a professional website that showcases his services with testimonials from satisfied clients. He can no longer rely solely on his company's branding, he has to invest in his own. Mark planned to launch his website by the end of the second month and establish a presence on social media platforms relevant to his industry.

Step 3: Networking and outreach

Mark already has a leg up. In his 15 years as a salesperson, he had managed to build an extensive network, all he would need to do is reach out to them. He would also expand his network by attending industry conferences and local business events. He sets a goal to attend at least two networking events each month and decides to leverage his past successes to build credibility. He also created an elevator pitch that succinctly described who he is and the value he brings as a sales consultant.

During that period, Mark also developed a targeted sales strategy. He defined the specific services he was going to offer and set quarterly sales goals for himself by breaking down his overall target into manageable chunks. He found that if he secured three new clients per quarter, each contributing at least $15 000, then he would exceed his annual goal.

Step 4: Cultivating confidence

By creating a detailed plan, Mark was already addressing his lack of confidence. Defining what it is that we need to do to achieve success goes a long way to increasing confidence. Mark also needed to seek out mentorship, and reached out to seasoned consultants to get guidance and advice. He was already experienced in his field, he didn't need technical guidance, but he needed help learning how to run a consultancy. A mentor would also help him to stay persistent. He would have someone to talk to about the challenges he met, who would have the experience to help. A mentor would help make Mark accountable and set him up to take the leap.

A New Sales Consultant

Four months later, Mark was on his last day at his job. He had already given his resignation but remained in his position to help the company find a replacement for him. He sat at his kitchen table, a sense of satisfaction washing over him as he reviewed his progress. The changes he had implemented since embarking on his journey to become a sales consultant were substantial. Each step of his action plan had brought him closer to his goals, and he could see the fruits of his labor.

In the first few weeks after launching his business, Mark had invested significant time in market analysis. He reached out to former clients, gathering invaluable feedback that helped him refine his services. By the end of the first month, he had identified three primary areas where his expertise could add value: sales training for teams, market analysis, and strategic planning for new product launches. These offerings set the foundation for his new brand.

Mark had also launched a professional website that showcased his services and included testimonials from satisfied clients. The website was sleek and user-friendly, reflecting the professionalism he wanted to convey. Within the first month of its launch, he had started to receive inquiries from potential clients, which validated his decision to take this leap. He felt a surge of confidence every time he checked his email and found a new message from a prospective client.

He also actively engaged with fellow professionals, sharing his insights and listening to their challenges. This outreach resulted in forming new connections and he secured his first consulting client within three months— an up-and-coming pharmacy looking to enhance its sales strategies. That initial contract brought in $15,000, which was a significant boost to his confidence and income.

After that contract, Mark handed in his resignation and became a full-time sales consultant. He began conducting workshops, helping sales teams improve their techniques and understanding market dynamics better. His workshops were well-received, and word of mouth quickly spread within the industry. By the end of the six-month mark, he had onboarded three more clients, each bringing in additional revenue and solidifying his reputation.

Mark loved that he was now able to keep a balanced schedule. By this time his twins had arrived and he could afford to spend time with Jessica and their kids. As he entered the final quarter of the year, Mark reviewed his financials and found himself pleasantly surprised. He had not only met but exceeded his goal of $150,000 annual income. With his diligent efforts, he had generated approximately $165,000, with bonuses exceeding his expectations.

Like it was for Mark, sales can be a way to take back control of your career. It can be a way to achieve your FUM© lifestyle sooner than you are poised to, if you are bold enough to take the leap.

Key Takeaways

- As you transition into sales, calculate your risk. Create a plan that will guarantee a smooth transition.
- Your background in the industry provides a unique advantage. Use it to build credibility.
- Develop a clear and concise elevator pitch that articulates your passion for sales and highlights how your skills align with each role you desire. Use it as you build your brand.
- When your environment changes significantly to affect your goals, adapt and find ways to still meet your sales targets.

CHAPTER 3

UNCHARTED – GETTING INTO SALES FROM AN UNRELATED FIELD

"The only way to make sense out of change is to plunge into it, move with it, and join the dance." – **Alan Watts.**

Recent data and trends show that there is a growing interest in transitioning into sales from other careers. Many people are moving towards sales roles because of career flexibility, earning potential, and the broader acceptance of non-linear career paths.

The sales industry offers a range of positions for people of varying experience levels, from entry-level roles such as Sales Development Representatives with an average salary of $50,304 to executive-level roles such as Chief Sales Officers earning up to $360,000 annually. This range of opportunities makes sales an attractive option for career changers seeking growth potential without needing advanced degrees or certifications.

Besides, the sales industry is attractive because you can transfer skills from any other field to succeed. People from diverse career backgrounds can leverage their previous experiences effectively in a sales environment. In a post-pandemic, remote-work world, more and more people are expressing interest in transitioning to sales. Sometimes, this transition is prompted by an internal desire to do things differently or achieve certain goals. Other times it is prompted by circumstances outside of your control. In Lisa's case, it was both.

Lisa Ramirez was once a rising star in the world of professional gymnastics, leaping, twisting, and flipping her way into the hearts of fans around the globe. At just 22, she had already graced the Olympic stage, snagging a silver on the balance beam (where she had, against all odds, managed to remain upright after a particularly enthusiastic dismount), and a gold in team events, where her teammates often joked that she was the "human defibrillator", she just brought everyone back to life with her dazzling routines.

With a lifetime of dedication to gymnastics, Lisa had woven her identity around her sport. Gymnastics wasn't just what she did; it was who she was. She could talk about the intricacies of a vault, or the finesse required for a floor routine for hours. Her mother would often say she was a lot like a "human sports encyclopedia," which is just a fancy way of saying she was a gym nerd. But then, during a training session leading up to a major competition, disaster struck. A poorly timed landing during a practice routine sent her spiraling down; not in a dramatic, slow-motion way that could make for a great highlight reel, but in the "oh no, my ankle!" kind of way that echoed through the gym. The diagnosis was a severe ankle injury, requiring extensive rehabilitation and leaving her sidelined for at least a year.

At first, Lisa thought she was just experiencing a minor inconvenience. "A year off? No problem!" She told herself, with the kind of optimism that comes from years of landing on one's feet, literally. But as the reality set in, she felt the ground beneath her shift. The initial shock wore off like a bad spray tan, revealing the starkness of her new reality. Without the daily grind of training, the thrill of competition, and the camaraderie of her fellow gymnasts, Lisa found herself grappling with an unexpected void. What would she do next? Was she destined to become the world's most overqualified couch potato?

As she shuffled through the days, still in her compression socks (which did not match her image as an Olympic gymnast), her mind raced with questions. Could she ever return to gymnastics? Would she trade her leotards for sweatpants forever? How could she leverage her experience and passion in a new way? She pictured herself at a party, awkwardly mingling while trying to explain how she once could do a backflip without breaking a sweat, but was now reduced to navigating the complexities of online shopping for compression sleeves.

Despite her concerns, Lisa had always harbored an interest in the business side of sports— management, marketing, and athlete representation. Yet it was a field she had never seriously considered pursuing. The thought of trading her mat for a desk felt surreal. Could she really leave the flips and tumbles behind? Could she make a career out of talking about the very world that had once defined her?

In the depths of her existential crisis, Lisa turned to her trusty sidekick— her cat, Flip. Sitting on her couch with Flip sprawled across her lap, she tried to brainstorm ideas for her next chapter. "What do you think, Flip? Sports management? Athlete coaching?" She mused, only to be met with a yawn and a slow blink that felt suspiciously like judgment. "You think I should just stick to cat videos instead?" She chuckled, wondering if that might be a more viable career path.

As she contemplated her next steps, the realization dawned on her: she wasn't just an athlete, she was a passionate advocate for her sport. Perhaps this was her opportunity to build something new, something that could bridge the gap between athleticism and business. After all, every gymnast knew that sometimes you had to fall before you could fly. With a mixture of determination and humor (and a little help from Flip's unwavering support), Lisa decided it was time to turn the page on this new chapter.

Changing Course

As Lisa navigated the rocky road of injury recovery, the emotional and financial toll hit her like an unexpected splashdown in the pool. The once-cozy cushion of her savings began to dwindle faster than she could say "back handspring." Medical bills started piling up like dirty laundry after a week of intense training— suddenly overwhelming, and just as smelly. Every time she opened a new bill, she half-expected to find a tiny gymnastic figurine alongside the figures, just as a cruel reminder of what she could no longer afford.

With her competitive career seemingly at an end, Lisa faced a full-blown identity crisis. What was she without her sport? The gold medals? The adoring fans? The endless supply of leotards? The thought of being forgotten haunted her like a particularly clingy ex, always lurking in the back of her mind. "I'm Lisa the gymnast! Not Lisa the girl who can't even jump over a coffee table!" She lamented, staring at the empty mat that used to be her sanctuary. She began to wonder if she should start introducing herself as "Lisa, the former human tornado."

Feeling isolated in her metaphorical bubble of despair, she reached out to her friends and fellow athletes for support. Most of them were still training or competing, their lives moving forward while hers felt like a slow-motion replay of a disaster sequence. The sense of urgency washed over her like a cold shower at 5 a.m.; she needed to take control of her situation, stat!

That's when Lisa had a revelation: she needed a mentor, someone with the experience to help her navigate this new path. She imagined herself sitting across from a wise sage of sports management, perhaps a figure cloaked in a gym mat, handing her pearls of wisdom like "How to Build a Career Without Flipping" or "Surviving Life After the Olympics."

With her connections in the gymnastics world, Lisa began her quest to find the perfect mentor. She recalled Maria, an old coach who had transitioned into sports management. "If she can do it, maybe I can too!" Lisa thought, envisioning a bright future filled with contracts, sponsorships, and maybe even a few funny cat videos thrown in for good measure.

You are a lot like Lisa if you feel stuck in your current career and your dreams seem distant. For you, sales can be a way to redefine yourself. It can be a different identity. It can be a way to recover after an unexpected setback or a way to grow in a different, more authentic way.

With a mix of determination and desperation, Lisa hit the ground running, or limping, more accurately. She sent out emails, made phone calls, and even tried to decipher the mystical world of LinkedIn connections, all while dodging Flip, who seemed to think every computer cable was a personal attack. If there was a chance to learn and grow, she was ready to leap— perhaps not quite as gracefully as before- but certainly with plenty of heart (and a touch of humor). It was time for

Lisa to reclaim her narrative, and she wasn't about to let a little setback stop her from spinning her story into something extraordinary.

The Action Plan

Lisa reached out to Maria who graciously agreed to help. Over coffee, Lisa shared her concerns and ambitions. Maria encouraged her to leverage her knowledge of the gymnastics world and her personal experiences to help other athletes navigate their careers. Together, they outlined an action plan. This is what it looked like:

1. Catalog your interests and strengths - Lisa made a list of her interests, including sports management, athlete advocacy, and mentorship. She recognized her strengths in communication and empathy, both vital for working with athletes.
2. Build a network - With Maria's guidance, Lisa began networking with professionals in the sports management field. She already had some networks, but most of them still saw her as an athlete. She needed her networks to support her transition. She attended conferences, joined online forums, and connected with people on LinkedIn, focusing on building relationships with those who could offer insight and opportunities.
3. Acquire skills and refine knowledge - Lisa enrolled in online courses about sports management, marketing, and contract negotiation. This not only filled her time during recovery but also helped her gain essential knowledge for her future business.
4. Develop a business plan - Inspired by her mentor, Lisa started drafting a business plan for her own sports management company. She envisioned a firm that would help athletes like her-

self transition to life after sports, focusing on personal branding and career development.
5. Financial planning - To support her new venture, Lisa began saving money, working part-time as a gymnastics coach to supplement her income while she built her company.

Growing into Herself

Months later, Lisa's hard work began to pay off. She successfully launched her sports management company, "Beyond the Mat," which offered services like career coaching, branding workshops, and contract negotiation for athletes. Through her networking efforts, she secured her first clients, young gymnasts who admired her accomplishments and wanted guidance in navigating their own careers.

The business was growing steadily, and Lisa found joy in helping others avoid the pitfalls she had encountered. She became a sought-after speaker at sports conferences, sharing her journey from athlete to entrepreneur. As her company thrived, she forged valuable partnerships with sports brands and local gyms, expanding her influence in the industry.

Lisa's injury, which had felt like the end of her gymnastics career, became a catalyst for a new and fulfilling life chapter. She transformed her passion for sports into a thriving business, proving that even in crisis, opportunity awaits. Her story can be yours too. You too can catalog your transferable skills and figure out a plan that, with the help of a mentor, can turn you into a salesperson.

Key Takeaways

- Taking calculated risks will often lead to new opportunities but will also mean stepping outside your comfort zone.

- Every experience, even those in seemingly unrelated fields, can offer valuable skills for salespeople. Take the time to identify and articulate these skills to make them relevant to your sales career.
- Continuously seek education and training opportunities to enhance your qualifications. This not only boosts your confidence but also makes you a more attractive candidate.
- Every salesperson's transition is different. Sometimes the switch into an expert salesperson will not be a straight line.

CHAPTER 4

SELLING AGAINST ALL ODDS - FROM EX-CON TO SALESPERSON

"It is not whether you get knocked down, it's whether you get up."
– **Vince Lombardi.**

Sometimes, our biggest failures in life pave the way to our greatest successes in sales. When we experience extremely traumatic things, our knee-jerk response is often to block them out. We want to bury them deep in our unconscious mind so that we don't have to relive the pain. Yet, that is often counterproductive. If we can sift through the pain, the trauma and the ugliness long enough, we can find golden lessons that transform our lives in positive ways. We can find opportunities to replace destructive values with good ones.

We can move out of these negative, life-defining situations, harness the tools in the Devil's Dealbook that we already possess, and cultivate the rest to create a better life for ourselves. If that sounds like you, you can use sales to change your life. If you have, like our penultimate protagonist Josh, gotten into an unfortunate situation, sales can be your way out.

This is Josh's situation. He finds himself in jail after a series of poor life choices, so that when he leaves, he has to start life from scratch. Without networks to rely on or a good reputation to start from, and with limited financial resources to get started, all he has is his *ambition* to make a better life for himself.

Josh was just a kid when life threw him a curveball so big it felt like he was playing in a different league. At 16, he found himself unexpectedly promoted to fatherhood when his girlfriend, who he swore was just "the one" for the week, announced she was pregnant. Suddenly, the weight of the world— along with a toddler-sized dose of responsibility—landed squarely on his shoulders.

With no money and little support, Josh felt like a deer caught in the headlights of a runaway minivan. Desperate to provide for his baby and still somehow be "cool," he made a series of spectacularly poor choices. Surrounded by a neighborhood where quick cash was the norm, Josh thought he could make a fast buck by selling drugs.

What began as a "brilliant" idea to fund diapers and baby formula quickly spiraled into a lifestyle that could only be described as chaotic. Imagine a teen whose idea of multitasking involved folding laundry while watching YouTube videos on how to sell drugs. Spoiler alert: it doesn't work out well.

Before long, a deal went sideways faster than a malfunctioning shopping cart. The flashing lights of police cars lit up the night, bathing his neighborhood in a surreal glow reminiscent of a bad reality show. Arrested for possession and distribution, Josh faced a three-year sentence. He traded in fatherhood for the confines of a cell, where his biggest concern would be whether he could snag the top bunk.

Inside, the reality of his choices hit hard. Initially, he grappled with regret, like a fish trying to remember how to swim after jumping out of the bowl. But as the days turned into weeks and the weeks into months, he discovered an unexpected refuge: the library. Yes, you heard that right, a prison library, where the only thing more surprising than a self-help book was the sheer number of people actually trying to improve themselves.

With time to kill and nowhere else to turn, Josh dove into books like a kid on a summer day diving into a pool, hesitant at first but then fully submerged. He devoured everything he could find about cars, engines, and performance upgrades. The smell of motor oil and the roar of an engine became his escape. He envisioned a world where he could transform clunkers into racing machines, and who knows, maybe even impress his kid with something more exciting than a plastic rattle.

His fascination with cars grew, and the library became his sanctuary. Instead of plotting his next move in a drug deal, he was now plotting how to soup up a '92 Honda Civic. Sure, he was still stuck in prison, but at least he had dreams.

The Turning Point

Determined to turn his life around, Josh devised a plan that was equal parts ambition and teenage daydream. When he was finally released early for good behavior he jumped right into action. He sought out opportunities to learn more about cars and landed a spot as an apprentice at a local auto shop, where the only drugs involved were the caffeine-fueled variety from the shop's coffee machine.

It wasn't glamorous; his first task was sweeping floors while dodging grease stains that could double as modern art. But he soaked up every bit of knowledge like a sponge in a car wash. From oil changes to performance tuning, he was eager to prove he could turn his life around, and maybe even fix that rusty old truck that had been languishing in the shop's back lot since the last ice age.

Initially, Josh faced skepticism from coworkers who saw him as just another kid with a past. They wondered if he was genuinely committed or if he was simply there for the free donuts. But with each completed task, each satisfied customer, and each cringe-worthy dad joke, he began to rebuild his reputation. "Why did the car break up with its girlfriend? It couldn't find the right brake!" became a staple in the shop, much to everyone's eye-rolling dismay.

The only problem Josh was having was that he still couldn't afford to support his child, who was now two years old. His paycheck, though earned through honest work, barely scraped the surface of living expenses. The truth was, while he was learning the ins and outs of engines, his wallet felt more like a bottomless pit than a flourishing bank account.

With mounting bills and the ever-looming cost of baby supplies, Josh realized that his current gig wasn't going to cut it. Diapers weren't getting any cheaper, and the baby formula could probably be used as currency in some circles. He needed more money, and fast. He thought about getting a second job, but the idea of juggling shifts between the auto shop and a late-night gig at a fast-food joint didn't seem ideal, he'd barely have time to see his kid.

That's when it hit him: he could leverage the skills he was developing into something bigger. After all, cars were more than just machines, they were a passion for many people. What if he could help others find the perfect vehicle, maybe even some souped-up dreams, while also making a decent living? He'd always had a knack for chatting people up and getting a sense of what they wanted, whether it was a new exhaust system or the right set of tires.

Josh decided to dip his toes into sales, taking the plunge into the world of car salesmanship. Sure, he had a rocky past, but he knew firsthand what it was like to be on the other side of the counter, feeling overwhelmed by options and unsure of what to choose. With his unique experiences, he could bring a relatable, honest approach to the sales floor. "No high-pressure tactics, just me telling you whether your dream car is a beauty or a lemon," he chuckled to himself.

With a few connections he had made at the auto shop, Josh began reaching out to local dealerships to see if they had openings for sales positions. He was ready to pitch his story, after all, who wouldn't want to hire a guy who had gone from the inside of a cell to the inside of a car? He felt like a phoenix rising from the ashes, but instead of wings, he was armed with knowledge about horsepower and a strong desire to provide for his child.

As he filled out applications and brushed up on his sales techniques, he realized that this could be his ticket not just to financial stability, but also to a future where he could truly support his kid—not just as a dad, but as a role model who had turned his life around. And if that meant throwing in a few dad jokes along the way, well, that was just part of the deal. After all, what was life without a little humor, especially when it came to navigating the twists and turns of fatherhood and a new career?

Creating a Plan for the Future

This was his action plan for getting out of his difficult financial situation:

1. Cataloging his skills

Josh started by identifying the transferable skills from his apprenticeship at the auto shop, such as customer service, product knowledge, and communication. He also recognized his strengths in building rapport and understanding customer needs. His goal was to secure a sales position at a car dealership within three months of starting so that he could earn enough to support his child.

2. Researching and developing skills

Josh started to research local car dealerships to learn about their sales processes, customer demographics, and popular vehicles, and familiarized himself with current trends in the automotive market. He was too broke to enroll in courses to help him to that end, but he approached an ex-convict facility close to him and they gave him some resources. He read as many of these books as he could get his hands on.

3. Networking to build connections

Josh did not have much to go on in the way of relationships before his incarceration, but he had formed some at the auto shop. He decided to reach out to the connections made there, including mechanics and salespeople, for advice and potential job leads. One of them was open to the idea and offered Josh more guidance than he had dared to expect. He was connected to car enthusiast meetups and local business associations to meet professionals in the automotive and sales industries. Jude became his mentor. He advised Josh to create an online presence as well, so Josh created a LinkedIn profile highlighting his journey and aspirations in sales. There, he started connecting with local dealership managers, sales trainers, and automotive professionals.

4. Applying for jobs and gaining experience

Josh started sending out his resume. He tailored it to emphasize customer service experience from the auto shop and any relevant skills learned during his apprenticeship. He was careful to highlight his determination and unique background as a selling point. His applications were for entry-level sales positions at local dealerships, focusing on those with a reputation for training and development. He just wanted something to help him get a foot in the door.

5. Building a personal brand

In the meantime, Josh was sharing his story and promoting his brand everywhere he got a chance to. He wanted to develop a personal brand that reflected his journey and his mission in sales. His tagline became, "your relatable car guide— helping you find the perfect ride with no pressure." He used social media as much as he could to showcase his expertise.

Becoming a car salesperson

After diligently following his action plan, Josh finally landed a job he wanted. The dealership he landed a position with was bustling, filled with the hum of conversation, the scent of fresh coffee, and the gleaming shine of cars ready for their new owners. It was a far cry from his previous life, but it felt like a fresh start, like a pit stop before the finish line of a race he was determined to win.

Josh's first week was a whirlwind. He spent hours shadowing seasoned salespeople, absorbing every tip and technique. At first, he felt like a fish out of water— there were acronyms to learn, financing options to understand, and an unspoken hierarchy among the sales team that was more complicated than a car's engine. But he was undeterred. He leaned on his background, connecting with customers in a way that felt genuine and relatable.

During his second week, Josh got his first taste of success. A young couple walked in, looking overwhelmed by the choices. Sensing their anxiety, he approached them with his signature mix of charm and humor. "Don't worry, I'm here to help you find your perfect ride— no fireworks involved!" They laughed, and the ice was broken.

With his knowledge of cars and his newfound sales techniques, Josh was able to guide them through the lot. By the end of their visit, they drove away in a sleek sedan, and he earned his first commission check. It wasn't a fortune, but to Josh, it felt like a trophy for his hard work. He could already picture how he'd use that money to buy some toys for his son.

As weeks turned into months, Josh's reputation at the dealership began to grow. He became known not just for his impressive sales numbers, but for the personal touch he brought to every interaction. Customers appreciated that he listened to their needs and offered solutions rather than pushing for a sale. His quirky sense of humor— "Remember, a car is like a relationship. If it makes you feel bad, it's time to break up!"— made him a hit on the showroom floor.

His manager took notice of his dedication and customer rapport. He was a rising star. His colleagues would often say of him, "if you need a pep talk, just ask Josh. He'll make you feel like you can conquer the world, or at least the car-buying experience!"

Of course, with each successful sale, Josh's financial situation improved. He diligently saved his commissions, working towards stability for himself and his son. He was no longer just getting by; he was building a future. Soon, he could afford to buy a small used car for himself, allowing him to better juggle work and parenting duties. He felt a sense of pride every time he buckled his son into the car seat, this was a tangible symbol of his progress. Maybe one day, Josh would reach his larger goal of owning his own dealership. For now, he was well on his way.

Key Takeaways

- Let your enthusiasm for helping others and your positivity shine through in your interactions. Positivity is a great tool that attracts clients and builds rapport.
- Focus on establishing trust and credibility through consistency and authenticity. Your reputation will grow as you gain experience and demonstrate your commitment to your work.
- Utilize the resources you have available to you. No place or resource is too small to be a starting point.

CHAPTER 5

REINVENTING YOURSELF – A RETIREE'S GUIDE TO SALES

"Every success story is a tale of constant adaptation, revision and change." – **Richard Branson.**

Up to this point, it is clear that we all come into sales from incredibly different places. We start out young and inexperienced, or we have experience of other fields. We can also start out at a period when society would have us retire out of an official career. Research has shown many retirees going back to work for different reasons; often for financial reasons, social engagement, or the desire to stay active.

According to AARP in 2024, approximately 20% of Americans over the age of 65 are either working or actively looking for work, a trend expected to grow in the coming years. Many retirees are opting to return to work due to insufficient retirement savings and their desire to be less of a burden on others, or simply to keep themselves engaged and purposeful. Sales roles, with their flexible hours and potential for commission-based earnings, present an appealing option for older workers seeking a second career or supplemental income. There is a market for retirees to sell insurance, especially in events for seniors.

And since experience in other fields often translates well to sales- particularly in industries like real estate, insurance, or consulting, where interpersonal skills and industry knowledge are crucial- sales is doubly as enticing for retirees. A report from Harvard Business Review highlights that older workers often excel in sales because of their experience in handling customer relationships, understanding complex products, and maintaining patience during long sales cycles.

If you are one such person who dreams of re-entering the workforce, then Grace's story will likely resonate. Grace lives in a mobile home in Dorking, Surrey, surrounded by the familiar yet heavy silence that has settled in since Neil – her husband - passed. At 67, she is trying to adapt to a life she never anticipated, a life without her partner of over 30 years. The small space feels both cozy and constricting, filled with memories that tug at her heartstrings. Photographs of their adventures together hang on the walls as mementos of the laughter and love they shared, but sometimes she gazes around and gets an overwhelming sense of loss.

Every morning, she wakes up with the sun streaming through the curtains, casting soft shadows on the walls. She stares at the ceiling for a moment, gathering her thoughts. "Today is a new day," she tells herself, but the words feel hollow. After nearly three years of balancing a busy chauffeur company while caring for Neil, the sudden emptiness is suffocating. "I was up before dawn, managing bookings and drivers," she recalls, the memory flooding back. The hustle and bustle of her previous life seems so far away now. She had envisioned retirement as a chance to finally breathe, but instead, she finds herself grappling with loneliness and financial strain.

She pours herself a cup of tea, the warm aroma filling the air. On some days she remembers Neil's favorite mug, the one with the silly cat on it. She picks it up, running her fingers over the familiar shape, and feels a pang of sadness. Since Neil passed away in February, she has struggled to find her footing. Looking for a distraction, she took a part-time job at the local kitchen canteen, pouring coffee and serving meals to customers. The job keeps her mind busy, but it's not enough to ease the weight of her financial concerns. After losing Neil, she wasn't entitled to any allowances. With her pension, she is left with £720 a month, and it disappears quickly after bills and food.

Every week, she feels the pinch as rising costs gnaw at her limited budget. As she sits at her small kitchen table, the light glinting off the edge of her unpaid bills, she worries about the future. It feels as if the walls are closing in, reminding her of the life she used to have, a life filled with plans and dreams that now feel so distant.

Often, when Grace is getting ready for her shift, the thought of rushing around waiting tables, fills her with dread. She has always prided herself on being adaptable, but the demands of the job are taking a toll on her aging body. The constant standing and scurrying around exacerbate the arthritis creeping into her joints. She winces as she stretches, her knees protesting the movement. "Some days, I feel more like a weary soldier than a spirited retiree," she mutters to herself.

Because the local bus service is unreliable, she has to maintain her old car, which is yet another burden on her limited income. She feels the weight of it all— every trip to the mechanic, every time the engine sputters, and every time she fills up the tank. "Why is everything so expensive?" She wonders, feeling defeated. The freedom she once associated with driving has turned into a financial strain, leaving her feeling tethered rather than liberated.

On most days, she arrives at the kitchen canteen and the sound of laughter and chatter envelops her like a warm blanket. She loves those mornings. She enjoys interactions with regulars, but sometimes she often feels invisible among the bustling crowd. "How are you today, Grace?" A familiar face will ask, and she forces a smile, her heart not quite in it. "Oh, you know, just getting through the day," she will reply, trying to sound upbeat.

Grace continues to serve the meals, and while her mind keeps busy, her body starts to ache. The clattering of dishes and the hum of conversation create a rhythm that is comforting, yet exhausting. She often takes a moment to lean against the counter, catching her breath. The arthritis in her knees and back causes shooting pains that remind her she can't rely on her health forever. "I was always so active," she thinks, recalling the long walks she and Neil used to take in the countryside, hand in hand, chatting about everything and nothing.

As she wipes down tables at the end of the day, her thoughts drift to the future. She knows she needs to make changes, but where to start? The idea of downsizing to a smaller place or even relocating crosses her mind, but the thought of leaving their home— the place filled with shared memories— feels unbearable. "What would Neil have wanted?" She asks herself, wishing for his guidance at this turbulent time.

Each day blends into the next, a series of tasks that leave her feeling more isolated. In the evenings, when she settles into her favorite chair, a well-worn spot where she used to curl up with a book while Neil watched TV, she feels restless. The loneliness creeps in like an unwelcome guest and she fights it with small rituals— watering her plants, rearranging the flowers on the table, or going for a short walk, despite the chilly air. Something has to give.

What Grace does not yet realize is that she could set up a different life for herself through sales. In her work at the chauffeur company, she already developed many of the tools in the Devil's Dealbook. There, she learnt how to *persevere* through unwanted outcomes. She learnt how to *persuade* people toward different causes. Through caring for Neil, she had learnt *empathy*. At the kitchen canteen, she was already learning the value of a *positive attitude*. She was *ambitious*. She was already many steps ahead of many salespeople at the point they start their sales journey.

Heeding the Call to Sales

It was a particularly hectic afternoon at the canteen, the kind of busy that had Grace rushing from one end of the kitchen to the other. She was pouring coffee, serving plates, and smiling at the regulars when she overheard a conversation at a nearby table. Two women were deep in discussion about their insurance plans, their voices rising and falling with concern and uncertainty. "I just don't understand what's covered," one of them said, her brow furrowed in worry. The other nodded, sharing similar frustrations, and Grace felt a familiar tug in her heart.

The way they spoke, full of doubt and anxiety, struck a chord in her. She realized that navigating such decisions could be overwhelming, especially for those who had never dealt with it before. In that moment, a flicker of recognition sparked in Grace. "What if I could help people like them?" She thought, suddenly seeing the potential to use her own skills to make a difference.

After her shift, Grace returned home, the weight of her situation pressing down on her like a heavy blanket. She felt trapped in a cycle of grief and financial insecurity, yet, the conversation she had overheard lingered in her mind. She had always prided herself on being adaptable and empathetic, traits that could be valuable in a field where people often needed guidance and support. Could she possibly channel her communication skills into a career in sales, particularly in insurance?

Later that week, while sorting through old boxes in the attic, Grace stumbled upon some dusty notes from a sales workshop she had attended years ago. She remembered signing up out of sheer curiosity, intrigued by the idea of working in sales. As she flipped through the pages, her heart raced with a sense of nostalgia. The notes were filled with tips on understanding customer needs, building relationships, and the art of persuasion. "Could I really do this?" she wondered.

Suddenly, she could picture herself meeting with clients, discussing their needs, and helping them navigate the confusing world of insurance. The idea of working in a field that offered a service to people, especially to those who might feel lost, seemed like the perfect fit. Grace imagined herself reassuring a young couple, guiding them through their options, helping them feel secure in their decisions.

But as quickly as the excitement bubbled up, doubts crept in. What if she didn't have the courage? She also knew she didn't possess the specific industry knowledge needed to succeed. "What if I fail?" she whispered to herself.

Grace sank into her chair at the kitchen table, the notes still clutched in her hands. She felt torn; on the one hand, there was the tantalizing prospect of a new career that wasn't physically demanding, and on the other, the nagging fear of stepping into the unknown. She knew she needed to make a change, to find a way out of her current predicament, but could she really leap into something so different at this stage of her life?

Still, the more she thought about it, the more the idea of selling insurance appealed to her. It would keep her engaged, give her a sense of purpose, and offer a financial boost that her current job simply couldn't provide. The image of the two women at the canteen swirled in her mind, and she felt a yearning to make a difference in their lives.

Making the Leap

With some resolve, Grace decided to make a plan. To successfully transition to an insurance salesperson, here is what Grace would need to do. These steps are based on the tools inside the Devil's Dealbook:

Step 1: Update her industry *knowledge*

The insurance industry is complex and ever evolving. Retirees need to familiarize themselves with various insurance products, regulations, and market trends. Online courses and certifications are valuable resources one can use to get started. According to the Insurance Information Institute, nearly 12% of jobs in the insurance sector are projected to be unfilled due to a shortage of qualified candidates. This figure indicates a significant opportunity for retirees to enter the field. Grace definitely has a chance; she could learn the specific insurance offerings to sell in order to carve out a new career for herself.

Step 2: Find a *mentor*

Having a mentor can make a substantial difference in navigating a new career path. Research shows that mentoring can increase job satisfaction and retention rates. Grace would need a mentor to help make the things she learns more real. She would have to leverage her existing networks and explore professional organizations related to insurance to find an appropriate mentor. Networking events, both in-person and virtual, can facilitate connections with experienced professionals willing to share insights and guidance.

Step 3: Define her goals

You need clear, achievable goals to stay focused and motivated. According to a study by the Dominican University of California, people who write down their goals are 42% more likely to achieve them. Grace would have to outline both her short-term goals (e.g., completing a specific course or securing a mentor) and long-term goals (e.g., obtaining a job in insurance sales or setting up a consultancy). By breaking these goals into manageable steps with specific timelines, she could track her progress and maintain a sense of purpose.

Step 4: Create a brand

Building a credible brand is essential in sales and especially in today's digital age. Retirees like Grace do well to update their online profiles to reflect their new career goals and highlight relevant skills gained from previous employment. This would require an effort to learn how to use *social media and technology*. Even if not creating her own website, Grace would need some online presence- according to LinkedIn, 90% of recruiters use the platform to find candidates. Joining industry-related groups on social media could also provide networking opportunities and facilitate connections with potential employers.

The Outcome

Over several months, Grace committed herself to learning and growing, transforming her life in new ways. Grace began by enrolling on in-person courses that covered the fundamentals of insurance products, regulations, and sales strategies. Each lesson helped her understand the intricacies of the industry. She dedicated several hours a week to studying, often sitting at her small kitchen table with a cup of tea, surrounded by notes and textbooks. The excitement of acquiring new knowledge reignited her passion for learning, making her feel vibrant and engaged once more.

Finding a mentor proved to be one of the most impactful steps she took. Grace reached out to a former colleague from her days managing the chauffeur company. This contact- Fiona- had transitioned into insurance sales years earlier and was eager to help. They planned weekly phone calls which became a cornerstone of Grace's development. Fiona taught Grace the nuances of selling insurance, shared practical tips for building client relationships, and encouraged Grace to embrace her unique strengths— her life experience and ability to empathize with clients.

As she gained *confidence*, Grace set clear goals for herself. She crafted a timeline, setting milestones like completing her first insurance certification exam and attending local networking events. With the help of Fiona, she also figured out what her financial goals were, to ensure that her target income would not only support her living expenses but also allow for some personal interests and activities. She wanted to create a balanced financial picture that reflected both her needs and her dreams. She was defining her FUM© lifestyle.

First, Grace calculated her essential monthly living expenses, and found she needed £1,100 which included:

- Housing (mobile home lot rent) - £400
- Utilities (electricity, water, gas, internet) - £150

- Groceries - £200
- Transportation (fuel, insurance for her car) - £100
- Health Insurance - £150
- Miscellaneous (clothing, personal care) - £100

In addition to her essential expenses, Grace wanted to set aside some funds for her gardening supplies, books, travel needs and savings. She did her calculations and found that figure to be £500. This meant that every month, to live her ideal life, she needed £1,600. This brought it to an annual figure of £19,200.

With her goal of earning at least £40,000 per year set, Grace could clearly see that her earnings would not only cover her living expenses but also provide her with a comfortable cushion for her interests and investments. She figured it was not too late to leave her grandkids a small inheritance and that is what the surplus would go toward funding.

Grace also began to establish her professional presence online. She created a LinkedIn profile that highlighted her new career aspirations and the skills she was developing. Gradually, she connected with other professionals in the industry, joining groups that focused on insurance sales.

After several months of hard work, Grace felt like she could officially call herself an insurance sales consultant. The sense of accomplishment washed over her like a warm embrace. She only needed to make her first sale to prove it to herself.

This sale came unexpectedly. One afternoon, she received a call from a young mother looking for guidance on insurance options for her growing family. The young mother had learnt about Grace from one of her networking events. Grace listened carefully, understanding the importance of this decision for the woman's peace of mind. She offered compassionate advice and presented options that fit her budget and needs. By the end of the conversation, the mother was relieved and grateful. When she agreed to a policy, Grace felt a surge of pride.

As the weeks rolled on, Grace continued to build her client base, often receiving referrals from satisfied customers. The financial rewards began to alleviate the stress that had weighed heavily on her since Neil's passing. Each commission cheque brought her closer to feeling secure again, allowing her to enjoy small pleasures like treating herself to a nice meal or saving for a little getaway. She was well on her way toward her FUM© lifestyle.

Key Takeaways

- Your years of life and work experience are invaluable assets. Use them to build rapport with clients; your unique insights and understanding can provide a level of trust and connection that other competitors may lack.
- Consider your age and lifestyle when setting your work demands.
- Use your passion for helping others to connect with clients on a deeper level. It can lead to stronger relationships and greater success in sales.
- Keep updating your skills to stay relevant in your industry.

PART IV

PUTTING IT ALL TOGETHER - UNLOCKING YOUR SALES POTENTIAL

"God didn't make Rambo. I made him." – **Colonel Trautman.**

"A good mentor will inspire you to push and break barriers, they will develop you and expand your perception. They will chip away at your edges until you are perfect." – **Bobby Rakhit.**

A top-notch salesperson is a coveted role. I know this from my personal experience and from research. Throughout this book, you have read stories of people who transformed themselves into great salespeople, you have read my personal journey through sales and you have interacted with all the tools inside the Devil's Dealbook.

You have the knowledge. How you proceed from here depends on how well you integrate this knowledge. That's the purpose of this section. It is a self-help section intended to help you gauge exactly where you are in terms of all the tools inside the Devil's Dealbook so that you can know how to proceed.

The same way Colonel Trautman ensured the evolution of Rambo from an average joe to a full-blooded Green Beret combat soldier, is the same way this section of the book will transform you into a great salesman if you dare to be honest. Each question will reveal a thing or two about where you are on your journey. If you are honest with yourself, you will get a thorough picture of where you stand and where to go next from there.

CHAPTER 1

ARE YOU FIT FOR SALES?

"Knowing yourself is the beginning of all wisdom."–**Aristotle.**

*I*n sales, as in life, knowing where you are is the first step to moving forward. When you take the time to understand your current situation, you gain control over your journey. You get the clarity that allows you to make deliberate decisions, reducing chaos and helping you cultivate a sense of purpose.

By recognizing where you stand right now, you can identify what you want to achieve and where you're headed. This knowledge enables you to set meaningful goals that align with your dreams. Whether it's reaching a sales target or enhancing your skills, clear goals give you something to aim for.

Secondly, with a solid grasp of your circumstances, you can commit to specific actions and habits. This isn't just about making promises; it's about holding yourself accountable. Knowing where you are helps you take responsibility for your actions so that you can steer out of situations you don't want to be in, and toward the future you desire.

As you reflect on the questions in this section and the insights from your evaluation, it's essential to recognize that selling is more than just a profession, it's a personal journey that intertwines with who you are at your core. The way you approach sales reflects your values, beliefs, and experiences. Every conversation you have, every pitch you make, and every relationship you build is a manifestation of your unique identity.

Think about it: when you're selling, you're not just offering a product or service; you're sharing a piece of yourself. Your passions, your empathy, and your authenticity shine through in your interactions. When you genuinely connect with others, you're not just closing a deal, you're forging relationships that can transform your career and impact lives.

Sales is inherently relational. You're not merely engaging in transactions, you're participating in conversations that can inspire change, solve problems, and create value. The more you tap into your personal journey, the more you'll find that your sales approach becomes an authentic extension of who you are. Your personal story, your struggles, and your triumphs all inform how you connect with clients and prospects.

Consider the moments when you've felt most successful in sales. Often, those moments stem from being true to yourself, when you've shared your enthusiasm, demonstrated your knowledge, or shown vulnerability in the face of challenges. This authenticity resonates with others, creating trust and rapport that are essential in sales.

In sales, your individuality is your greatest asset. It is the canvas for your expression and creativity. Each client interaction is an opportunity to showcase your unique perspective and insights. Since sales is a personal journey, this chapter will help you figure out whether sales is really for you.

Are You Fit for Sales?

Instructions: Read each statement carefully and rate yourself on a scale from 1 to 5, where:

5 = Strongly Agree

4 = Agree

3 = Neutral

2 = Disagree

1 = Strongly disagree

1. I am a person that is always trying to find the best price before making a purchase.

    - 5
    - 4
    - 3
    - 2
    - 1

I love money.

- 5
- 4
- 3
- 2
- 1

I am ambitious and constantly seeking to improve.

- 5
- 4
- 3
- 2
- 1

I enjoy competition and always strive to win.

- 5
- 4
- 3
- 2
- 1

I communicate well with people.

- 5
- 4
- 3
- 2
- 1

I am good at building and maintaining relationships.

- 5   • 4   • 3   • 2   • 1

I make friends easily.

- 5   • 4   • 3   • 2   • 1

I am never scared to interact with people, even in places where I don't know anyone.

- 5   • 4   • 3   • 2   • 1

I am extroverted (energized by social interactions).

- 5   • 4   • 3   • 2   • 1

I can travel alone comfortably.

- 5   • 4   • 3   • 2   • 1

I bounce back quickly after rejection.

- 5   • 4   • 3   • 2   • 1

I prefer working independently.

- 5   • 4   • 3   • 2   • 1

Understanding Your Score

As you read the interpretation of your scores, bear in mind that there is nothing right or wrong with your answers. This is not that kind of test. The questions you have answered were simply meant to help you understand yourself, not define you. The idea is that from an informed place, you have options.

1. 50-60: You're a hunter

If you scored between 50 and 60, you have a strong killer instinct that makes you exceptionally suited for any sales role, even aggressive sales roles. Hunters thrive in competitive environments, where the thrill of the chase drives them to pursue new clients relentlessly. Your ability to engage with prospects and turn leads into sales is a core strength.

You enjoy the challenge of outperforming others and often set ambitious goals for yourself. Rejection doesn't deter you; instead, it fuels your determination to succeed, and you actively seek out opportunities, often taking the initiative to network and connect with potential clients. As a hunter, you can excel in sales roles in new business. You are well suited for entrepreneurial types of sales ventures, for example you can work in a startup or an existing company that is looking for organic growth or expand into new areas or territories. Basically, anything that taps into your hunger for money is a great fit for you. Hunters excel in commission-based roles and are not scared of risk

In sales, the ability to hunt and secure new business is crucial. Just as in nature, those who can adapt and thrive in competitive settings are more likely to succeed. Embrace your strengths and consider pursuing roles like business development or direct sales, where your skills can shine.

2. 30-49: You're a farmer

If your score was between 30 and 49, you possess valuable qualities that can make you successful in sales, particularly in roles that involve nurturing and managing relationships. You have an innate ability to build and maintain long-term connections, which is an essential trait for cultivating client loyalty. Your skills in this area make you well-suited for environments where success is measured over time through the cultivation of trust, satisfaction, and mutual respect.

You excel at listening to clients and responding thoughtfully to their needs. This trait helps you uncover the underlying concerns of your clients and offer solutions that truly meet their expectations. You're invested in ensuring your clients feel valued and understood. This approach helps you build deep-rooted trust and loyalty, which, over time, can lead to repeat business and strong referrals.

While hunters are essential for growing a business, farmers are crucial for ensuring their sustainability. Your score suggests that you are more inclined toward this way of being. This is a strength, as customer retention and repeat business are often more profitable in the long run than constantly pursuing new prospects. It is okay to be more focused on delivering value over time and ensuring that clients continue to feel engaged and supported.

With your skillset, roles such as account management, customer success, or relationship management would be excellent fits. In these roles, you'll be able to leverage your ability to nurture existing client relationships while helping clients achieve their long-term goals. Your focus on client satisfaction can translate into ongoing loyalty, upselling opportunities, and continued business growth.

In salary-based sales roles, where the emphasis is more on managing accounts and maintaining relationships rather than closing new deals constantly, you can thrive. Your steady approach ensures that your clients' needs are met, and that they feel cared for, which is critical for keeping them as long-term partners.

While you excel in the nurturing side of sales, there may come a time when you desire to broaden your skill set and become more of a "hunter." Hunters tend to take more risks by pushing for new opportunities, entering new markets, or closing deals faster. If you find yourself interested in expanding your role, you can increase your appetite for calculated risks by deliberately seeking out opportunities that involve higher stakes or new challenges.

You can begin by asking for more responsibility in your current position. Perhaps you could take on additional clients or explore new areas within your existing client base. This can be a great way to gradually ease into more risk-heavy roles while still maintaining the relationships you've worked hard to cultivate.

Consider finding a mentor who has successfully navigated both the farmer and hunter approaches in sales. A mentor can provide guidance on how to balance relationship-building with more aggressive, risk-oriented strategies. They can also help you identify any barriers that may be holding you back from stepping into a more high-stakes sales role.

As a farmer, your natural inclination may be to minimize risk, but as you grow in your career, embracing calculated risks is crucial to advancing. Taking risks doesn't mean acting recklessly; it's about weighing potential outcomes, understanding the variables, and making informed decisions that push you out of your comfort zone. For instance, you might decide to target a more competitive market, pitch a larger deal, or expand your role to include new responsibilities.

Risk management is all about understanding the landscape and taking measured steps toward growth. It's important to assess when the time is right to push for new opportunities, while still maintaining the strong relationships you've worked to establish. Balancing these two aspects— risk-taking and relationship management— is a skill that can be developed over time. With time and intentional effort, you can expand your skills and adapt to different roles, including those of a hunter, without losing sight of your core strengths as a farmer.

3. Below 30: Sales may not be for you

If your score was below 30, it might indicate that you are not as naturally inclined toward high-pressure sales situations or the competitive environment that typically defines the world of sales. That's okay; sales is not for everyone, and recognizing this is an important step in developing self-awareness and understanding where your strengths truly lie. Acknowledging that sales may not be your forte is not a weakness, but rather a sign of maturity and clarity about what you want in your career.

Before diving into alternative career paths, it's worth noting that communication is an essential skill in every role, and in many ways, we are always selling ourselves. Whether it's convincing a colleague to collaborate on a project, persuading a manager to approve an idea, or negotiating with a vendor, we are constantly engaging in forms of persuasion and communication. These are the foundational skills that underpin success in virtually any professional environment. In essence, everything we do in life requires us to communicate, to advocate for ourselves, and to influence others in one way or another. The degree to which we need to do this may vary by role, but the skill set is universal.

In sales, this concept is amplified because the job revolves around convincing others to buy a product, service, or idea. However, even if you don't thrive in traditional sales, effective communication such as understanding needs, building relationships, and advocating for solutions is still a vital skill that can serve you well in other areas. So, don't worry that you're lacking in something essential; rather, consider how your current communication strengths might serve you in different contexts.

If you find yourself feeling anxious in high-pressure sales situations or uncomfortable with competitive, results-driven environments, it may be a sign that your talents lie elsewhere, in roles that align better with your natural inclinations, preferences, and strengths.

Chances are, you are more comfortable in environments that require collaboration, critical thinking, and problem-solving. You might find more satisfaction in roles that allow you to work at your own pace, explore new ideas, and engage in more analytical or creative tasks. For example, if you're someone who enjoys tackling complex problems, thinking through solutions, and working with detailed information, you might excel in roles like project management, where you can focus on coordinating teams, planning initiatives, and managing timelines rather than closing deals, research or analysis and so forth.

You want roles that allow you to leverage your strengths, without the high-stakes pressure often associated with sales quotas or direct client persuasion. You can still make a shift toward sales or a more client-facing role, but it will require deliberate effort and stepping outside your comfort zone. You'll need to work on building your communication skills and developing a higher risk tolerance. Sales requires confidence in your ability to engage with others, handle objections, and take calculated risks. These are areas where you can grow over time with focus and support.

One way to transition into sales or a more client-focused role is to start small. Ask for new responsibilities within your current role, which involve client interaction or communication. Perhaps you could take on a project that requires you to lead a team or present an idea to upper management. These small steps can help you build confidence in your communication abilities and expand your comfort zone gradually.

A mentor can be incredibly helpful in this process. If you're interested in moving into a more sales-oriented role, find someone who has experience in that field and can offer advice, feedback, and guidance. A mentor can help you identify areas where you can improve — whether it's your confidence, persuasion techniques, or ability to manage risk.

Remember, just like in nature, not every role is meant for everyone, and that's a good thing. By focusing on the roles where you can truly excel you can create a fulfilling and successful career without forcing yourself into a mold that doesn't fit. The key is to find your niche, where your skills and strengths shine. And if, at some point, you do decide to venture into sales or a more client-focused role, know that with intentional effort, mentorship, and a willingness to step out of your comfort zone, you can develop the skills necessary to succeed.

CHAPTER 2

WHAT'S IN YOUR HAND? - DO YOU HAVE THE TOOLS IN THE DEVIL'S DEALBOOK?

"If you spend too much time thinking about a thing, you'll never get it done." - **Bruce Lee.**

"It is not enough to "think positive," because most of who we are might reside subconsciously. We need to enter into the operating system of the subconscious mind and make permanent changes where those programs exist." – **Joe Dispenza.**

Now that you have a broad scheme of what you are, do you have the tools to excel there?

Sales is often viewed through a narrow lens associated with pressure, quotas, and competition. However, the moment you shift your mindset about sales, you unlock a transformative potential that can ripple through both your professional and personal life.

Sales is about connection, understanding, and providing value. When you embrace this perspective, it becomes less about transactions and more about relationships. This internal shift allows you to see each interaction as an opportunity to help others rather than merely a chance to close a deal. This has been one of the major arguments of this book.

When you approach sales with a mindset centered on service and connection, you naturally become more empathetic. This shift fosters deeper relationships with clients and colleagues as you prioritize understanding their needs and challenges. As you cultivate these authentic connections, you not only enhance your sales performance but also enrich your personal interactions. The skills you develop translate seamlessly into your everyday life, making you a more relatable and approachable person. This section is meant to help you evaluate your skill set.

Instructions: For each question below, rate yourself on a scale from 1 to 5, where:

5 = Fully

4 = Mostly

3 = Moderately

2 = Slightly

1 = Not at all

Ambition

1. Do you have long term goals that you actively pursue?

- 5
- 4
- 3
- 2
- 1

How driven are you to achieve your goals and to advance in your career?

- 5   - 4   - 3   - 2   - 1

Are you primarily driven by internal motivations rather than external reward?

- 5   - 4   - 3   - 2   - 1

Persuasion

2. Do you feel confident when presenting your ideas to others?

- 5   - 4   - 3   - 2   - 1

How effective are you at convincing others to see your point of view or take action?

- 5   - 4   - 3   - 2   - 1

How often do you consider your audience's needs and perspectives when communicating?

- 5   - 4   - 3   - 2   - 1

Networking

3. How comfortable are you with building and maintaining new professional relationships?

- 5   - 4   - 3   - 2   - 1

How likely are you to follow up with people you meet?

- 5   - 4   - 3   - 2   - 1

Do you share valuable resources and information with your network?

- 5   - 4   - 3   - 2   - 1

Confidence

4. How confident do you feel in your abilities when interacting with people that you don't know?

- 5   - 4   - 3   - 2   - 1

How aware are you of your body language and how often do you use it to convey confidence?

- 5   - 4   - 3   - 2   - 1

How comfortable are you advocating for yourself and your needs?

- 5   - 4   - 3   - 2   - 1

Knowledge

5. How well do you understand your product/service, industry trends, and market dynamics?

- 5   - 4   - 3   - 2   - 1

Do you have a strong desire to learn new things and expand your knowledge?

- 5   • 4   • 3   • 2   • 1

Do you engage in critical thinking and analysis when processing new information?

- 5   • 4   • 3   • 2   • 1

Empathy

6. How effectively do you understand and relate to other people's emotions and needs?

- 5   • 4   • 3   • 2   • 1

How attentive are you to nonverbal cues and body language when interacting with others?

- 5   • 4   • 3   • 2   • 1

Do you make an effort to see things from other people's perspectives?

- 5   • 4   • 3   • 2   • 1

Passion

7. How passionate are you about what you do?

- 5   • 4   • 3   • 2   • 1

When working on what you do, do you lose track of time because you are so engaged?

- 5
- 4
- 3
- 2
- 1

How willing are you to invest time and effort into the thing you love, even if it means making sacrifices?

- 5
- 4
- 3
- 2
- 1

Persistence

8. How willing are you to follow up and keep trying, even after setbacks or rejections?

- 5
- 4
- 3
- 2
- 1

Do you reach out for support when you need it rather than give up on your goals?

- 5
- 4
- 3
- 2
- 1

How often do you see tasks to completion after they become challenging?

- 5
- 4
- 3
- 2
- 1

Technology and media

9. How comfortable are you with using technology and tools (e.g., CRM software, analytics)?

- 5
- 4
- 3
- 2
- 1

How adept are you at using social media for networking, branding, and lead generation?

- 5
- 4
- 3
- 2
- 1

Do you actively stay updated on the latest technology trends and advancements?

- 5
- 4
- 3
- 2
- 1

Interpret Your Score

Add up your scores for each tool and for all of them combined and use the following guidelines to understand what they mean for you.

Ambition

11-15 - Your ambition is strong! You actively pursue long-term goals and are driven to achieve success in sales. Keep harnessing this energy to inspire others and drive results.

6-10 - You have some ambition, but may not be fully committed. Focus on setting actionable steps to advance your career and enhance your sales performance.

Below 5 - You may lack clear long-term goals in your sales career. Consider defining specific objectives to boost your motivation and drive.

Persuasion

11-15 - You are a persuasive communicator! Your confidence and consideration for your audience make you effective in convincing clients to your way of thinking. Leverage these skills to close more deals.

6-10 -You have a moderate level of persuasion skills. Continue to refine your ability to present ideas and engage your audience, as this will significantly impact your sales success.

Below 5 -You might struggle with confidence to persuade others. Consider practicing your presentation skills and understanding your audience needs to improve your effectiveness.

Networking

11-15 - You excel at networking! Your comfort in building relationships and sharing information positions you as a valuable contact in your industry. Use this to expand your client base.

6-10 - You have a decent grasp of networking but could improve in maintaining relationships. Make it a habit to connect regularly and share valuable resources with your network.

Below 5 - Building relationships may feel uncomfortable for you. Focus on initiating conversations and following up with contacts to strengthen your network.

Confidence

11-15 - You demonstrate high confidence in sales! Your ability to convey assurance and engage with clients will set you apart. Keep showcasing this trait in all interactions.

6-10 - Your confidence is developing, but there's room for growth. Continue to practice self-advocacy and reinforce positive body language to build rapport with clients.

Below 5 - You may lack confidence in your sales abilities. Consider engaging in training or mentorship to enhance your self-assurance and body language awareness.

Knowledge

11-15 - Your knowledge is a significant asset! You clearly understand your product and industry, which helps build trust with clients. Continue to share insights to establish yourself as a thought leader.

6-10 - You possess a reasonable level of knowledge but should aim to expand further. Engaging in continuous learning will enhance your sales discussions and decision-making.

Below 5 - You may need to deepen your understanding of your product and industry. Invest time in learning and stay informed about market trends to boost your credibility.

Empathy

11-15 - Your empathetic skills are strong! You effectively relate to clients, making them feel valued. Use this ability to enhance customer loyalty and satisfaction.

6-10 - You show some empathy, but there's potential for greater connection. Make an effort to recognize nonverbal cues and adjust your approach based on clients' perspectives.

Below 5 - You might find it challenging to relate to clients' needs. Practice active listening and focus on understanding their emotions to improve client relationships.

Passion

11-15 - Your passion is infectious! You deeply care about your product and the sales process, which energizes your interactions and can significantly impact your sales success.

6-10 - You have a moderate level of passion. Consider sharing your enthusiasm more with others, as this can help motivate your team and attract clients.

Below 5 - You may not feel strongly about your product or the sales process. Explore what aspects of your work excite you and reignite that passion to drive your performance.

Persistence

11-15 - Your persistence is commendable! You are willing to follow up and seek support, which is crucial in sales. Keep pushing through challenges to achieve your goals.

6-10 - You demonstrate a fair amount of persistence but could improve your approach to challenges. Setting incremental goals can help maintain your motivation through tough times.

Below 5 - You may struggle with setbacks and give up easily. Focus on building resilience and develop strategies to bounce back from rejection in your sales efforts.

Technology and media

11-15 - You are tech-savvy! Your ability to leverage sales technology and social media positions you well for success in today's digital landscape. Continue to explore innovations that can enhance your sales approach.

6-10 - You have a reasonable level of comfort with technology but could improve. Actively seek out new tools and trends that could enhance your sales strategy.

Below 5 - You may feel uncomfortable using sales technology. Invest time in training or resources to become more adept, as technology is essential for modern sales success.

Combining Your Scores

1. 108-135: Strong skill set

If you scored between 108 and 135, you possess a robust set of sales skills and tools, indicating a high level of competence in various aspects of sales. This level of proficiency allows you to navigate complex sales environments with confidence and effectiveness.

You can adjust your approach based on client needs and market changes. You think critically about your sales strategies, enabling you to anticipate challenges and seize opportunities. You excel at engaging clients and persuading them to make decisions that align with their needs.

Seek leadership positions or complex sales projects that push you out of your comfort zone. This will further hone your skills and demonstrate your capabilities. You should also consider mentoring others. Sharing your knowledge with less experienced colleagues can reinforce your understanding and position you as a leader in your organization. Stay updated on industry trends and best practices by attending workshops, webinars, or pursuing advanced certifications. This commitment to growth will solidify your status as a top performer.

2. 81-107: Developing skill set

A score between 81 and 107 means that you have a solid foundation in sales, demonstrating competence in several areas. However, there are specific skills that you could develop further to enhance your overall effectiveness and boost your performance.

You deliver reliable results but may lack the flair or assertiveness seen in top performers. You show openness to feedback and are keen to develop your skills further. You have the ability to connect with clients but may not fully leverage these relationships for long-term success.

Use your self-assessment results to pinpoint specific skills that need improvement. For example, if persuasion is a weaker area, consider enrolling in a persuasive communication workshop. Create measurable, achievable, relevant goals for skill development. You can, for example, aim to attend one networking event per month to improve your networking abilities. Regularly solicit feedback from peers and supervisors to identify blind spots in your performance thenuse this input to make targeted improvements.

3. Below 81: Emerging skill set

You may be new to sales or feel unsure about your abilities. This score is an opportunity for self-discovery and growth. You are beginning to understand your strengths and weaknesses in sales, but you hesitate to take risks or engage with clients due to a lack of confidence. You show a willingness to learn and grow, even if you're unsure where to start.

Reflect on the skills that interest you the most. Focus on these as areas for development. Look for workshops, online courses, or mentorship programs that can help build your confidence and skill set. Consider joining sales training programs that focus on foundational skills. You can also engage in role-playing exercises with peers or practice networking in informal settings to build your confidence gradually.

Remember, every expert was once a beginner. Embrace this phase as a crucial step in your journey. Celebrate small victories and remain open to learning and adapting as you grow in your sales career.

CHAPTER 3

IT IS NOT SET IN STONE

*"I can't change the direction of the wind, but I can adjust my sails to always reach my destination." -***Jimmy Dean.**

The results from the self-help chapters are just snapshots of where you are right now, not a final verdict on your abilities or future.

Personal growth, evolving circumstances, and targeted effort can shift your trajectory in the sales landscape. This chapter explores how you can move between these categories, what factors might cause you to shift downward, and actionable steps to enhance your skills and adaptability.

Moving Up the Categories

- Becoming a farmer if you were 'not fit for sales'

If you find yourself categorized as "not fit for sales," it's essential to recognize that this label doesn't define your potential. Many have successfully transitioned into sales by focusing on relationship-building skills. If you desire to make the shift, begin with self-reflection. Identify your strengths and interests. Consider what aspects of sales resonate with you. Take into account your results of the Chapter two above–

which sales tools do you already possess? You may not have them to the level that you desire, but you know where you are beginning from.

Once that's done, figure out the skills you want to develop and enroll in workshops or courses that focus on them, whether that be communication, empathy, and/or customer service. Look for resources that emphasize active listening and problem-solving. While at it, seek out mentorship. A mentor will be able to shape you into a farmer. They would be able to see the person you could become way more than you may see it yourself, the way Colonel Trautman did for Rambo and Colin Rodgers did for me.

Where you can, volunteer for sales-related tasks. Seek opportunities within your current role or organization to assist in client interactions or sales presentations. This exposure will build your confidence and skills gradually. Connect with experienced sales professionals and watch them work. Observe their way of being, from how they present themselves, to how they communicate and so forth. See if you can spot the differences that make them the person you want to become. Whenever possible, join sales-focused groups or associations to interact with peers who can share their experiences.

- Moving from farmer to hunter

If you found yourself in the farmer category, don't think for a second that you're limited to nurturing existing relationships. You have the ability to cultivate ambition and persistence— qualities that can help you become a successful hunter too. It may feel daunting, but with practice, you can learn to seek out new opportunities and step outside your comfort zone.

To do this, you must be proactive. You have to set ambitious goals to begin cultivating the hunter instinct. Challenge yourself with specific targets which push you beyond your current comfort zone. Aim for new client acquisition or higher sales quotas. You don't have to quit your current role, but you can expand your responsibilities. You also need to increase your risk appetite and start taking calculated risks in your approach to sales. This could involve pursuing leads that seem challenging or initiating conversations with high-profile prospects. The more you do it, the better you will become.

Regularly solicit feedback from your peers and mentors. Learn how successful hunters operate and adapt those strategies to fit your style. Consider your results for the sales tools exercise. For which specific tools did you score low? Those are the ones you especially need to grow. Look for roles or projects within your organization that involve prospecting or lead generation; these experiences will help you develop the hunter instinct.

Leverage your network. Use your professional connections to find mentors, seek advice, and explore new opportunities. Networking can open doors you might not have considered.

If you scored in the hunter range, that's fantastic! You possess the killer instinct and skills that make you a natural at pursuing new clients. But remember, there's always room for growth. Even the best hunters can enhance their relationship-building skills and develop a deeper understanding of their clients' needs. Embracing some 'farmer' qualities will make you an even more versatile salesperson.

Change won't happen overnight. It will require effort, perseverance, and a willingness to learn. There will be challenges along the way, but every step you take toward improving your skills is a step toward achieving your goals. Embrace the journey, celebrate small victories, and don't hesitate to ask for help when you need it.

You've got this. Your potential is not fixed; it's a canvas that you can paint however you like.

Moving Down the Categories

As it turns out, it is possible to move down the categories. Changes in your environment can knock you down from a hunter to a farmer, or from a farmer to someone who isn't fit for sales.

From Hunter to Farmer

If you find yourself dropping from the hunter category, several factors may be at play:

1. You may be consistently failing to meet targets which can erode your confidence. Each missed goal might make you question your abilities, leading to a more cautious approach and a shift toward being a farmer.
2. It could be that your work environment lacks encouragement or resources, and you may feel isolated in your efforts. This can diminish your killer instinct, making you hesitant to pursue new leads or take risks.
3. Perhaps you lost momentum. Sales requires a proactive approach. If external factors slow your momentum— such as market downturns or reduced demand for your product— you might find it challenging to maintain the hunter instinct.
4. It could also be that you encounter personal challenges, such as health issues or significant life changes, and they impact on your performance and motivation, causing you to retreat from high-pressure sales environments.

To prevent moving down into the farmer category, you have to proactively refocus on your targets. Regularly remind yourself of the goals you're working toward. Reevaluate your strategies and refocus on high-priority prospects. Set small, achievable milestones to rebuild your confidence after setbacks and invest in your resilience; sales is an emotionally taxing profession and it's easy to become disheartened by missed targets or slow periods. Embrace the fact that setbacks are part of the journey. Use them as opportunities to learn, improve, and re-energize.

It is also okay to step away from being the mentor to become a mentee when you need to so that you reorient yourself. It will give you new perspectives, resources, and techniques to keep your momentum going. Even during market downturns or tough times, find new ways to keep moving forward. Diversify your approach, explore new channels for prospecting, and stay proactive about seeking new opportunities.

Always remember that your professional life is often an extension of your personal life. If your personal life is suffering, your professional life bears the brunt. Take time to manage stress, focus on self-care, and address any personal challenges that might impact your professional performance.

From Farmer to 'Not Fit for Sales'

In the same way, farmers can experience shifts downward, especially if they face challenges that impact their ability to nurture relationships effectively:

1. The demands of maintaining client relationships can lead to burnout. If you feel overwhelmed, you may withdraw from your role, which can hinder your effectiveness.
2. Significant life changes like health issues, family responsibilities, or emotional stress, can impact your performance and

motivation. These challenges might cause you to retreat from relationship building, leaving you feeling unfit for sales altogether.
3. If your company shifts focus away from your strengths or if market dynamics change significantly, you might find yourself struggling to adapt. This can lead to feelings of inadequacy and a reassessment of your sales roles.

To avoid slipping out of the farmer category, it's important to stay self-aware and address potential risks before they become bigger problems.

Make a point to regularly assess your workload. Whenever you're feeling overwhelmed, assess your responsibilities and look for areas where you can delegate or streamline your tasks. Don't let burnout sneak up on you — regularly check in with yourself to ensure you're not taking on too much at once. Maintain your physical and mental well-being and always seek professional development. If the market dynamics or company focus changes, invest in learning new skills or expanding your expertise. Don't allow yourself to stagnate, instead, keep growing to remain relevant in your role and ensure you're bringing value to your clients.

In both scenarios— whether you are a hunter striving to avoid shifting into a more cautious farming role or a farmer concerned about losing your fit for sales— the key is constant self-assessment and adaptation. Stay alert to your internal and external environments and how they might be affecting your performance. Regularly evaluate your approach, mindset, and personal well-being. Make adjustments where necessary but always stay focused on your core strengths and the areas where you can grow.

In other words, adjust your sails to the wind. Sales is dynamic, and maintaining the right mindset and skill set requires a commitment to continuous improvement. By proactively addressing the challenges that can lead you to move down a category, you'll ensure that you remain in the ideal position for growth and success.

PART V

THE SALES COMMANDMENTS

*A*s you consider the sales commandments in this chapter, there are two things to keep in mind:

1. Gap analysis is a vital tool that you use at every stage of the sales process, before, during, and after your meetings with clients.

Before you even step into a meeting, conducting a gap analysis allows you to assess where your products or services fit the client's needs. By researching your offerings and comparing them with industry standards and competitor solutions, you can identify the unique value propositions you bring to the table. This preparation not only helps you understand the product better but also equips you with insights that can tailor your pitch to align perfectly with what the client is looking for.

During the meeting, gap analysis becomes a dynamic tool for identifying areas where you can assist the client. You get to actively listen and ask probing questions, so that you can uncover pain points, unmet needs, and opportunities for improvement. This real-time analysis allows you to adapt your approach, highlight relevant features of your product, and position your solution as the ideal fit for their challenges.

After the meeting, gap analysis helps you evaluate how well your product met the client's expectations. Reflecting on any shortcomings or areas for improvement can inform your future strategies and enhance your offerings. By understanding where the gaps were, you can make necessary adjustments, whether that involves refining your product, enhancing your pitch, or improving customer support. This continuous improvement loop not only strengthens your product but also builds trust and rapport with your clients.

2. You are selling yourself, not just the product.

You get nowhere in life if you only sell the product, you risk becoming merely a product vehicle. Your goal should be to enhance your personal brand during the meeting by focusing on finding the best solution that fits the client's needs. This approach not only builds credibility but also helps you gather insights that can inform future product improvements. By prioritizing your personal brand and focusing on the client's needs, you not only elevate your sales approach but also cultivate meaningful relationships that can drive your success for years to come.

Make sure you sell yourself and integrate gap analysis into every stage of your sales process.

That said, here are the sales commandments:

Prep Like a Pro

1. Prep for success. Knowledge is power! Research your products and services inside and out. Put yourself in your customers' shoes to truly understand their needs. Preparation breeds confidence.

2. Look the part. First impressions matter. Keep yourself well-groomed and presentable. Good hygiene and a polished appearance can make a world of difference.
3. Take the first step. Reach out to those who can help you achieve your dreams. The first move is often the hardest but is crucial for growth.
4. Stay ahead of the curve. Keep your finger on the pulse of industry trends. Being in the know positions you as a credible resource and prepares you for client inquiries.
5. Welcome the challenge. Embrace competition. It's your chance to shine and showcase your unique strengths. Use your knowledge to stand out from the crowd.
6. Be ready for anything. Always prepare for those unexpected moments, whether it's an impromptu pitch in an elevator or a casual café chat. Flexibility can turn surprises into golden opportunities.
7. Know your customer. Deeply understand your demographic. Identify their needs and what they currently use, then educate them on the superior options you provide.
8. Don't put all your eggs in one basket. Relying too heavily on a specific piece of business? Think again! Pursue all qualified prospects with gusto, you never know which ones will come through.
9. Avoid procrastination. Opportunity waits for no one! Act early and decisively. While you're thinking things over, circumstances can shift beneath you- seize the moment.

Shine During the Show

1. A smile, a compliment, or a well-timed joke can break the ice even with the toughest clients. Build rapport through positive energy— it's contagious.
2. Keep it fun. Don't bore your clients to tears, keep your conversations lively and engaging and avoid jargon that sounds like a lullaby. A sprinkle of humor and charm can go a long way.
3. Make it a win-win. Remember, a successful sale benefits both you and your client. Focus on crafting solutions that meet their needs while hitting your goals. It's all about synergy.
4. Build relationships, not just sales. Remember, you're not just selling a product; you're fostering relationships based on trust, respect, and mutual benefit.
5. Attention to detail is key. Double-check your presentations, spelling, and calculations. Professionalism speaks volumes.
6. Present with confidence. Effective body language and eye contact can seal the deal. Practice regularly to keep your delivery sharp.
7. Convince with value. If you want to sell your services, show your customers their worth. Demonstrate how your offerings save them time and money, make it irresistible.
8. Don't let moments of anxiety hold you back. Face your fears head-on; pushing through discomfort can lead to amazing opportunities.
9. See the sale. Customers don't make sales, you do. Visualize the sale before it happens. If you can see the customer owning your product, you're already halfway there.

10. Be time efficient. Today's buyers are in a hurry. Be upfront about how much time you'll spend with them and bring up price early in your presentation to avoid surprises later.

Wrap It Up Right

Closing the Meeting

1. Before concluding, recap the main takeaways from the discussion. This reinforces your understanding of the client's needs and solidifies the next steps. Whether it's sending additional information or scheduling a follow-up meeting, you need to make sure your expectations are aligned.
2. Rejection? No Biggie. Don't take "no" personally. View rejection as a chance to learn and grow. It's not about you, it's a steppingstone to greatness. Don't let setbacks or others' opinions slow you down. Keep your eyes on the prize and move forward with confidence.
3. Look for the gaps. Ask your prospects for their honest opinion about your products. Figure out what improvements you can make and if possible, do so. If not, recommend a product that better fits their needs, even if it is not yours. Make it a relationship. You may benefit from a future word of mouth.
4. Always go for the close. Hopefully this is a successful sale, but it could also be the start of a positive and long-lasting relationship. Until the transaction is closed in one of these ways, you've provided no value to your client. Don't shy away from closing, handle objections with confidence and persistence.
5. At the end of the meeting, inquire if they know anyone else who might appreciate your product. A simple question can lead to new opportunities and expand your network.

After the Meeting

1. Send a thank-you email that summarizes the key discussion points and reiterates your value proposition. This keeps you top of mind and reinforces your professionalism. Include helpful resources or insights related to their needs, to make your communication valuable and memorable.
2. Schedule informal coffee meetings or check-ins to strengthen your connection. Building rapport outside of formal meetings fosters trust and can lead to more opportunities.
3. Go back to your product development team and share insights gathered from the meeting. Collaborate on ways to enhance your offerings based on client feedback.
4. Never give up. Persistence is your secret weapon. Embrace challenges with determination and a sense of humor, resilience often paves the way to success.
5. Own your results. Remember, you're the captain of your own ship. Don't blame others for your successes or failures. Take ownership and drive your journey.
6. Always keep a quantitative record of your meetings. Follow up in good time and remember contract expiry dates, logistics and key dates.
7. Take time to analyze what went well and what didn't. Use this reflection to refine your approach, enhance your product, and improve your overall sales strategy.

References

Alexander, R. (2024, February 28). *Frank Lucas – The true story of the American gangster.* Biographics. https://biographics.org/frank-lucas-the-true-story-of-the-american-gangster/

Ayaz, I. (2024, August 25). Volkswagen Emissions Scandal (2015): The deception that rocked the auto industry. *Medium.* https://medium.com/be-open/volkswagen-emissions-scandal-2015-the-deception-that-rocked-the-auto-industry-ebb7631f0ee0

Barsade, S. G. (2002). The Ripple Effect: Emotional Contagion and its Influence on Group Behavior. *Administrative Science Quarterly, 47*(4), 644–675. https://doi.org/10.2307/3094912

Better Business Bureau study: Online shopping scams flourish on social media during pandemic | Carson City Nevada News - Carson Now. (n.d.). https://www.carsonnow.org/story/12/05/2021/better-business-bureau-study-shopping-scams-flourish-social-media-during-pandemic?page=3

Biography.com Editors. (2021, May 27). Jordan Belfort. *Biography.* https://www.biography.com/business-leaders/jordan-belfort

Bybee, N., CPA. (2023, February 25). *The growth of Airbnb during the pandemic.* https://www.linkedin.com/pulse/growth-airbnb-during-pandemic-nathan-bybee-cpa

Coolidge, T. (2024, March 7). *MLMs vs. Pyramid Schemes: One Is Legal, But the Other Could Land You in Prison.* Coolidge Law Firm. https://coolidgelawfirmaz.com/mlms-vs-pyramid-schemes/

CoSchedule. (2024, October 9). *The History of Marketing: How Strategies have changed*. CoSchedule Blog. https://coschedule.com/marketing/history-of-marketing

Curcic, D. (2023, September 13). *Jordan Shoes Statistics*. RunRepeat - Athletic Shoe Reviews. https://runrepeat.com/jordan-shoes-statistics

Day, M. (2022, March 31). Trust in Influencer Marketing Report 2022 - Net Influencer. *Net Influencer*. https://www.netinfluencer.com/trust-in-influencer-marketing-report/

Dealer, T. D. M. P. (2016, January 14). Why do 70%of lottery winners end up bankrupt? *Cleveland*. https://www.cleveland.com/business/2016/01/why_do_70_percent_of_lottery_w.html

Dupont, L. (1995). L'Américanitéin Quebec in the 1980s: Political and cultural considerations of an emerging Discourse. *The American Review of Canadian Studies, 25*(1), 27–52. https://doi.org/10.1080/02722019509481785

Eime, R., Sawyer, N., Harvey, J., Casey, M., Westerbeek, H., & Payne, W. (2014). Integrating public health and sport management: Sport participation trends 2001–2010. *Sport Management Review, 18*(2), 207–217. https://doi.org/10.1016/j.smr.2014.05.004

Emler, R. (2018, December 13). *Vijay Mallya: The rise and fall of "the king of good times" - The Drinks Business*. The Drinks Business. https://www.thedrinksbusiness.com/2018/12/the-rise-and-fall-of-vijay-mallya/

Endly, T. (2024, September 12). Inheritance Statistics US - Trends, and impact of Wealth transfer. *https://endly.co*. https://endly.co/inheritance-statistics-us/

Eyal, N. (2024, October 21). *The morality of manipulation*. Nir And Far. https://www.nirandfar.com/the-art-of-manipulation/

Faces of economic mobility. (2013, September 17). The Pew Charitable Trusts. https://www.pewtrusts.org/en/research-and-analysis/data-visualizations/2013/faces-of-economic-mobility

Federal Reserve Economic Data | FRED | St. Louis Fed. (n.d.). https://fred.stlouisfed.org/

Gartner Says 80% of B2B Sales Interactions Between Suppliers and Buyers Will Occur in Digital Channels by 2025. (n.d.). Gartner.com. https://www.gartner.com/en/newsroom/press-releases/2020-09-15-gartner-says-80--of-b2b-sales-interactions-between-su

Global inequality - inequality.org. (2024, August 20). Inequality.org. https://inequality.org/facts/global-inequality/

Goetz, L. (2022, December 28). *Who is Sheryl Sandberg?* Investopedia. https://www.investopedia.com/articles/insights/051416/sheryl-sandbergs-success-story-net-worth-education-top-quotes.asp

Griggs, T. L., J. Casper, W., & T. Eby, L. (2013). Work, family and community support as predictors of work–family conflict: A study of Low-income workers. *Journal of Vocational Behavior, 82*(1), 59–68. https://doi.org/10.1016/j.jvb.2012.11.006

Hayes, A. (2024, October 3). *Law of Diminishing Marginal Returns: Definition, example, use in Economics.* Investopedia. https://www.investopedia.com/terms/l/lawofdiminishingmarginalreturn.asp

Hotten, R. (2015, December 10). *Volkswagen: The scandal explained.* BBC News. https://www.bbc.com/news/business-34324772

Industrialization, labor, and life. (n.d.). https://education.nationalgeographic.org/resource/industrialization-labor-and-life/

Li, C. (2006). The confucian ideal of harmony. *Philosophy East and West, 56*(4), 583–603. https://doi.org/10.1353/pew.2006.0055

Lioudis, N. (2024, October 7). *The collapse of Lehman Brothers: a case study.* Investopedia. https://www.investopedia.com/articles/economics/09/lehman-brothers-collapse.asp

Lubbock, J. (1870). Prehistoric Times, as illustrated by Ancient Remains, and the Manners and Customs of Modern Savages. *Notes and Queries, s4-V*(106), 53. https://doi.org/10.1093/nq/s4-v.106.53a

Luthans, J., Youssef, F., & Avolio, K. (n.d.). Meta-Analysis of the impact of positive psychological capital on employee attitudes, behaviors, and performance. *Human Resource Development Quarterly*, *22*(2), 157–162. https://doi.org/10.1002/hrdq.20070

Marc. (2022, June 12). *The history of marketing*. Marketing Museum. https://marketing.museum/marketing-history/

Martin, J. (2024, September 23). 18 Cyberbullying Facts & Statistics (2024). *Exploding Topics*. https://explodingtopics.com/blog/cyberbullying-stats

Mesoamerican writing systems: propaganda, myth, and history in four ancient civilizations. (1993). *Choice Reviews Online*, *30*(11), 30–6247. https://doi.org/10.5860/choice.30-6247

Mitchell, T., & Mitchell, T. (2024, May 31). *1. Trends in income and wealth inequality*. Pew Research Center. https://www.pewresearch.org/social-trends/2020/01/09/trends-in-income-and-wealth-inequality/

Moran, V. (n.d.). *The fall of the greats – The Blockbuster Story | MS&E 238 Blog*. https://mse238blog.stanford.edu/2018/07/vmoran/the-fall-of-the-greats-the-blockbuster-story/

Msod, M. G. M. (2021, February 7). *5 Scientific Studies that Prove the Power of Positive Thinking*. https://www.linkedin.com/pulse/5-scientific-studies-prove-power-positive-thinking-mark-guidi

Occupational Employment and Wage Statistics. (2023). US Bureau of Labor Statistics. https://www.bls.gov/oes/current/oes_nat.htm#41-0000

Petrecca, L. (2024, August 21). *How to overcome 7 inheritance obstacles*. AARP. https://www.aarp.org/money/budgeting-saving/info-2024/overcoming-inheritance-challenges.html

ReminderMedia. (2024, July 19). *A (Very) brief history of sales | ReminderMedia*. ReminderMedia | Impress and Stay Top of Mind With All of Your Contacts on Autopilot. https://remindermedia.com/blog/sales-is-the-only-thing-since-1986/

Rollin, J. (2022, November 16). *2015 FIFA corruption scandal | Explained, Qatar, & 2022 World Cup*. Encyclopedia Britannica. https://www.britannica.com/event/2015-FIFA-corruption-scandal

Rothman, L. (2016, January 21). The short, chaotic history of the De-Lorean. *TIME*. https://time.com/4180894/delorean-history/

Santiago, E., & Santiago, E. (2024, March 12). The HubSpot Blog's 2024 Social Media Marketing Report: Data from 1400+ Global Marketers. *The Hubspot Blog*. https://blog.hubspot.com/marketing/hubspot-blog-social-media-marketing-report

Satell, G. (2021, December 10). A look back at why blockbuster really failed and why it didn't have to. *Forbes*. https://www.forbes.com/sites/gregsatell/2014/09/05/a-look-back-at-why-blockbuster-really-failed-and-why-it-didnt-have-to/

Scott, E., PhD. (2024, January 30). *Understanding the law of attraction*. Verywell Mind. https://www.verywellmind.com/understanding-and-using-the-law-of-attraction-3144808

Smith, C., & Smith, C. (2024, July 17). *Apple*. DMR. https://expandedramblings.com/index.php/by-the-numbers-amazing-apple-stats/

Sprout Social. (2024, February 28). *#BrandsGetReal: What consumers want from brands in a divided society*. https://sproutsocial.com/insights/data/social-media-connection/

Teo, J. (2023, January 30). Action plan to help older Singaporeans live well as they age and work longer. *The Straits Times*. https://www.straitstimes.com/singapore/health/national-plan-to-help-older-singaporeans-live-well-as-they-age-and-work-longer

The Editors of Encyclopaedia Britannica. (2024, September 29). *Renaissance | Definition, Meaning, History, Artists, Art, & Facts*. Encyclopedia Britannica. https://www.britannica.com/event/Renaissance

The employee experience: Culture, engagement, and beyond. (n.d.). Deloitte Insights. https://www2.deloitte.com/us/en/insights/focus/human-capital-trends/2017/improving-the-employee-experience-culture-engagement.html

The History and Evolution of Sales. What did the first sales look like and what do they look like today? (2024, April 11). Lectera Magazine. https://

lectera.com/magazine/articles/the-history-and-evolution-of-sales-what-did-the-first-sales-look-like-and-what-do-they-look-like-today

Weber, M. (1976). *The Agrarian sociology of Ancient civilizations.* http://ci.nii.ac.jp/ncid/BB17826571?l=en

Whitehouse, N. J., & Kirleis, W. (2014). The world reshaped: practices and impacts of early agrarian societies. *Journal of Archaeological Science, 51,* 1–11. https://doi.org/10.1016/j.jas.2014.08.007

Whittaker, C. R., Sabloff, J. A., & Lamberg-Karlovsky, C. C. (1976). Ancient civilization and trade. *The Economic History Review, 29*(3), 518. https://doi.org/10.2307/2595323

Witters, B. M. P. J. a. D. (2024, October 17). Daily loneliness afflicts one in five in U.S. *Gallup.com.* https://news.gallup.com/poll/651881/daily-loneliness-afflicts-one-five.aspx

Wong, J. C. (2019, March). *The Cambridge Analytica scandal changed the world – but it didn't change Facebook.* The Guardian. Retrieved July 6, 2024, from https://www.theguardian.com/technology/2019/mar/17/the-cambridge-analytica-scandal-changed-the-world-but-it-didnt-change-facebook

World Population Clock: 8.2 billion people (LIVE, 2024) - Worldometer. (n.d.). https://www.worldometers.info/world-population/